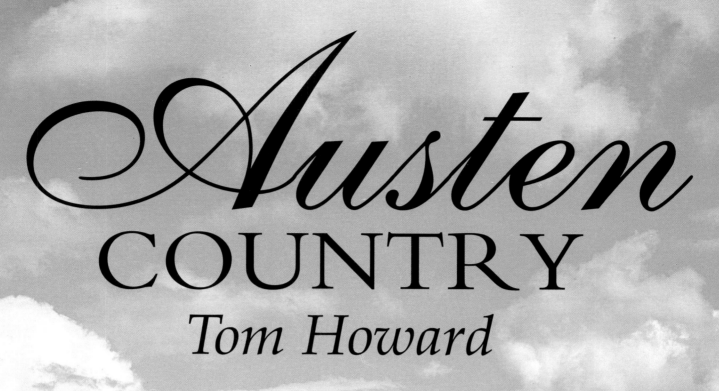

Austen
COUNTRY
Tom Howard

SMITHMARK

PHOTOGRAPHIC ACKNOWLEDGEMENTS
Jacket front cover main picture: Derek Forss Photography
Jacket front cover black and white inset:
Hulton Deutsch Collection
Back cover: Derek Forss Photography

Inside pages
Bridgeman Art Library
40 bottom, 52

Comstock Photo Library
26-27, 28, 38 bottom, 40 top, 47

John Crook
77 both, 80

Edifice
10, 11, 12, 13, 15, 16, 17, 18 both, 19, 21, 22-23, 24, 29, 43, 48 bottom, 49, 62 both, 64, 65, (Sarah Jackson) 46 both, 48 both top, 73 bottom, 75, (Philippa Lewis)

Derek Forss Photography
4-5, 35, 44 top, 55, 56, 57, 73 top

Jarrolds Publishing
36, 37, 38 top, 44 bottom, 58, 59, 60, 61

A.F. Kersting
2-3, 25, 30, 31, 32, 33, 34, 42-43, 45, 51, 53, 54, 66, 69, 74, 78, 79

National Building's Record
72

Clare Pawley
70 both, 71

Malcom Porter
Map on pages 8-9

Sarah Jackson would like to thank: Penelope Hughs Hallett; Mrs Joyce Brown, The Jane Austen Society, Steventon; Mr Tom Carpenter, Jane Austen Memorial Trust; Mr & Mrs Robert French-Blake, Ibthorpe House, Ibthorpe, Hampshire; Mr & Mrs Christopher Scott, Ashe Park

Pages 2-3: Looking eastwards to the Medway Valley from Wrotham Water, near Wrotham. These pages: The Royal Crescent, Bath, Avon.

This edition first published in the United States in 1995 by SMITHMARK Publishers Inc., 16 East 32nd Street, New York, NY 10016.

SMITHMARK books are available for bulk purchase for sales promotion and premium use. For details write or call the manager of special sales, SMITHMARK Publishers, 16 East 32nd Street, New York, NY 10016; (212) 532 6600.

Produced by: Regency House Publishing Limited
The Grange, Grange Yard, London, SE1 3AG.

ISBN 0-8317-1854-4

Printed in the U.A.E.

10 9 8 7 6 5 4 3 2 1

CONTENTS

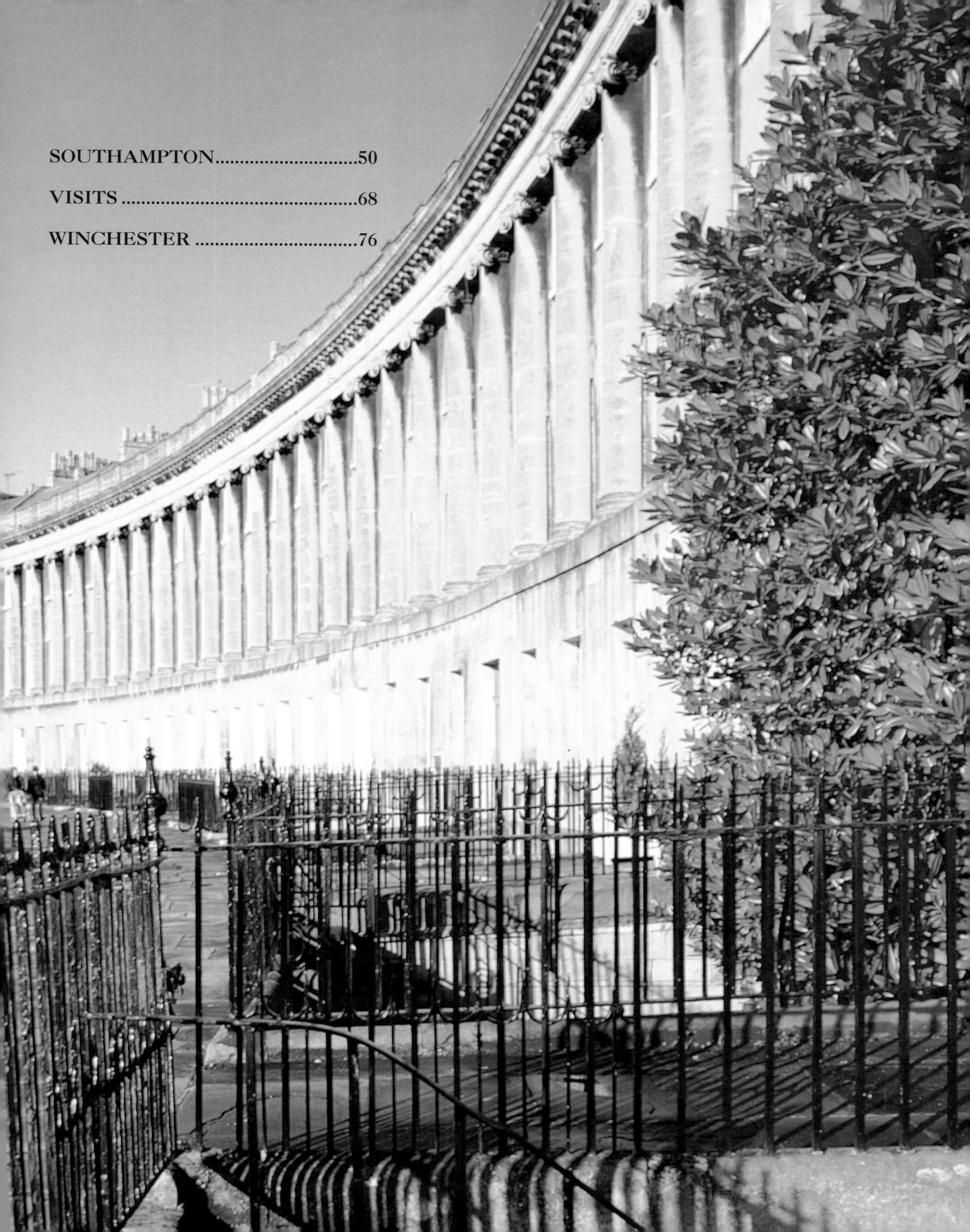

INTRODUCTION

Jane Austen's novels were not great romantic sagas or picaresque adventures. Neither were they examinations of the great moral issues of her time. They were minutely-observed portraits of middle-class English provincial life. She was wise enough to write about what she knew best, and portrayed each of her characters with incomparable wit, delicacy and wry humour.

That her work is so highly regarded and attracts such enthusiastic readership to this day can be attributed to the quality of her writing. To read her novels is to vividly imagine oneself the confidant of each of her characters, eagerly absorbing all the neighbourhood gossip from an endlessly fascinating raconteur. So close is the narrator's voice that it seems perfectly natural when, in the middle of *Sense and Sensibility*, for just one sentence, she adopts the personal pronoun.

The most successful novelist of his day, Sir Walter Scott, was enviously to declare:

'That young lady had a talent for describing the involvements, and feelings, and characters of ordinary life, which to me is the most wonderful I ever met with. The Big Bow-wow strain I can do myself like any now going: but the exquisite touch, which renders ordinary commonplace things and characters so interesting, from the truth of the description and the sentiment, is denied to me.'

Anthony Trollope and Alfred, Lord Tennyson were other literary admirers, and E.M. Forster, whose early 20th century novels were deeply concerned with the middle-class psyche, declared: *'She is my favourite author! I read and re-read, the mouth open and the mind closed. Shut up in measureless content, I greet her by the name of most kind hostess, while criticism slumbers.'*

She did have her detractors. Elizabeth Barrett Browning and Charlotte Brontë for instance, considered her to be of limited talent and, though her novels were generally well received on publication (the Prince Regent is said to have kept a complete set in each of his several residences), it was not until many years after her death and the publication of her nephew's biography of her life that she began to attract a following and the reputation of a classic writer that goes with her name today.

Jane Austen lived through very dramatic times: the French Revolution and the American fight for independence were taking place when she was a child, followed by the Napoleonic Wars in which her brothers saw service as sailors with the British Navy. In India, Britain was beginning to establish her Imperial power. At home, the enclosure of common land by the propertied gentry was changing the countryside and worsening the lot of the labouring countryman while steam-power, canals and industrialization were changing the economic pattern still further. Though by background a high Tory, she makes frequent criticism of blatant self-interest and exploitation, but her concern is with relationships and behaviour on a personal level, rather than with wider

OPPOSITE

A portrait of Jane Austen by Cassandra Austen, sketched in 1810. Although used as the main source for the prettified portrait accompanying James Edward Austen-Leigh's 1870 *A Memoir of Jane Austen*, and presumably regarded by the family as acceptable, it may not be a particularly good likeness, though one can well imagine this to be a person of sharp wit and perception. James Edward describes her as *'very attractive; her figure was rather tall and slender ... a clear brunette with a rich colour; she had full round cheeks, with mouth and nose small and well-formed, bright, hazel eyes, and brown hair forming natural curls round her face'.*

events and politics. These things play little part in her writing, but they are part of the background to them, as they were part of the background of her contemporary readers. To quote Sir Walter Scott again:

'The subjects are not often elegant, and certainly never grand; but they are finished up to nature, and with a precision which delights the reader.'

That precision is concentrated on conversation and behaviour. Jane Austen wastes few words describing the workings of the outside world, except where they have some bearing on the personality or station of her characters. There are no detailed text pictures of architecture or landscape which can pinpoint the precise identity of the locations she may have had in mind when writing about them.

Many of the scenes of Jane Austen's novels are set in well-known places: London, Bath, Portsmouth, Lyme Regis, but the country houses and small villages are given fictional names. However, she clearly wrote from her own experience, drawing closely on places that she knew, though she often combines elements of several actual locations to produce a setting for her story. In *Mansfield Park* she placed the scene of the action in Northamptonshire, a county she did not know, and while writing the novel requested in a letter to her sister: 'If you could discover whether Northamptonshire is a country of Hedgerows I should be glad'. However, she was able to draw upon knowledge of the country mansion her brother had inherited from adoptive parents and many other grand houses to create Sir Thomas Bertram's residence: but it is more usual for her to use familiar locales.

You will not find pictures of Northamptonshire in the pages that follow but, as this book explores her life, her

homes and travels, you will find many photographs of places familiar to Jane Austen as they exist today. Two centuries have wrought great changes but it is still possible to view them as a background to her life and a further dimension to her work.

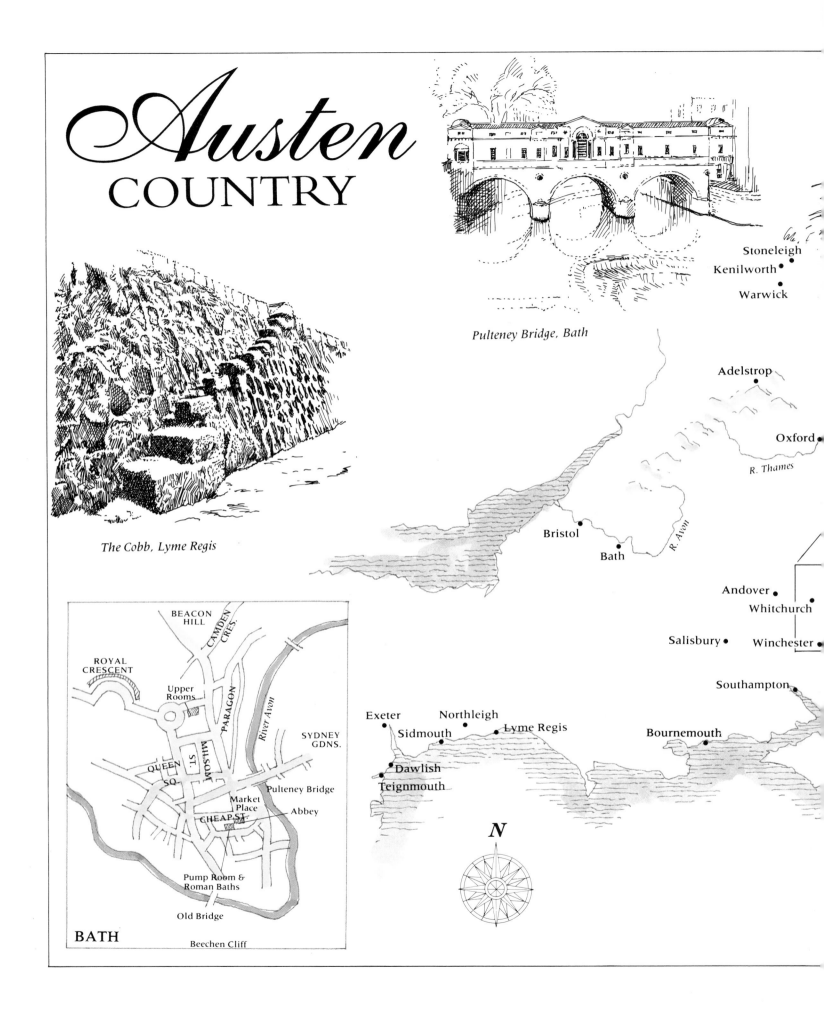

Austen COUNTRY

Pulteney Bridge, Bath

The Cobb, Lyme Regis

Stoneleigh

Kenilworth

Warwick

Adelstrop

Oxford

R. Thames

Bristol

R. Avon

Bath

Andover

Whitchurch

Salisbury

Winchester

Southampton

Exeter

Northleigh

Sidmouth

Lyme Regis

Bournemouth

Dawlish

Teignmouth

BATH

BEACON HILL

CAMDEN CRES.

ROYAL CRESCENT

Upper Rooms

PARAGON

River Avon

SYDNEY GDNS.

MILSOM ST.

QUEEN SQ.

Pulteney Bridge

Market Place

CHEAP ST.

Abbey

Pump Room & Roman Baths

Old Bridge

Beechen Cliff

N

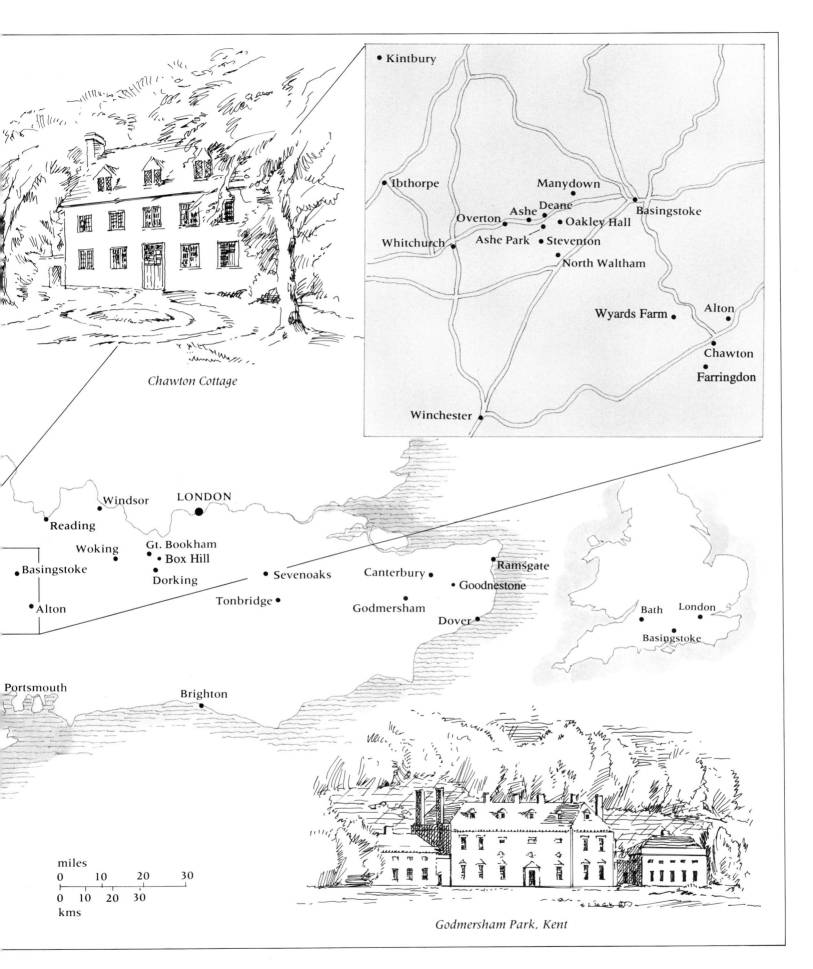

Chawton Cottage

Kintbury

Ibthorpe

Manydown

Deane

Overton Ashe

Basingstoke

Oakley Hall

Whitchurch Ashe Park Steventon

North Waltham

Wyards Farm Alton

Chawton

Farringdon

Winchester

Windsor LONDON

Reading

Woking Gt. Bookham

Box Hill

Basingstoke Dorking Sevenoaks Canterbury Ramsgate

Goodnestone

Tonbridge Godmersham

Alton Dover

Bath London

Basingstoke

Portsmouth Brighton

miles
0 10 20 30

0 10 20 30
kms

Godmersham Park, Kent

STEVENTON

A pump in a field at Steventon. A metal replacement of an earlier wooden pump is all that remains of the rectory where Jane Austen was born, the house being demolished in the 19th century not very long after her death.

Jane Austen was born in the rectory of Steventon, a village in the English county of Hampshire on 16 December 1775. Her father, George Austen, was descended from a family who had been clothing manufacturers in Kent, in the south-east of the country, in the middle ages. Some of its members had become wealthy landowners but he came from a less prosperous branch, some of whom had entered the professions. His father was a surgeon, an occupation of little social status at that time, and an uncle was a solicitor. George was orphaned when he was six years old and his uncle sent him to school at Tonbridge and then on to St. John's College, Oxford, where he obtained a scholarship. After a period spent teaching at his old school, he returned to Oxford and took Holy Orders. Clergymen were not then paid by the central church authority but received an income from the rents, tithes and any other profits accruing to the benefice which had usually been given by the founder who established the church or were the gift of other benefactors. This gave the founder's inheritors, whether by descent or purchase, the right to choose the incumbent; one of George Austen's richer relatives, his uncle, Francis, owned the gift of the living at Steventon and in 1761 he presented it to him. His uncle also bought him two other livings in the neighbouring parishes of Ashe and Deane to add further to his income, once the present incumbents had died.

Jane's mother, Cassandra Leigh, whom George married in Bath in 1764, came from a family which could trace its roots back to the Norman conquest. One ancestor had been Lord Mayor of London in the time of Elizabeth I, and a great-aunt had married the Duke of Chandos. His wife's branch of the family was settled at Adelstrop in Gloucestershire while a junior branch had their country seat at Stoneleigh Abbey in Warwickshire. Cassandra was brought up at Harpsden in the Thames Valley not far from Windsor, where her father was rector, holding the living of All Soul's College, Oxford where he had been a Fellow. She may have met her husband at Oxford where her uncle Theophilus, was Master of Balliol. A decade earlier, her brother James had inherited an estate at Northleigh, Oxfordshire, from another relation, adopting their surname of Perrot as a condition of his inheritance.

By comparison with some members of their families, Jane's parents were 'poor relations', but they were by no means impoverished, having had good education and important 'connections'. Her father's annual income was between £500 and £600 but he added to this by taking boys of good family as paying pupils to be tutored and live as members of his household. The first of them was probably the son of Warren Hastings, the British administrator in India, though there is no surviving proof of this, and others included the son of Lord Portsmouth whose country seat was within a few miles at Hurstbourne Park. With the help of a paid foreman he also ran the rectory lands as a farm thus providing some further income as well as helping to feed the family and servants.

There were already five elder brothers and a sister when Jane was born in 1775: James (born 1765), George (1766), Edward (1768), Henry (1771), Francis (1774), Cassandra (1775), and Charles was to follow four years later. Little is known about George, apart from a reference in a letter of 1770 in which Mrs. Austen mentions that he was prone to fits. Was he handicapped in some way, and perhaps deaf? Many years later Jane writes of being able to speak to the deaf with her fingers. He lived until 1838, but maybe not as part of the household. Edward became a landed gentleman, adopted by his wealthy uncle and taking his surname of Knight; two brothers went into the church and two into the Navy; Cassandra did not marry but stayed at home. The lives of this large family could not have failed to interact with Jane's, widening her knowledge of the world and extending her range of acquaintances.

The England of 1775 was still ruled by George II. The Boston Tea Party which sparked the fight for American Independence had taken place only two years earlier and the slave trade still flourished from English ports. Though steam power had been used to pump water out of mines since the beginning of the century, James Watt's improvements to the steam engine, which were to make it the driving force of the next century, and Richard Arkwright's patent for his water frame both date from 1769. The building of the first iron bridge was to come ten years later. But the technical changes brought about by the Industrial Revolution, which took place during her lifetime, were more noticeable in the North and Midlands

than in the area frequented by Jane Austen. In her milieu, social status was firmly based on property rather than commerce. However, a comparable revolution was taking place on the land of which she, and therefore her characters, would have been well aware. The old medieval system of common land and the farming of strips in larger shared fields was already being swept away in the reign of Elizabeth I. But by the last quarter of the 18th century many successive Acts of Parliament were forcing the enclosure of the land by purchase or exchange of territory as decreed by Parliamentary Commissioners to enable the big landowners to make the transition to new agricultural methods.

The approach to Steventon Church, where Jane Austen's father was rector for 40 years.

The site of Steventon rectory. The house was near the road, approached by a 'sweep', a curving drive big enough to accommodate carriages, from a gate in an wooden fence of open palings. A trellis arch framed the front door, which led straight into the parlour. Jane and Cassandra shared a bedroom and a sitting-room on the first floor, where they had bookshelves and space for Jane's piano and writing desk. The Reverend Austen had a book-lined study overlooking the garden at the back of the house, where two wings extended to the rear.

There were 1,300 Enclosure Acts between 1760 and 1801, when the General Enclosure Act simplified the procedures involved, and a further 1,000 in the next two decades. As a contemporary verse put it:

They hang the man and flog the woman
That steals a goose from off the common
But leave the greater criminal loose
That steals the common from the goose.

Enclosure meant that land could become the property of the individual, thus changing the face of society to this day. It changed the landscape too, for as fields were enclosed, woodlands and wastes disappeared and a new pattern of hedges, walls, fences and roads took shape. Together with the fashionable new landscaping of parkland in the style of Capability Brown, emulating the idealized landscapes of Claude and Poussin, this created what many think of as the natural appearance of the English countryside: a prospect which itself saw rapid change two centuries later with the grubbing up of hedgerows to create the larger fields required by highly mechanized farming methods.

Agricultural techniques apart, the growth of arable crops as winter feed for cattle brought fresh instead of salt meat for winter meals and a reduction of scurvy and other skin diseases – though a preference for more highly refined flour, instead of wholemeal, was to prove bad for health and teeth. Not that the increasing number of landless labourers could afford such luxuries.

The establishment of passenger services on steam-hauled railways did not begin until a decade after Jane Austen's death, but canals and improved river navigation were already having their effect and bringing great improvement to both roads and road transportation services. This made it much easier to travel about the country, especially on the new turnpike roads that were being built in such numbers at the time and for which travellers were expected to pay a toll. Travel over long distances was not a thing to be taken lightly, especially by ladies of refinement, but visits to London, to fashionable watering places, or to stay with friends in their country houses were becoming more a question of expense than availability of transport. The Austens lived in a small village but they were by no means cut off from the world. News travelled quickly along the highways, whether of foreign wars or private gossip.

As babies, all the Austen children were put out to a wet-nurse who lived a mile away in Deane. This was a common practice among gentlefolk at this time and, although not under the same roof, they were not cut off entirely from their parents, for one or other made a daily visit to see them. Once weaned, the babies would have been returned to the rectory.

While she was still a very little child, two of Jane's brothers, James and Edward, both left home. James, aged 14, went up to Oxford to become a

Founder's Kin scholar (through his mother's family connections) at his father's old college, St. John's. Edward went to live with the Knight family (whose heir he later became) at Godmersham Park in Kent. George too, may not have been brought up at home. Though Frank was nearer to Jane in years she seems to have been closest to Henry and Cassandra. Henry was her favourite brother and Cassandra her immediate role model. 'If Cassandra were going to have her head cut off, Jane would insist on sharing her fate', was the way Mrs. Austen put it. So much so, that when Cassandra was sent away to school in 1782, six-year-old Jane went too. The school was run by Mrs. Cawley, the widow of an academic and sister of their mother's brother-in-law, Edward Cooper. They were soon

The ground behind the rectory rises and the terrace which formed the Austens' 'Wood Walk' can still be discerned. This was set out as a shrubbery with occasional seats or benches. In *Northanger Abbey* Catherine Morland enjoys rolling down just such a green slope as that which descended to the house.

joined there by their cousin Jane Cooper.

The following year Mrs. Cawley relocated her school to Southampton, and it was there that an epidemic of a condition called 'putrid throat', a septic throat characteristic of typhus fever, broke out. This was a common infection which the Austens had unhappily already experienced – it had killed Warren Hastings's little boy, aged six, when he was in their charge. Jane Cooper informed her mother in a letter and Mrs. Cooper and Mrs. Austen collected their daughters and took them home as soon as possible. The girls survived but Mrs. Cooper herself caught the infection and died of it.

The girls did not return to Southampton. Another school was found: the Abbey School in Reading, located in the gatehouse of Reading Abbey. From an account left by a pupil who attended this school a little after Jane Austen, it was an easy-going establishment where, provided pupils appeared at mealtimes and put in an hour or two's study with their tutor in the morning, they were free to spend the rest of the day as they wished. Certainly, when Jane's brother Edward called to see them together with Jane Cooper's brother and a party of friends, the girls were given leave to join them in a meal at a local inn.

Jane continued at the Abbey until she was 11 and was then taught at home by her father. She learned French, a little Italian, read the classics – and contemporary fiction. Her mother probably supervised her sewing and embroidery (at which she became most proficient) and other feminine accomplishments. She also learned to play the piano and as she grew older took great pleasure in dancing.

The vicar's family took an active part in local life. The boys were keen sportsmen. When he was seven years old, Francis had bought himself a pony on which he regularly went hunting and little Charles was soon infected with the same enthusiasm. However, by the time Jane was living at home, Francis was already at the Royal Naval College, Portsmouth, where Charles followed him in 1791, though of course they did come home on leave from time to time.

The Austens were on receiving terms with families in the locality who were rather more prosperous than themselves and, as the girls grew up, they received many invitations to attend both private and public balls. They also mounted theatrical performances at home in the barn behind the house at midsummer and in the dining-room in winter. These seem to have begun in 1784 with a performance of Richard Brinsley Sheridan's *The Rivals* and to have sporadically continued until 1790. (Later, Jane's memories of them provided her with useful material for some of the scenes in *Mansfield Park*).

Her brother James wrote prologues for some of these performances and Jane appears to have assisted with them. Composing rhymed charades was also a family pastime to which Jane contributed. At 12 years old she was the busy author of stories and amusing sketches, frequently dedicated to friends or family members, which sometimes parodied popular contemporary novels. However, they were not particularly well-regarded. In a family such as hers, such talents and pursuits were not considered exceptional. Up at Oxford her brother James founded and edited a journal: *The Loiterer*. Henry later wrote for it and he and Charles were both versifiers. Cassandra, according to Jane herself was 'the finest comic writer of the age' (though nothing survives to prove it!). Later a niece began to send

The lane which led from the rectory to Steventon church was not much more than a rutted track when the Austens lived here. In bad weather they would wear pattens to keep their feet out of the mud – clog-like overshoes with iron rings beneath to walk on and raise the sole out of the dirt. In dry weather they would use a path straight from their garden to the church.

her own stories, seeking her opinion of them, and a nephew wrote the first biography of his Aunt Jane. By 1793 she had copied some of these early writings into notebooks which still survive, entitled *Volume the First*, *Volume the Second* and *Volume the Third*. A comic *History of England*, *Love and Friendship*, a novel in letter form parodying popular romances, and the rather more ambitious but incomplete *Catherine* are all among these early pieces.

In 1791, Jane's brother Edward, having been sent on the Grand Tour to Europe rather than to university, married Elizabeth Bridges, daughter of a wealthy landowner of Goodnestone, Kent and they set up home at Rowlings

quite close to her own family and his adoptive parents at Godmersham. James, after a time as Fellow of his old Oxford college, became a clergyman and, in 1792, moved back nearer to Steventon as curate to the parish of Overton. That same year he married, his wife Eliza bringing £100 a year to add to his own income of £200, and they moved into the rectory which went with the living at Deane which had been bought for his father. This had been occupied by the widow of Rev. Nowys Lloyd and her daughters, but they now moved to Ibthorpe, some miles to the west enabling him to take up residence.

The Lloyds were close friends of the Austens, as too were the family of the

Ashe House, home of the Reverend Isaac Lefroy and his family. Mrs. Lefroy became Jane's close friend: her death following a fall from her horse in 1804 came as a great shock. This was where she met Tom Lefroy (see pages 18-19). The youngest of the Lefroy boys married Jane's niece Anna. Usually the double doors between the dining- and morning-rooms were opened to allow plenty of room for dancing, but a letter of 1800 describes a lively party of 14 taking place in the study, the dining-room being out of action because a storm had blown down the chimney. It had also played havoc with the elms at Steventon rectory. Ashe House ceased to be the local rectory in 1905.

Rev. George Lefroy who held the adjoining living in the parish of Ashe. Among the local gentry the Austens were also well acquainted with the Bigg-Withers of Manydown Park, the Bramstones of Oakley Hall, the Harwoods of Deane House, the Holders of Ashe Park, the Portals of Freefolk, and on an even grander level with Lord Bolton of Hackwood, Lady Dorchester of Greywell (later of Kempshott) and the Portsmouths, to whose son Mr. Austen had been a tutor.

A guest at Steventon in 1792 was Jane Cooper, who stayed there between the time of her father's death in August and her marriage in December. Another was Eliza de Feuillide, daughter of the Rev. Austen's sister,

Philadelphia. Her father, now deceased, had met and married her mother in India, where they met Warren Hastings and his wife who proved themselves to be generous friends. They had often stayed at Steventon before Eliza was sent to Paris to complete her education and where she met her husband, a French aristocrat, the Comte de Feuillide. She returned to England when she was expecting a baby and, especially after her mother's death in 1791 she, with her son, were often at Steventon again.

In France, the Revolution was building up to the execution of Louis XVI at the beginning of 1793. The Comte returning to France in an attempt to sort out his own affairs and

Ashe Park, home of local friends the Holders, is a large, red-brick mansion dating back to the reign of James I. 'To sit in idleness over a good fire in a well-proportioned room is a luxurious sensation,' Jane Austen wrote after a November evening spent there in 1800.

salvage what he could of his estates, foolishly supported the Marquis de Marboeuf who had been charged with failing to cooperate with the State over food production. He became further embroiled in the affair and was guillotined early in 1794. The political upheavals in France may not have troubled the consciences of the landed British aristocracy but they were certainly well informed of the French situation and were keeping a close watch for signs of creeping egalitarism in their own country. The execution of such a close relation must have brought the reality of the Terror dramatically to the consciousness of the family in their country vicarage.

The following year brought another family tragedy: the death of James's wife Anne. His little daughter, two-year-old Jane Anna Elizabeth, was taken across from Deane to Steventon to be brought up by her grandparents and aunts. Happier news arrived of the acquittal of Eliza's family's benefactor, Warren Hastings, impeached by the British Parliament in 1788 for alleged corruption in his administration of India and now released after a trial lasting seven years.

There were also developments in the Austen sisters' own private lives. Cassandra was becoming attached to a young clergyman, Thomas Fowle, the brother of Mrs. Lloyd's son-in-law. In

RIGHT
Though the coaching inn where the
Austens used to collect their mail
now stands near a busy motorway,
most of the local roads still pass
through peaceful countryside.

fact she had known Tom since childhood; he had been a pupil of her father's
at Steventon before she went away to
school. They became engaged in 1795
but Jane began a flirtation with another
Tom, an Irish cousin of the Lefroy
family at Ashe Rectory.

It is not clear how serious Jane's
involvement with the handsome young
Irishman was. Letters surviving from
the time reveal that Jane wrote regularly to Cassandra when they were
apart; but her references to Lefroy are
extremely flippant and light-hearted.
Both Cassandra and Mrs. Lefroy were
concerned and gently warned her
against involvement for both were
lacking in financial resources even
though Tom Lefroy was clearly over-
ambitious. This rather suggests that she
ran a serious risk of disappointment,

BELOW
The Winterborne Valley near
Ibthorpe to which the Lloyd family
moved after leaving the rectory at
Deane.

but her outward defence of the liaison bears all the hallmarks of a person nursing a real but self-acknowledged 'impossible' affection.

In the first of her letters to survive, dated 9 January 1796, Jane replied to her sister, who was staying with her fiancé's family at Kintbury in Berkshire:

'You scold me so much ... that I am almost afraid to tell you how my Irish friend and I behaved. Imagine to yourself everything most profligate and shocking in the way of dancing and sitting down together. I can expose myself, however, only once more, because he leaves the country soon after next Friday, on which day we are to dance at Ashe after all. He is a very gentleman-like, good-looking, pleasant young man, I assure you. But as to our having ever met, except at the three last balls, I cannot say much; for he is so excessively laughed at about me at Ashe, that he is ashamed of

coming to Steventon, and ran away when we called on Mrs. Lefroy a few days ago ...

' ... he has but one *fault, which time will, I trust, entirely remove – it is that his morning coat is a great deal too light. He is a very great admirer of Tom Jones* [the title character in the novel by Henry Fielding], *and therefore wears the same coloured clothes, I imagine, which he did when he was wounded ...'*

A week later she writes:

'Tell Mary that I make over Mr. Heartley ... to her ... and ... all my other admirers ... as I mean to confine myself in future to Mr. Tom Lefroy, for whom I do not care sixpence ...

'At length the day is come on which I am to flirt my last with Tom Lefroy, and when you receive this it will be over. My tears flow as I write at the melancholy idea.'

Serious or not – and the Lefroy family later tended to believe that

Ibthorpe House, the new home of Martha Lloyd, her mother and sisters which Jane was often to visit.

Thomas *had* behaved rather badly as far as she was concerned – there had definitely been a strong attraction there. A nephew, who questioned Lefroy in old age reported that 'he did not state in what her fascination consisted, but he said in so many words that he was in love with her, although he qualified his confession by saying that it was a boyish love.' Whether or not hearts were broken, there was to be no future for this relationship. Tom Lefroy eventually made a suitable marriage and went on to pursue a legal career, eventually becoming Lord Chief Justice of Ireland.

Neither was Cassandra's happiness to last. Tom Fowles already had a living in Wiltshire and despite the promise from Lord Craven of a better one in the future, in Shropshire, it was not felt that his income could not yet support them. With some reluctance he accepted an invitation from Craven to go out to the West Indies as chaplain of his regiment in the hope that this would enable the couple to save money for their marriage.

He sailed in 1796 to commence his duties but on arriving at his destination went down with yellow fever and in 1797 died in Santo Domingo, the old island of Hispaniola which is now split between Haiti and the Dominican Republic. Cassandra was no doubt distraught when the news arrived. But as Jane related to Eliza Fowle (married to Tom's brother), Cassandra 'behaves with a degree of resolution and propriety, which no common mind could evince in so trying a situation.' It cannot have been much of a consolation that Craven regretted that he had sent a betrothed man abroad, neither was the £1,000 bequeathed to her by Tom – though in later years the income from it became a useful addition to the family finances. Cassandra never married and

there is no report of her even considering the possibility of matrimony again.

However, there *were* Austen marriages that year. James was married to Mary Lloyd and Henry to his cousin Eliza, the Comtesse de Feuillide. Not that either wife was a first choice. James had first asked Eliza to become his second wife – but she refused him, not being particularly eager to become a parson's wife. Henry had been engaged in a flirtation with another woman, but perhaps without serious intentions, before he became engaged to Eliza, who was ten years his senior.

Jane persevered with her writing. It is not easy to assign accurate dates to particular works for she often made later amendments to her earlier writings. *Catherine*, which was written for the most part when she was 16, contains a reference to a book not published until 1809. Between 1794 and 1796 she completed *Elinor and Marianne*, a novel written as a sequence of letters which was complete enough to be read aloud to the family. (This story was later to be re-worked as *Sense and Sensibility*.) Another novel in letter form, *Lady Susan,* survives only in a clean copy written on paper bearing a watermark dating it to 1805. It was, in fact, written earlier, probably before Elinor and Marianne.

In the autumn of 1796, Jane began a new novel which she called *First Impressions* (later to become *Pride and Prejudice*). It was finished by the following August and her father thought so highly of it that he made an attempt to get it published, describing it as a three-volume novel of about the length of Fanny Burney's *Evelina*. The publisher promptly rejected the offer to read the manuscript. Jane's letters show that her intimates did not share the publisher's lack of interest but were eager to read and re-read it over the following years.

Jokingly she accused Martha Lloyd of being 'very cunning, but I saw through her design; she means to publish it from memory, and one more perusal must enable her to do it.'

While close members of the family were aware of all this literary activity, they did not wish the world at large to know. James's little daughter Anna, who became a great favourite of her Aunt Jane, heard Cassandra laughing as Jane read out parts of her work to her and soon became familiar with the story and its characters; but she was forbidden to divulge the secret. Anna herself began to compose stories, dictating them to her aunt: a copy still survives of a play written out for her by Jane.

In November 1797, Mrs. Austen took Jane and Cassandra on a visit to Bath, where it is likely that they stayed with Mrs. Austen's brother James Leigh Perrot and his wife. James had

Oakley Church, from the grounds of Oakley Hall.

Oakley Hall, now housing Hilsea College, was home to the Bramstons, another house which Jane knew well as a visitor. Here, she wrote to her sister in 1800, *'We did a great deal – ate some sandwiches all over mustard, admired Mr. Bramston's transparencies, and gained a promise ... of two roots of heartsease, one all yellow and the other all purple ...'*

adopted the surname Perrot on inheriting his great-uncle Perrot's estate in Oxfordshire. Although their main home was at Scarlets, in Berkshire, the Leigh Perrots spent half the year at Paragon Buildings in Bath. They too, were childless, and it was expected that they would make James Austen their heir. This may have been Jane's first visit to the city; if so, it was to be the first of many.

About this time Jane seems to have returned to *Elinor and Marianne* changing it from its letter form and incorporating her experiences of Bath: however, it was still many years from publication. We do not know its exact form when she felt it to be complete or put it aside to begin work on another story *Susan* (no connection to the earlier *Lady Susan*.) This was somewhat different from her other books in that it was a deliberate burlesque of the 'gothick' novel, no doubt influenced by the publication of Mrs. Radcliffe's *The Mysteries of Udolpho* in 1794. It was probably largely completed in 1799, and although in her introduction of 1816 Jane says it was 'finished' in 1805, it seems to have had much less revision than the other redrafted novels.

At the end of August 1798, Jane and Cassandra went with their parents to visit their brother Edward at Godmersham, the house and estate in Kent of which he had become the owner when his adoptive mother, Mrs. Knight, moved to White Friars in Canterbury the previous year. They made numerous visits to the houses of Edward's local friends and relations and Cassandra stayed on when the others returned to Steventon in October so that when Jane wrote to her during their separation, it is an indication of the busy social life in which she was involved at home.

Tom Lefroy is by no means for

gotten. Reporting a visit from Mrs. Lefroy she says:

'... of her nephew she said nothing at all ... she did not once mention the name ... to me, and I was too proud to make any enquiries; but on my father's afterwards asking where he was, I learnt that he was gone back to London on his way to Ireland, where he is called to the Bar and means to practise.'

She compares the pattern of life at Steventon vicarage with that at Godmersham:

'We dine now at half after three, and have done dinner I suppose before you begin. We drink tea at half after six. I am afraid you will despise us. My father reads Cowper to us in the evening, to which I listen when I can. How do you spend your evenings? I guess that Elizabeth [their brother's wife]

Deane House from Deane churchyard. This was home to the Harwood family, who often invited their friends, the Austens, to visit and to attend the balls they gave in their elegant mansion.

works [needlework]*, that you read to her, and that Edward goes to sleep.'*

She writes of dining with neighbours, and entertaining at home and of balls at Manydown and Kempshott Park. The Christmas Ball at Manydown was

' ... very thin, but by no means unpleasant. There were thirty-one people, and only eleven ladies out of the number, and but five single women in the room. Of the gentlemen present you may have some idea from the list of my partners – Mr. Wood, G. Lefroy, Rice, a Mr. Butcher (belonging to the Temples, a sailor and not of the 11th Light Dragoons), Mr. Temple (not the horrid one of all), Mr. Wm. Orde (cousin to the Kingsclere man), Mr. John Harwood, and Mr. Calland, who appeared as usual with his hat in his hand, and stood every now and then behind Catherine and me to

be talked about and abused for not dancing. We teased him, however, into it at last ... There were twenty dances, and I danced them all, and without fatigue ...'

At Lady Dorchester's, though hardly the belle of the ball she:

'spent a very pleasant evening, chiefly among the Manydown party. There was the same kind of supper as last year, and the same want of chairs. There were more dancers than the room could conveniently hold, which is enough to constitute a good ball at any time.

'I do not think I was very much in request. People were rather apt not to ask me till they could not help it; one's consequence, you know, varies so much at times without any particular reason. There was one gentleman, an officer of the Cheshire, a very good-looking young man, who, I was told,

Jane and Cassandra were 'perfect beauties, and of course gain hearts of dozens'. We can imagine Jane, just 23, as lively, attractive and flirtatious. A clerical friend of Mrs. Lefroy, the Rev. Samuel Blackall, was eager to make her better acquaintance at this time but his pomposity ruled out any hope of Jane being interested in a proposal. It is frustrating that we have no satisfactory portrait of her. Cassandra made a sketch (see page 7) from which an engraving was made for Edward Austen-Leigh's 1870 *A Memoir of Jane Austen* but it was only guardedly endorsed by the Austen relations so cannot be considered a good likeness. Brother Henry, in a biographical note published with *Northanger Abbey*, and written after her death, gave a more staid picture:

'Of personal attractions she possessed a considerable share. Her stature was that of true elegance. It could have been increased without exceeding the middle height. Her carriage and deportment were quiet, yet graceful. Her features were separately good. Their assemblage produced an unrivalled expression of the cheerfulness, sensibility, and benevolence, which were her real characteristics. Her complexion was of the finest texture. It might with truth be said, that her eloquent blood spoke through her modest cheek.'

This, perhaps, is Jane in her mature years and it certainly does not convey the true vivacity that comes through in her letters and novels.

In the spring of 1799, Jane was again enjoying the lively atmosphere of Bath. Edward Austen-Leigh was being troubled by incipient gout and had decided to try the waters as a cure. Accompanied by his wife and two eldest children, his mother and Jane, he took a house in Queen Square. The following year, while Cassandra was on a visit to Godmersham and Jane was staying with

Steventon Church dates back to the 12th century. Here, both Jane's father and her brother James preached as rectors, followed for a short time by brother Henry until her nephew William Knight was ready to take over the living. Beside the church was the home of the Digweeds, but the ancient manor house was destroyed in a 20th-century fire and only a Victorian block of servants' quarters survives.

wanted very much to be introduced to me; but as he did not want it quite enough to take much trouble in effecting it, we never could bring it about ...'

The mother of writer Mary Russell, whose family had been at the rectory before the Lefroys and then lived in nearby Alresford, described Jane Austen to her daughter as 'the prettiest, silliest, most affected, husband-hunting butterfly'. Cousin Eliza reported that the Lloyds at Ibthorpe after attending a ball, their parents decided to abandon Steventon and retire to Bath. The Rev. Austen was 70, but the decision seems to have been a sudden one for there had been plans to alter the Steventon garden. It is said that when Jane arrived back home, accompanied by Martha Lloyd, she was greeted by the news and promptly fainted with shock.

The interior of Steventon church.

BATH

Jane Austen had certainly enjoyed the shops, the entertainments and social life of her previous visits to Bath but she was very attached to the Hampshire home where she was born and grew up. Though she may not have had so strong an aversion to the city as her character Anne Elliot in *Persuasion* who persisted 'in a very determined, very silent, disinclination for Bath', she was not entirely happy with the move. James was set to take over his father's duties but he already had a well established household, and since the cost of transporting furniture and effects to Bath would be high it was decided to sell or leave behind many of their possessions. These included 500 books from the library and Jane's own pianoforte.

Jane tried her best to be enthusiastic about the imminent removal, putting on a brave front as soon as she had recovered from the news. By the beginning of 1801 she is writing to Cassandra:

'*My mother looks forward with as much certainty as you can do, to our keeping two maids — my father is the only one not in the secret. We plan having a steady cook, and a young giddy house-maid, with a sedate, middle-aged man, who is to undertake the double office of husband to the former and sweetheart to the latter. No children of course to be allowed on either side ...*

'*My mother bargains for having no trouble at all in furnishing our house in Bath — and I have engaged for your willingly undertaking to do it all. I get more and more reconciled to the idea of our removal. We have lived long enough in this neighbourhood, the Basingstoke balls are*

Pulteney Bridge and the Avon. The crescent of buildings just below the church on the hill is the Paragon.

Arriving in Bath.
'*When Lady Russell ... was entering Bath on a wet afternoon, and driving through the long course of streets from the Old Bridge to Camden-place, amidst the dash of other carriages, the heavy rumble of carts and drays, the bawling of newsmen, muffin-men and milkmen, and the ceaseless clink of pattens, she made no complaint. No, these were noises which belonged to the winter pleasures; her spirits rose under their influence; and, like Mrs. Musgrove, she was feeling, though not saying, that, after being long in the country, nothing could be so good for her as a little quiet cheerfulness.*
'*Anne did not share these feelings. She persisted in a very determined, though very silent, disinclination for Bath; caught the first dim view of the extensive buildings, smoking in rain, without any wish of seeing them better; felt their progress through the streets to be, however, disagreeable, yet too rapid; for who would be glad to see her when she arrived? And looked back, with fond regret, to the bustles of Uppercross and the seclusion of Kellynch.*'
Persuasion

FAR LEFT
The Paragon. Uncle James Leigh Perrot and his wife had lodgings at number 1 on the slope above Walcot Street and the Avon. Jane Austen came to stay with them there.

LEFT
Laura Place, an address which Jane Austen thought would be far too expensive for the family!

BELOW
The Countess of Huntingdon's chapel in the Paragon.

*certainly on the decline, there is something
interesting in the bustle of going away, and
the prospect of spending future summers
by the sea or in Wales is very delightful ...
It must not be generally known, however,
that I am not sacrificing a great deal in
quitting the country – or I can expect to
inspire no tenderness, no interest in those
we leave behind.'*

Where in Bath were they to live? 'In
what part of Bath do you mean to place
your bees?' writes Jane to Cassandra.
'We are afraid of the South Parade's
being too hot.'

At the beginning of May, Jane and
Mrs. Austen went to stay with the
Leigh Perrots in the Paragon in Bath to
begin their hunt for a house. Mr.
Austen went off to visit Edward in Kent
and then to London and Cassandra visited the Lloyds at Ibthorpe and the
Fowles at Kintbury, so deciding where
to live was largely left to them.

Jane wasted no time in beginning the
search. The day after her arrival she
walked to the Pump Room with her

uncle and looked at two houses in
Green Park Buildings on the way back,
'one of which pleased me very well'. A
week later she attended the last ball of
the season:

*'I dressed myself as well as I could, and
had all my finery much admired at home.
By nine o'clock my uncle, aunt and I
entered the rooms and linked Miss
Winstone on to us. Before tea it was rather
a dull affair; but then before tea did not
last long, for there was only one dance,
danced by four couple. Think of four couple,
surrounded by about an hundred people,
dancing in the Upper Rooms at Bath!*

*'After tea we cheered up; the breaking
up of private parties sent some scores more
to the ball, and tho' it was shockingly and
inhumanly thin for this place, there were
people enough to have made five or six very
pretty Basingstoke assemblies ...'*

The tail end of the season was not
providing the glamour and excitement
which one might expect of a fashionable
spa and which would have added con-
siderably to the social round. The night

after the ball was even more disappointing:

'Another stupid party ... perhaps, if larger they might be less intolerable, but here there were only just enough to make one card table, with six people to look on and talk nonsense to each other.'

Then came news of the sale of their possessions at Steventon rectory: eight guineas for tables, eight for Jane's pianoforte and sixty one and a half for three cows being some compensation for the low figure raised by the furniture; and their books apparently sold well too. Their severance from the old home now felt final. The search for the new one continued: 'The houses in the streets near Laura Place I should expect to be above our price,' Jane wrote to Cassandra, and it was at the opposite end of Great Pulteney Street, in Sydney Terrace, facing Sydney Gardens that they eventually took a house. Sydney Gardens, on the opposite side of the Avon from the centre of town, was then on the outskirts and

Royal Crescent, by John Wood the Younger, dates from 1767. It forms a 180-metre (600-foot) elipse of 30 houses, its 114 Ionic columns beneath a single cornice.

Queen's Square, where Edward Austen took number 13 in 1799 and Jane and her mother spent a midsummer holiday with him. It was built by John Wood the elder as his first great project in Bath, beginning in 1729. Jane found the view 'far more cheerful than the Paragon.'

RIGHT
14 Alfred Street. The iron balconies, railings and lamp holder at the entrance, with snuffers for the linkman's torches on either side, are typical of Bath.

overlooked open countryside. The Austens rented the house from the end of May 1801 and the family was reunited there in June.

Bath, when Jane Austen knew it, was no longer the highly fashionable resort it had been when Sheridan set his sparkling comedies there. The Prince Regent's interest in Brighton had made it more attractive to fashionable society since he had had the Royal Pavilion built in 1782 (rebuilding it in its present oriental style in 1817). It was closer to London and offered the diversions of a seaside town. Bath was fast becoming a health spa rather than a pleasure resort. It was a centre of solid respectability, eminently suitable for retirement homes for clergymen such as the Rev. Austen. A fitting resort for

the older generation, though still offering many attractions for the younger relatives who might visit or accompany them, it was no longer the magnet for the highly sophisticated upper classes which it had been when Beau Nash presided as the main arbiter of taste.

Bath takes its name from a bathing place fed by the hot springs which still bubble out of the earth beneath the modern Pump Room. Since long before the Romans came to Britain, the waters have seeped down through the earth where they have been heated to a temperature of 46.5 C (120 F) before being forced upwards and emerging at the rate of about 1,137,000 litres (250,000 gallons) a day. Here, where the mineral-laden water stained the earth red and where considerable heat was produced even when the land was frozen solid in winter, the Celts of Iron Age Britain worshipped their sun god Sul.

Legend has it that the discovery that water from Sul's spring had healing

Abbey Square with the façade of the Pump Room on the left. The Greek inscription on the architrave can be translated 'Water is best'.

properties was made about 500 B.C. by a prince called Bladud, according to legend the father of Shakespeare's King Lear, who was banished from court for being a leper. Farmers in the Avon valley took pity on him and gave him work as a swineherd. One day he noticed that some of his pigs, who were affected with a skin disease, were wallowing in the hot mud around the spring to emerge suddenly cured. He too, entered the muddy waters and his leprosy was cured. He returned to his father's court and, when he in turn became king, founded a city where the springs rose from the earth.

City or not, the mineral springs were known long before the Romans arrived following the invasion by the armies of the Emperor Claudius in A.D. 43. When the Romans came they probably set up a military fort by the loop of the Avon where the trackway from Wales to London and the ancient Fosse Way crossed. But with their realization of the benign medicinal properties of Aquae Sulis an important centre was born with recreational baths on a major scale. By the last quarter of the first century, Bath had its first stone buildings. The Roman city was not large – about 9 hectares (22 acres) and everything was dwarfed by the baths, which were the largest of their kind in western Europe. There were three great plunge and swimming baths. The largest, now

OPPOSITE
Bath Abbey.
There was a Benedictine monastery here in Saxon times followed after the Norman conquest by the huge cathedral. The present church, no bigger than the Norman nave, dates from the beginning of the 16th century.

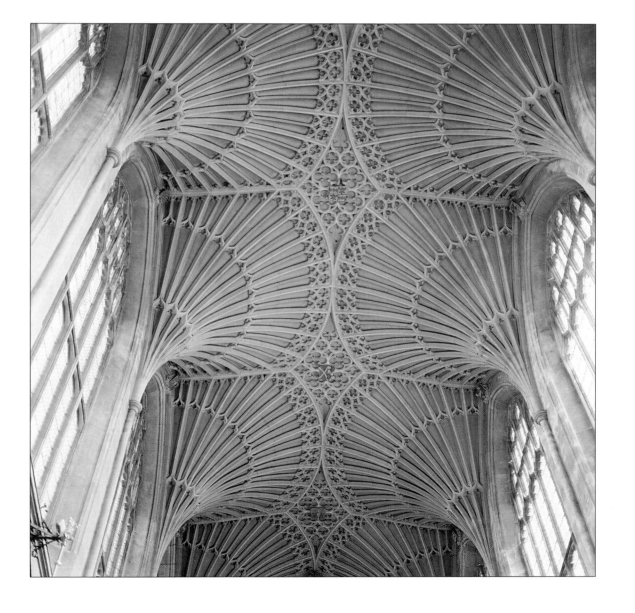

The fan-vaulted roof of Bath Abbey.

OPPOSITE
The Great Bath, the heart of the
ancient bath complex. The pillars
and statues above the parapet are
late 19th century work, not Roman.
Only the square pillar bases
and the bath itself are ancient
though the lead lining of the bath
itself survives.

the Great Bath, was at first open to the air with alcoved colonnades, but later it was roofed by a great tunnel vault with a span of over 10 metres (35 feet) with open lunettes at each end to allow steam to escape. Later, there were hot baths of the hammam type at both ends of the building, though it is not known whether there were any included in the original building.

The Celtic goddess Sul became assimilated with the Roman Minerva and as Sul-Minerva became the presiding spirit of the temple. Its pediment with a disc bearing the head of Sul surrounded by Gorgon-like hair or flames and the flowing robes of the supporting Victories makes this the masterpiece of Romano-Celtic sculpture in Britain. It was supported on columns with fine-cut capitals and entablature and there was a restrainedly beautiful cult statue of the goddess of which the gilded-bronze head survives. One votive dedication discovered in the excavations suggests that Gallic sculptors were among those working here for it bears the inscription

of a stone-mason from the neighbourhood of Chartres in modern France. Many other fine examples of provincial Roman art have been found in Bath. Among them are figured panels of the four seasons, a coping depicting a mastiff biting a stag, a pewter candelabra in the form of a stag and a pewter figure of a water deity with a painted beard and moustache, similar to the shield of the pediment bearing an ambiguous head of what is possibly Sul-Minerva but which might perhaps be another deity.

It was not only work that brought foreign artists and craftsman to Bath. The spa attracted pilgrims and those seeking to be healed of their bodily ills. Excavations enable the modern visitor to see the sacrificial altar sited on the precinct of the temple, and the steps which led up to the temple itself. In the museum can be seen the votive offerings, coins, inscriptions, memorials and artefacts which were found. Almost nothing of this was known to Jane Austen. It had lain buried for more than a thousand years. Workmen digging a

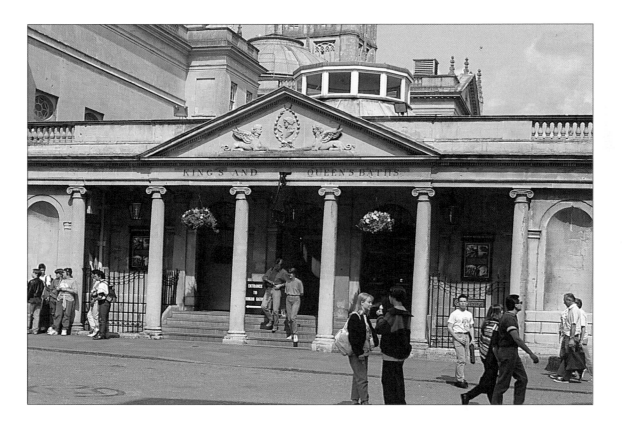

The entrance to the King's and
Queen's Baths.

sewer in Stall Street had unearthed the head of the statue of Sul-Minerva in 1727 and more discoveries were made in the 1750s; but it was not until 1878 that the city engineer, investigating a leak under the King's Bath, discovered the great Roman Bath, still lined with lead from the Mendip Hills. Lead was a metal with which the Romans were familiar but in Bath they found an unusual mineral, a curious black fuel burning on the altars of the goddess 'which did not waste away but turned to

RIGHT
A carving of a river or sea god found on the temple site.

LEFT
The Great Bath was probably used
for both immersion and swimming.
The stone platform (left foreground)
makes an effective diving board.

with the withdrawal of the Romans, there would have been no experienced engineers sufficiently capable of carrying out repairs to structural damage which led to the sinking of masonry and cracking of columns. The once famous watering place became buried beneath layers of earth and the fine Roman town forgotten.

The hot springs were rediscovered in the 12th century and, by the 16th century, three baths were in use: the medieval Cross Bath (in Bath Street), the nearby Hot Bath and the King's Bath by the Pump Room. Those with skin complaints used the Cross Bath: the King's Bath tended to be more frequented by gentlefolk.

It was the visit of Anne of Denmark, the consort of James I, early in the 17th century which began the development of Bath as an increasingly popular resort for the rich and ailing. The waters were being recommended for drinking as well as bathing – the royal physician at the court of Charles II even prescribed them. In the same reign, diarist Samuel Pepys, who tried the waters in 1668, saw the crowd of people in the King's Bath, and thought 'it cannot be clean to go so many bodies together in the same water.'

At some point the waters gained a reputation for making barren women fertile and James II's childless queen, Mary of Modena, made a visit and spent some time in the Cross Bath, after which she conceived. There was much celebration and a pillar was erected in the centre of the bath.

A visit from Queen Anne really put Bath on the map as a fashionable venue and, during the 18th century the town rapidly expanded, its population increasing from not much more than 3,000 to ten times that amount by the time the Austens took up residence at Sydney Terrace. Not long after Queen

stony lumps': Somerset cannel coal.

Rome withdrew many of its legions from Britain after A.D. 383 and by 410 Britain had ceased to be part of the Roman Empire. Aquae Sulis was by then fortified with a defensive wall, built towards the end of the Roman period: but the pattern of Roman life had begun to disintegrate, though it was not until 550 that Aquae Sulis was engulfed by the spread of the invading Saxons. A change towards a wetter climate was responsible for flooding the baths and,

BELOW
Inside the Pump Room the waters
could be sampled from a fountain
in the centre of the long wall. In the
alcove to the left stands a statue of
Beau Nash above a clock made by
Thomas Tompion, who presented it
to the city in 1709, together with a
sundial to check its accuracy. The
alcove at the opposite end has a
gallery for musicians. Today, there
are sedan chairs in the room. In
Jane Austen's time the streets
would have been full of them,
a pair of chairmen, front and
rear carrying them by the shafts
to transport their client about
the town.

Anne's visit, Daniel Defoe was describing Bath as 'the resort of the sound as well as the sick, and a place that helps the indolent and the gay to commit that worst of all murders – to kill time.'

The focus of the life of fashionable Bath was a man called Richard Nash who arrived in 1705 and made a huge win of £1,000 at the gaming tables. In his 31 years he had been at Oxford, in the Guards and enrolled at the Inner Temple he had failed to achieve any distinction: but in Bath he became Master of Ceremonies for the Corporation, officiating from the time of Queen Anne through the reigns of the first two Georges.

'Beau' Nash, as he became known, made Bath synonymous with good taste and high fashion, drawing the élite of English society to take the waters and attend the balls and assemblies which he organized. He ensured that the Corporation kept the roads in good repair, the streets paved and provided with lamps. He issued licences to carriers of sedan chairs and endeavoured to control their prices; he forbad the wearing of swords inside the city, banned riding boots from the ballrooms and prohibited smoking in the public rooms as a habit disrespectful and unpleasant to the ladies. He encouraged the building of the fine Assembly Rooms and engaged an orchestra of talented musicians from London. When he died, aged 87, in 1761 he had lost most of his money through debts and lawsuits and new legislation against public gambling put an end to the lucrative profits he had made from it. But, though he died in near poverty, the city gave him a magnificent funeral, in acknowledgement of its debt to him. Novelist and playwright Oliver Goldsmith, in the biography he published the following year declared that he had 'too much merit not to become remarkable, yet too much folly to arrive at greatness'. You can see his statue in the Pump Room and next to the Theatre Royal in Sawclose is the house in which he lived. It is now a restaurant named after his mistress, Juliana Papjoy.

The increase in the number of visitors to Bath was partly due to improvements in roads and transport and in its turn justified the rebuilding of the city in a grand style providing a standard of comfort worthy of the expectations of its fashionable new residents and visitors.

A largely Elizabethan town was swept away in a building boom inspired by Richard Allen, who arrived in Bath about 1710 as an assistant in the postal service. He was responsible for developing the nationwide postal routes, making himself a fortune in the process, and bought the Combe Down quarries south of the city to provide raw material for rebuilding. London architects had declared Bath stone useless, so to prove them wrong he built his own house in York Street and later his mansion, Prior Park, south of Bath. He built it in the Palladian style which was greatly enhanced by the beauty of the stone. The architect for both was John Wood, a Yorkshireman, who had been in Bath since 1727 and who, with his son, was responsible for Bath's classical appearance. His first major city project was Queen Square, begun in 1729. His masterpiece, the Circus, was not started until 1754, the year he died, and was completed by his son, also called John, who continued to transform the city with developments such as Royal Crescent and the Assembly Rooms.

In 1771, Pulteney Bridge was built to the design of Robert Adam, to link the city with the new suburb of Bathwick across the river, where Sydney Gardens were laid out in 1795. It was overlooking these classical

In the Pump Room.
'Mr. Tilney did not appear. Every creature, except himself, was to be seen in the room at different periods of the fashionable hours; crowds of people were every moment passing in and out, up the steps and down; people whom nobody cared about, and nobody wanted to see; and he only was absent. "What a delightful place Bath is," said Mrs. Allen, as they sat down near the great clock, after parading the room till they were tired; "and how pleasant it would be if we had any acquaintance here." '
Northanger Abbey

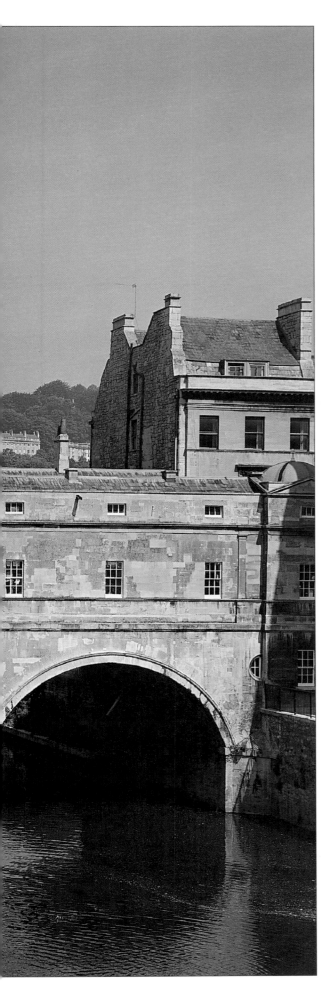

pavilions that the Austens took a house. The following year, higher up the hill above Royal Crescent, another Bath architect, John Palmer, started to build Landsdowne Crescent.

Bath at its zenith was the setting for plays by Richard Brinsley Sheridan, and novels by Tobias Smollett and Henry Fielding. Its heyday was long past when Jane Austen knew it and in describing some of its inhabitants she is gently critical of those who are not *quite* from the top drawer of fashion as they imagine themselves to be.

In several of her novels Bath plays a peripheral role and in two it is the main location. It is here that she sets more than half of *Northanger Abbey*, although, in its early form as *Susan*, it was probably written before her visit to Edward's family in 1799. She would no doubt have already heard much about life there and amendments based on her own experience may have been made before it was first offered for publication in 1803 to Crosby and Son. It was sold

ABOVE
The Circus, dating from 1745, was John Wood's masterpiece: it is 97 metres (318 ft) across, and built in three sections, each of eleven houses. The façades are embellished with tiers of Doric, Ionic and Corinthian columns and a frieze on the entablature of the ground floor tier features 365 motifs symbolizing the arts and sciences.

LEFT
Pulteney Bridge, built to the design of Robert Adam in 1771, links the centre of the city with the suburb of Bathwick with the gracious mansions at Laura Place (where Lady Dalrymple lived in *Persuasion*) via Great Pulteney Street (where Catherine Morland stays with the Allens in *Northanger Abbey*), to Sydney Gardens where the Austens decided to make their Bath home.

The New, or Upper Assembly Rooms were built by John Wood the Younger between 1769-71. They consist of two elegant blocks on Bennet Street and Alfred Street with the octagonal card room and antechambers between them, with the entrance portico and vestibule on the open piazza to the west. Harrison's Rooms, on the site of what are now the Parade Gardens between the Abbey and the River Avon, were the original Assembly Rooms, where Beau Nash presided. Jane Austen knew them as the Lower Rooms. Their prestige declined after the opening of the new Upper Rooms in 1771. The Upper Rooms are still the setting for balls, concerts and public events, as they were 200 years ago. They were restored by the National Trust in the 1930s, re-opened in 1938 but were gutted by incendiary bombs during one of the heavy air raids on Bath during the Second World War.

Restored to their former magnificence with their original chandeliers, which had fortunately been in store elsewhere during the war, they re-opened in 1963, the basement areas being turned into a Museum of Costume.

OPPOSITE
Sally Lunn's house (1482), the oldest in Bath, although its façade dates only from the 17th century.

RIGHT
Milsom Street, with Beechen Cliff in the distance. Then as now it was a smart shopping street. In *Northanger Abbey* the Tilneys lived there, while Edgar's Buildings, where Jane Austen's Thorpes had their home, faces its top end on the other side of George Street.

for £10, the arrangement being made by a Mr. Seymour, probably an associate of Henry Austen, who was placing the book on his sister's behalf. The publisher advertised it as a two-volume novel but it never appeared – perhaps he saw Jane's parody of the gothick novel, examples of which already featured strongly in his list, as an attack on the genre which was best suppressed.

There was great disappointment, even resentment, that it did not appear.

When, nearly ten years after her residence in Bath she wrote *Persuasion,* she set almost all the story in the city, creating a picture of life there which shows how clearly she remembered her years in the city.

Although the Austens had made their home in Bath, moving in 1804

'... the important evening came which was to usher her [Catherine] into the Upper Rooms. Her hair was cut and dressed by the best hand, her clothes put on with care... Mrs. Allen was so long in dressing, that they did not enter the room till late. The season was full, the room crowded, and the two ladies squeezed as well as they could. As for Mr. Allen, he repaired directly to the card-room, and left them to enjoy the mob by themselves. With more care for the safety of her new gown than for the comfort of her protegée, Mrs. Allen made her way through the throng of men by the door, as swiftly as the necessary caution would allow; Catherine, however, kept close at her side, and linked her arm too firmly to her friend's to be torn asunder by any common effort of a struggling assembly. But to her utter astonishment she found that to proceed along the room was by no means the way to disengage themselves from the crowd; it seemed rather to increase as they went on, whereas she had imagined that when once fairly within the door, they should easily find seats and be able to watch the dances with perfect convenience. But this was far from being the case, and though by unwearied diligence they gained even the top of the room, their situation was just the same; they saw nothing of the dancers but the high feathers of some of the ladies. Still they moved on – something better was yet in view; and by a continued exertion of strength and ingenuity they found themselves at last in the passage behind the highest bench. Here there was something less of crowd than below; and hence Miss Morland had a comprehensive view of the company beneath her, and of all the dangers of her late passage through them. It was a splendid sight and she began, for the first time that evening, to feel herself at a ball ...'

Northanger Abbey

RIGHT
Beacon Hill, the heights above the Paragon, where Jane Austen went walking on a summer day in 1799:

'We took a very charming walk from 6 to 8 up Beacon Hill, and across some fields to the village of Charlcombe, which is sweetly situated in a little green valley, as a village with such a name ought to be.'

Letter to Cassandra, 2nd June.

BELOW
Charlcombe Church dates back to Norman times and tradition says that it was once the mother church of Bath.

to 27 Green Park Buildings on the opposite side of the city, they did not spend all their time there. In the summer of 1802 they took a holiday at Dawlish and Teignmouth. In 1804 they stayed at Lyme Regis, and Jane made visits to James at Steventon, to Edward at Godmersham, to friends at Great Bookham and possibly to see her brother Frank at Ramsgate where he was in charge of raising defensive troops to face the possibility of French invasion.

During one of these holidays, Jane is thought to have formed a deep attachment to a young man whom she might have married if he had not died soon after the initial flowering of their acquaintance.

On one of her visits back to Steventon in 1802, while staying with the Bigg-Wither family at Manydown, Harris the 21-year old son of their host proposed to Jane, six years his senior, and was accepted by her. Next morning she changed her mind and insisted that her brother James drive them straight back to Bath.

LEFT
An evening view of Bath from the top of Beechen Cliff on the south of the city on the other side of the Avon, where Catherine, in *Northanger Abbey*, eventually walked with Eleanor and Henry Tilney and listened to their talk of landscape painting. Although Bath is now more extensively and densely built, there was then little building on this side of the river. Today, parks and trees retain some of the feeling of space and the open countryside beyond.

In *Northanger Abbey*, Jane Austen described Beechen Cliff as: '*that noble hill, whose beautiful verdure and hanging coppice render it so striking an object from almost every opening in Bath...*'

47

RIGHT
Camden Crescent, which Jane Austen calls Camden Place, is high above the city, beyond the Paragon and the Upper Rooms, though within a short stroll of them.

'Sir Walter had taken a very good house in Camden-place, a lofty dignified situation, such as becomes a man of consequence ... they had the pleasure of assuring her ... undoubtedly the best in Camden-place; their drawing-rooms had many decided advantages over all the others which they had seen or heard of; and the superiority was not less in the style of the fitting-up, or the taste of the furniture. Their acquaintance was exceeding sought after. Everybody was wanting to visit them. They had drawn back from many introductions, and still were perpetually having cards left by people of whom they knew nothing.'
Persuasion

TOP FAR RIGHT
The Holburne of Menstrie Museum, in Sydney Gardens, near the Austen house in Sydney Terrace, was a tavern with a ballroom, card rooms and coffee room when Jane Austen lived in a house overlooking the gardens. These were popular pleasure gardens, with music and fireworks to enjoy on gala nights.

Gay Street, where Jane lived for a few months at number 25 in 1805.

The families were close, the match seemed a good one: whatever had made Jane accept, then change her mind? She had known the young man for some years, even though she may never have thought of him as a future husband. 'Single women have a dreadful propensity for being poor – which is one very strong argument in favour of matrimony,' she wrote in one of her letters and perhaps she did feel that it was time to put an end to her spinsterhood. But why the panic next day? Could it be that she bitterly remembered her experience of the previous year? She may have thought of Cassandra, who seems to have rejected the idea of marriage to anyone else after the death of Tom Lefroy, thinking that no one could measure up to him: either of these factors may have caused her to change her mind.

In Bath in 1803 or 1804, Jane began *The Watsons*, a novel with a Surrey setting which she abandoned unfinished, perhaps because of the disruption in her life at this time: perhaps because she was not satisfied with it. She does not appear to have embarked on any new work for some years, disillusioned no doubt, by the non-appearance of her novel from Crosby and Company.

The move to Green Park Buildings brought the Austens closer to the Pump Room making it more convenient for Mr. Austen to take the waters, for he was intermittently troubled by a feverish complaint and was now unable to walk without a stick. They were not to be there long for on 19 January 1805 he felt unwell and, although next morning was fit enough to breakfast with the family, he collapsed and died the following day. He was buried in the crypt of St. Swithin's, at the corner of Walcot Street and the Paragon, the church where he had been married.

Mr. Austen's death left the family income sadly depleted. To supplement what little was provided for Mrs. Austen they used the interest which Cassandra received on her bequest from Tom Lefroy: but Jane had no resources of her own. Their brothers made contributions which brought their income up to about £460 per annum: £50 each from James, Henry and Frank and the balance from Edward. They moved to 25 Gay Sreet and reduced their staff from a man and two maids to just one maid – though the house itself was in a somewhat smarter district. Martha Lloyd's mother died in April and it was arranged that she should leave Ibthorpe and become part of the household, staying with them until her marriage as second wife to Francis in 1828.

The following year the Austens resided at another address in Trim Street and in June 1806, much to Jane's satisfaction, they left the city, travelling first to Clifton, then to Adelstrop, Stoneleigh Abbey and Southampton where they stayed with brother Frank and his wife in lodgings while looking for a house that they all could share.

'They made their appearance in the Lower Rooms; and here fortune was more favourable to our heroine. The master of the ceremonies introduced to her a very gentlemanlike young man as a partner; – his name was Tilney. He seemed to be about four or five and twenty, was rather tall, had pleasing countenance, a very intelligent and lively eye, and, if not quite handsome, was very near it. His address was good, and Catherine felt herself in high luck. There was little leisure for speaking while they danced; but when they were seated at tea, she found him as agreeable as she had already given him credit for being.'
Northanger Abbey

The Lower Rooms were destroyed by a fire in 1820. They stood near North Parade where gardens now slope down to the River Avon.

BELOW
Many Bath street names are elegantly carved directly on to the dressed stone.

SOUTHAMPTON

In January 1805 Jane wrote to her brother Frank, on *H.M.S. Leopard*, which she heard was due in Portsmouth, to inform him of their father's death and a week later to tell him that their mother had found a compass and sundial among her husband's possessions which she wanted him to have as a keepsake, such astronomical instruments being of particular use to a sailor. In Ramsgate, in 1803, Frank had met a young woman called Mary Gibson and became engaged to her, though his prospects were not then secure enough to embark on marriage; but marry they did in July 1806 in Ramsgate, and they then settled in Southampton where it was decided his mother, sisters and Martha Lloyd should come to live with them, Southampton being chosen for it proximity to Portsmouth and its convenience for him when ashore.

Francis Austen, 20 months Jane's senior, had progressed well in the Royal Navy. He had seen service in home waters, the Mediterranean and the East Indies, and had had the command of ships since 1798, having been made captain in 1800. He captured a French brig off Marseilles, helped blockade Cadiz, and in 1804 was appointed to *H.M.S. Leopard*, flagship of Rear-Admiral Louis, blockading Boulogne. In 1805 he was given *H.M.S. Canopus*, again with Louis, Nelson's second-in-command. But though he met Nelson on the *Victory*, and followed him across the Atlantic in pursuit of the French fleet, Nelson decided to send the *Canopus* to Gibraltar to take aboard water and provisions and caused Frank, much to his regret, to miss the Battle of Trafalgar. Now after taking part in the Battle of St. Domingo he was ashore, married, and waiting for a new posting.

On 10 October 1806, the Austen ladies moved into lodgings with Frank and Mary in Southampton. It took a little time to find a suitable house but they eventually decided to rent one of the largest houses in Castle Square in the north-east of the city. Their landlord was Lord Lansdowne, who had bought the square in which the remains of the keep of a Norman castle had stood, and had built for himself a turretted mansion rather like a Disneyland castle. Here he now lived with his new bride, a middle-aged, well upholstered and over-dressed Irish widow whose carriage, a phaeton was drawn by six or eight ponies

'each pair decreasing in size, and becoming lighter in colour, through all the grades of dark brown, light brown, bay and chestnut, as it was laced further from the carriage. The two leading pairs were managed by two boyish postillions.'

This is how James's son James Edward remembered them when he wrote his *Memoir* of his aunt. The comings and goings of their aristocratic neighbours and their fanciful home supplied plenty of scope for the Austen wit and sense of invention.

In February 1807, Jane wrote to Cassandra reporting that 'alterations and improvements ... advance very properly' and teasing her that if she did not come back to help with all the things they had to buy, Frank and Mary would deliberately get 'knives that will not cut, glasses that will not hold, a sofa without a seat, and a bookcase without shelves'.

There was a good size garden which ended at the old city wall which was easily accessible by steps allowing for walks along the fortifications. The garden was being

' ...put in order, by a Man who bears a remarkable good character, has a very fine complexion and asks something less than the first. The shrubs which border the gravel walk he says are only sweetbriar and roses, and the latter of an indifferent sort; – we mean to get a few of a better kind therefore, and at my own particular desire he procures us some Syringas. I could not do without a Syringa, for the sake of Cowper's Line. — We talk also of a Laburnam. — The Border under the Terrace Wall is clearing away to receive Currants and Gooseberry Bushes, and a spot is found very proper for Raspberries.'

All was ready for them to move in on 9 March.

Even in lodgings there had been visits from the James Austens and with Frank's naval contacts there were many new people to meet. 'Our acquaintances increase too fast,' wrote Jane early in the year. As well as private entertaining there were the Assembly Rooms and a theatre in Southampton, and balls were also held in the Long Room of the Dolphin Hotel. An increasingly active social life was developing and with Mary and Martha part of the household and available to keep Mrs. Austen company, it was

The Bargate, Southampton, the north entrance to the old walled town, was built by the Normans in the 12th century. The Austen house was not far away in Castle Square.

ABOVE
Arrivals entering the public
assembly rooms before a ball. The
picture is by Rolinda Sharples
(1794-1838).

easier for Jane and Cassandra to make visits to Edward at Godmersham, Henry in London and elsewhere.

Of course there were tedious acquaintances as well as lively ones, though Jane's letters seem to place an emphasis on the former appreciating them for their comic value:

' ... *at seven o'clock, Mrs. Harrison, her two daughters and two Visitors, with Mr. Debary and his eldest sister walked in; and our Labour was not a great deal shorter than poor Elizabeth's* [Mrs. Edward Austen had just given birth to her eleventh child], *for it was past eleven before we were delivered. A second pool of*

Commerce, and all the longer by the addition of the two girls, who during the first had one corner of the Table and Spillikens to themselves, was the ruin of us ...'

Thus she wrote to Cassandra on 1 October 1808. A party just before Christmas seems to have been a disaster too, for it

' ... *produced nothing more remarkable than Miss Murden's coming too, though she had declined it absolutely in the morning, and sitting very ungraciously and very silent with us from seven o'clock till half after eleven, for so late was it, owing to the chairmen, before we got rid of them.*

'The last hour, spent in a yawning and

A Ball in Southampton.

'*Our ball was rather more amusing than I expected. Martha liked it very much, and I did not gape till the last quarter of an hour. It was past nine before we were sent for, and not twelve when we returned. The room was tolerably full, and there were perhaps thirty couple of dancers. The melancholy part was to see so many dozen young women standing by without partners, and each of them with two ugly naked shoulders!*

It was the same room in which we danced fifteen years ago! I thought it all over – and in spite of the shame of being so much older [she was just short of her 33rd birthday], *felt with thankfulness that I was quite as happy now as then. We paid an additional shilling for our tea, which we took as we chose in an adjoining and very comfortable room. There were only four dances, and it went to my heart that the Miss Lances (one of them, too, named Emma!) should have partners for only two. You will not expect to hear that I was asked to dance – but I was – by the gentleman whom we met* that Sunday *with Captain d'Auvergne. We have always kept a bowing acquaintance since, and being pleased with his black eyes, I spoke to him at the ball, which brought on me this civility; but I do not know his name, and he seems so little at home in the English language, that I believe his black eyes may be the best of him ...*'

Letter to Cassandra
9th December 1808

The West Gate, Southampton, from inside the walls. The garden of the Austens' house was against the ancient city walls.

shivering in a wide circle around the fire, was dull enough, but the tray had admirable success. The widgeon and the preserved ginger were as delicious as one could wish.'

Only two weeks after they moved to Castle Square, Frank received the captaincy of *H.M.S. St Albans*, then at Sheerness, and consequently was not at home for the birth of his first child, Mary Jane, on 27 April. Soon he was off escorting vessels of the East India Company to China. The following year he was accompanying ships carrying troops to Portugal for the Peninsular War – and at the beginning of the next year was evacuating some of them after the Battle of Corunna and was at Spithead for their disembarkation. When he took lodgings more convenient for his duties in Yarmouth on the Isle of Wight, the Austen ladies and Martha

Lloyd were left with the large new house to themselves. It was too big and too expensive and a further move was discussed.

Edward came to the rescue. He had a suitable house near Godmersham, Kent and on his second estate near Alton, in the northern part of Hampshire there was another house which was available. They could have their choice. After much deliberation they chose Chawton Cottage in Hampshire.

In the autumn of 1808, Cassandra went to Godmersham to help her sister-in-law Elizabeth with the birth of her eleventh child, though she arrived just too late for the birth. When the baby was only ten days old, its mother died. Her eldest daughter, 15-year-old Fanny, of whom Jane was particularly fond, and the younger children were at

home but the two eldest sons were at Winchester School. They were taken to stay with James's children at Steventon and then to Southampton before returning to school.

Despite the sadness surrounding their visit Jane found her nephews engaging company, taking them on excursions, playing games of spillikins, bilboquet and cards, telling riddles and conundrums, making paper ships and bombarding them with horse-chestnuts brought from Steventon.

'We had a little water party yesterday; I and my two nephews went from the Itchen Ferry up to Northam, where we landed, looked into the 74 [naval vessel with 74 guns]*, and walked home ... I had not proposed doing more than cross the Itchen ... but it proved so pleasant, and so much to the satisfaction of all, that when we reached the middle of the stream we agreed to be rowed up the river; both the boys rowed great part of the way, and their questions and remarks, as well as their enjoyment, were very amusing ...'*

Netley Abbey, though they did not reach it on that occasion, was a favourite excursion, whether by water or by foot and ferry: a comfortable five kilometres (three miles) there and back. Another favourite walk was along the old town walls which edged the bottom of the Castle Square garden.

Jane seems to have liked the Southampton neighbourhood but the move to yet another new home after only two years does not seem to have disturbed her, once she knew that they were returning to the Hampshire countryside. Meanwhile, she determined to make the most of Southampton's attractions. At the beginning of December she wrote to

The Saluting Platform at Portsmouth. Jane probably went there to see her sailor brothers and their vessels. She sets part of *Mansfield Park* here.

Cassandra:

'A larger circle of acquaintance and an increase of amusement is quite in character with our approaching removal. Yes – I mean to go to as many Balls as possible, that I may have a good bargain. Everybody is very much concerned at our going away, and everybody is acquainted with Chawton and speaks of it as a remarkably pretty village; and everybody knows the House we describe ...'

There was one last ball in Southampton at the end of January:

'We were very well entertained, and could have staid longer but for the arrival of my List shoes to convey me home, and I did not like to keep them waiting in the cold. The room was tolerably full, and the Ball opened by Miss Glyn; the Miss Lances had partners, Capt. D'Auvergne's friend appeared in regimentals, Caroline Maitland had an officer to flirt with, and Mr. John Harrison was deputed by Capt. Smith, being himself absent, to ask me to dance. Everything went well you see, especially after we had tucked Mrs. Lance's neckerchief in behind, and fastened it with a pin.'

The anticipated return to a country home seems to have stimulated Jane's interest in writing again. Shortly before departing Castle Square, under the pseudonym Mrs. Ashton Davies, she wrote to Crosby and Company enquiring after the still unpublished *Susan* and offering a copy of the manuscript should the original have been lost and declaring that if the offer were unacceptable she would feel at liberty to offer the book elsewhere. Crosby wrote back that his company was not bound to publish the book but would take action if anyone else did, though she could buy back the manuscript for the same sum they had paid for it: £10.

Admiral Horatio Nelson's flagship *H.M.S. Victory*, on which he died at the battle of Trafalgar, in its dry dock in Portsmouth naval dockyard which features in *Mansfield Park*. Francis Austen served under Nelson and narrowly missed being at Trafalgar.

CHAWTON

Chawton Cottage was chosen for the Austen ladies' new home partly because the widowed Edward would in future be able to spend at least part of the year at Chawton Manor House, though it had been let until 1812. Another reason was that Henry had established a branch of his banking firm at Alton and his business would take him there. More particularly, perhaps, the balance of choice was tipped by a general affection for Hampshire – 'the Hampshire-born Austens' Jane called their branch of the family – and relative proximity to their old home and friends around Steventon,

Chawton Cottage, Jane Austen's house from July 1809. This is the garden side of the house.

'Chawton' Cottage, Jane Austen's home from July 1809. The front door opens straight into the living room. Edward had the window to the left blocked and turned into a bookcase, opening up a new window on the side wall.

where James still lived. They may also have thought that being on Edward's doorstep at Godmersham they would have been too drawn into the life of the big house rather than being able to revolve in a milieu of their own choice.

Chawton is a small village about a kilometre and a half (one mile) southwest of the town of Alton on the road to Winchester. The cottage, which had formerly been tenanted by Edward Austen's steward, was larger than the word suggests. Standing at the end of the village street, it was near the junction of the road to Gosport with the road from Southampton and Winchester to London. Indeed, it may

previously have been a coaching inn. A large pond (now drained) was set in the angle between the roads which carried a considerable amount of traffic. One of Jane's nieces later remembered how comforting it was 'to have the awful stillness of night frequently broken by the sound of many passing carriages, which seemed sometimes even to shake the bed': not a sentiment which most people would share today, but even Mrs. Austen seemed to have enjoyed the frequent traffic on the road outside.

Once the decision to come to Chawton had been made, the move could not be immediate but some changes were put in hand. Both sitting-

rooms had windows looking out onto the road, and that of the large room to the left of the front door was blocked up and the space turned into a bookcase, a new window being cut in the side wall to look out over turf and trees towards the fence and hedge which hid the Winchester road. The garden is smaller today but the house does not appear to be greatly changed.

At the beginning of December Jane was writing to Cassandra:

'We want to be settled at Chawton in time for Henry to come to us for some shooting, in October at least; not a little earlier, and Edward may visit us after taking his boys back to Winchester [at the start of the autumn term]; *suppose we name the 4th of September?'*

She was looking forward to the move, determined to buy a piano instead of renting one as she had in Bath and Southampton ' ... as good a one as can be got for thirty guineas, and I will practise country dances, that we may have some amusement for out nephews and nieces, when we have the pleasure of their company.' Mrs. Knight saw the bachelor rector of Chawton as a marriage prospect for Jane and she joked back 'depend upon it that I *will* marry Mr. Papillon, whatever may be his reluctance or my own.'

In fact they moved in in July, after

Chawton Cottage, the general living-room. Here Jane Austen is thought to have written many of her novels, probably working on the table with a sheet of blotting paper under which she could quickly hide the page if someone, unaware of her writing, surprised her. She wrote on small sheets of paper, folding ordinary sheets of writing paper in half until she had a number of them to make fascicles of 32, 48 or 80 pages, stitched to form small booklets to give her a sense of her novel coming into being.

Water for tea was heated in a copper kettle on the grate hob. The cupboards to the left of the fireplace were used for storing groceries such as tea and sugar which it was Jane's responsibility to order.

Chawton Cottage, the drawing-room. The pianoforte is similar to the one Jane Austen owned. She began each day with piano practice.

the month Frank and Mary's first son was born and Jane wrote a congratulatory verse which read:

'As for ourselves, we're very well;
As unaffected prose will tell. –
Cassandra's pen will paint our state,
The many comforts that await
Our Chawton home, how much we find
Already in it, to our mind;
And how convinced, that when complete
It will all other Houses beat
That ever have been made or mended,
With rooms concise, or rooms distended.
You'll find us very snug next year,
Perhaps with Charles and Fanny near,
For now it often does delight us
To fancy them just over-right us.'

There were six bedrooms, enough to house visiting relations, though Jane and Cassandra probably shared a bedroom. The building is an L-shape, the longer arm parallel with the road. The room to the right, looking from the road, was entered directly from the street. Here, a few months after they moved in, a traveller passing the window in a post-chaise reported to Mrs. Knight that he had seen 'the Chawton party looking very comfortable at breakfast'.

This is the room in which Jane was to return to her writing and much of her published work was written or revised here, on her mahogany desk by the front door or even on the dining-table. Though callers could see her writing through the window she insisted that the creaky door leading to the rest of the house should not be oiled so that she would have some warning of people coming in and could slip her writing out of sight under her blotting paper, thus keeping her writing a secret from strangers. The other front room, with its blocked window, was the more

Chawton Cottage. The bedroom which Jane Austen used, or perhaps shared with her sister Cassandra.

formal drawing-room. Upstairs, Jane's room was on the left at the top of the stairs; her mother had the room across the corridor with two large windows looking out onto the road. There were dormer-windowed rooms above and more rooms in the rear wing for Martha, the servants and visitors. There was a well in the yard behind and beyond that a bakehouse with an oven and a wash-boiler.

At Chawton, Cassandra and Jane became increasingly responsible for running the household. Mrs. Austen, now 70, devoted herself mainly to needlework and gardening. When both daughters were at home it was Jane's responsibility to make breakfast and to order tea, sugar and wine stores. Cassandra took care of everything else.

When Jane came down in the morning she would start the day by practising on her piano so as not to disturb the others later on. She would then put the kettle on and make breakfast. There were rustic benches in the garden for when they preferred to sit outside but in the afternoon, weather permitting, she and Cassandra would usually go for a walk, to shop in Alton, to visit a neighbour or to simply enjoy the countryside.

Chawton House – the 'Great House' as the Austens called it, is only a short way along the road towards Winchester. It is approached by a drive through its parkland, almost opposite the vicarage where the Papillons lived and who soon became friends, as did the Middletons who had the Great House on lease before Edward began to live there himself. Set in the park alongside the Great House is the church of St. Nicholas where the family regularly

RIGHT
The approach and Chawton House.

BELOW
Chawton House. An Elizabethan
house set in parkland, this was
owned by Jane Austen's uncle and
then by her brother Edward whom
he adopted as his heir. When Jane
knew the house, its stone walls
were hidden beneath a layer of
painted stucco.

worshipped and where Mrs. Austen and Cassandra were buried. Further in this direction and to the east is Upper Farringdon where the Rev. John Benn was rector. His daughter became a family friend and even had the first part of the newly published *Pride and Prejudice* read aloud to her at Chawton, though without the secret of its authorship being revealed.

Alton, not much more than ten minutes' walk from Chawton Cottage, would have been visited frequently for shopping. It still has many 18th-century frontages which Jane would have known, sometimes concealing much older buildings. There were old inns around the square and a church with a Norman nave and tower complete with amusing animal carvings. There was a skirmish here during the Civil War in

which a Royalist colonel was shot while standing by the pulpit: there are lead bullets still embedded in the tower. Close by, too, is Wyards Farm, where Jane's niece Anna came to live with her husband Ben Lefroy. But walks did not have to be combined with a visit or linked to a useful purpose; they could be taken for their own sake, in the woods of Chawton Park across the meadows and along the lanes of this charming countryside that Jane Austen loved.

Since they had neither horses nor carriage – though later there was a donkey cart, excursions on their own were restricted to within walking distance. For longer expeditions they relied on friends or family providing transportation. Cost, and the unsuitability of ladies travelling alone, prevented them from making too much use of public coaches or privately-hired carriages, but nevertheless, there were frequent visits to distant friends and relations.

At Chawton, Jane again took out her old novel, *Elinor and Marianne,* and began to rewrite it. We do not know what prompted her to do so. Perhaps the more relaxed atmosphere of country life re-awakened her creative urge, or maybe the negative behaviour of Richard Crosby and Company stimulated her to show them she *would* be published. However, according to Henry Austen, the family had some difficulty persuading her to publish the book that resulted: *Sense and Sensibility.* Henry placed it with Thomas Egerton of the Military Library, with an office in Whitehall, London, and probably advanced her the cost of publication. The arrangement was that she would pay the publishing costs and have the receipts less a commission to the publisher for handling publication. She was so sure that receipts would not cover the costs that she planned her accounts

The church of St. Nicholas, Chawton was remodelled by Victorian 'improvers'. The chancel and sanctuary are all that remain of the church where Mr. Papillon and Jane's brother Henry preached. The graves of Mrs. Austen and of Cassandra are in the churchyard.

in anticipation of a loss. To her suprise it made her a profit of £140. By April 1811 she was in London correcting proofs and the book was published that November. By then she was well into writing *Mansfield Park* but the success of *Sense and Sensibility* led her to put that aside to revise *First Impressions,* which was sold to Egertons outright for £110. Its author had hoped to get £150 but probably accepted the smaller sum to avoid giving Henry further trouble. It was published in January 1813 as *Pride and Prejudice* and gained excellent reviews.

In April 1813, Henry's wife Eliza died after a long and painful illness and Henry drove down to Chawton to take Jane back with him to London where she stayed for a few weeks, keeping him company and comforting him in his bereavement. She was back at Chawton in July when Edward and his family took possession of the Great House which had by that time been vacated by its tenants. In September she accompanied them back to Godmersham, though by then she had probably finished writing *Mansfield Park* which draws upon her experience of life in a big country house. Some of the people she met provided prototypes for characters in her next book, *Emma*, which she began in January at Chawton. She also made a trip to London in March when she possibly worked on the proofs of *Mansfield Park* which was published in May. (On the way from Chawton Henry read or had read to him the first part of either proofs or manuscript.) That August, brother Charles's wife died following the birth of her fourth child.

Emma was finished by the end of March 1815, inspired by a visit to her godfather at Great Bookham and an excursion to Box Hill. *Mansfield Park*

had sold out but Egerton decided against issuing a second edition. Consequently a new publisher was sought and Henry began negotiations with John Murray. Murray was only willing to pay £450 and to have the copyright of the two earlier books included. The bargaining was interrupted when Henry became seriously ill but it was finally agreed that the books would be published at the author's expense, less a ten per cent commission to John Murray.

Jane was in London looking after her brother and so met his doctor who also attended the Prince Regent. Through him she was able to visit Carlton House, the Prince Regent's residence, and was invited by the royal librarian to dedicate her next book to the Prince. Since she disapproved of

Old cottages at Chawton dating from 1550.

him she was not inclined to do so, until it was made clear that she did not have a great deal of choice in the matter. This had the effect of stirring a rather lethargic publisher into action and the book came out in December 1815 (though it bears the date 1816) and was well received. In London at the beginning of the month, awaiting its publication, she marked up revisions to the second edition of *Mansfield Park*, minor changes including new details in the Portsmouth scenes. This appeared in February 1816, but was a commercial failure.

Henry had recovered from his illness but was now beset by business worries of a much more disastrous kind. His bank collapsed and at the beginning of March he and his partners were declared bankrupt. His brother Edward lost £2,000, Mr Leigh Perrot £10,000, Charles Austen 'hundreds', and many other investors, including Henry's servants, lost smaller sums. Jane lost the profits from her writing which the bank was holding. The rich relations seem to have been able to absorb these losses and Henry himself began a new life by taking Holy Orders, being by the end of the year installed as curate to Papillon at Chawton. Charles had some further bad luck when his ship

Alton, the nearby town to which Jane Austen would walk to do her shopping. It still has many fine old inns and houses.

Phoenix was lost in a gale off Asia Minor and though the crew were saved he was faced with court martial.

Work on *Persuasion* had already begun at Chawton early in August 1815 and continued, but Jane's health was troubling her. She was tired and depressed and had rheumatic pains in her back. There were sometimes strange dark and light patches on her skin and the family's current problems did not help matters. At the end of April 1816, Cassandra took her to Cheltenham in the hope that the spa waters would alleviate her condition. They broke the journey at Steventon and at Kintbury, where Mary Jane Fowle later remembered that Jane 'went over the old places and recalled old recollections associated with them in a very particular manner' as if 'she never expected to see them again'.

Back at Chawton *Persuasion* was again resumed and completed, with some final rewriting of the penultimate chapter and parts of others. Henry had finally managed to recover *Susan* from Crosby, and Jane began to think of revising it, changing the heroine's name to Catherine, for another novel of the same name had appeared in 1809.

In September she was feeling sufficiently recovered for Cassandra to accompany James's ailing wife to Cheltenham. Jane was strong enough to spend a day at Alton and walk home by moonlight, but complained of her increased household responsibilities: *'Composition seems to me impossible, with a head full of joints of mutton and doses of rhubarb.'*

By the New Year she was developing ideas for another novel set in a seaside town, Sanditon, which was originally going to be called *The Brothers*. In the middle of March, Jane confided in her niece Fanny that 'Miss Catherine is put upon the shelve for the present ... but I have something ready for Publication, which may perhaps appear about a twelvemonth hence.'

On occasions when she was too weak to go out walking, Jane would take drives in her mother's donkey cart; to avoid the bother that all that involved she informed Fanny that she was going to ride the donkey. She had a saddle made and on 22 March enjoyed her first ride, with Edward and Cassandra walking beside her and Jane looking forward to repeating the experience. Any improvement was short-lived. A relapse seems to have been brought about by the death of Mr. Leigh Perrot, her mother's brother, and her concern at the discovery that his will did not make provision for Mrs. Austen as they had all expected.

Twelve chapters of the new book had been written before illness forced her to lay down her pen. She was tired, her muscles weak, and to abdominal pains were added nausea, vomiting and diarrhoea. From 13 April she abandoned her bed only to transfer to a sofa. There were periods when she felt better, when her head cleared and she had less pain, though she was feverish at night and tired during the day. But on 27 April she felt it was time to make her will: Cassandra was to inherit everything except for small bequests of £50 to Henry and £50 to his French housekeeper, who had lost her savings in his bankruptcy. Later she added a gold chain for her goddaughter Louisa Knight and a lock of hair for Fanny.

The Alton doctor was able to do little for her and, placing their confidence in a Winchester physician, Dr. Lyford, it was decided that she would be better there, where he would be on hand to afford her regular treatment.

VISITS

The Austen family had connections in several parts of the country. George Austen had come from a Kentish family and they still had relatives there. His uncle and benefactor Francis had by 1743 become rich enough to buy the Red House in Sevenoaks. Jane visited her great-uncle there in 1788, when she was 12 years old. Her father's second cousin, Thomas Knight, who adopted Jane's brother Edward as his heir, lived at Godmersham Park, about 13 kilometres (eight miles) southwest from Canterbury on the road to Ashford, and Edward, on his marriage, lived at Rowling, near his wife's family at Goodnestone House, 11 kilometres (six and three-quarter miles) east of Canterbury on the Deal road. Jane Austen was a guest at all these houses, and would have been a visitor at others in their neighbourhood. Jane went to see Mrs. Knight at her new home in Canterbury, to which she moved after Edward took over Godmersham. Jane would obviously have visited the Cathedral and seen the town as well as making frequent shopping trips there. Mrs. Knight's house was called White Friars, built on the site of the old friary, but has not survived: shops stand there today. When Jane's sailor brother Francis was in Ramsgate, she most certainly would have visited him there.

Mrs. Austen's family, the Leighs, had branches at Adelstrop, in Gloucestershire, and Stoneleigh, in Warwickshire, and visits were made to both, as well as to her brother James

Leigh Perrot who had inherited from another relative and added their family name to his. By the time Jane was born the Leigh Perrots had sold their estates in Oxfordshire and had a house called Scarlets at Hare Hatch in Berkshire. Jane probably visited there as a girl, as well as staying with her aunt and uncle at the house in Bath where they passed the winter.

Jane's brother Henry had a succession of London homes at which she stayed as a guest: her friend Catherine Biggs married the rector of Streatham, south of London and her niece Anna lived in Hendon, further to the north, after her marriage to Ben Lefroy. There were also other friends and relations living near London in the vicinity of Streatham and Hendon. At Great Bookham, not far from Dorking was her godfather Samuel Cooke and his wife who was Mrs. Austen's cousin.

Closer to home was Ibthorpe, to which the Lloyd family moved after vacating the rectory at Deane, and then there were all those local friends in the neighbourhoods of Steventon and Chawton where they would sometimes stay overnight: Manydown, for instance, was much closer to Basingstoke and meant a much shorter drive before bed after attending a public ball.

Some of these places find their way into Jane Austen's books, either under their own names or as the inspiration for her own inventions. Over two centuries there has been a great deal of change in both town and countryside, but, although urban development in particular has drastically changed the appearance of places she knew and a good many of the houses she stayed in have long disappeared completely, a number still survive, little altered from her own day.

A huge increase in urbanization and the building of modern road networks have brought change throughout the land but much of the countryside and parkland offers much the same pleasure to the walker that Jane Austen experienced, though changes in agriculture and forestry may have altered the

The saloon at Stoneleigh Abbey, Warwickshire. Jane visited Stoneleigh with her mother and sister after it became the property of the Reverend Thomas Leigh, Mrs. Austen's cousin. This magnificent sandstone mansion, built around the cloister of a 12th-century abbey, gave Jane further experience of a grand house from which to draw material for her novels. The immense west building, with pilastered front and much other new work, was built in 1720. The interiors were, and are, of great magnificence.

In the 18th century, Lyme Regis became a holiday resort and it was a favourite place of Jane Austen, who visited it in November 1803.

Anne Elliott at Lyme Regis in *Persuasion*.

'They were come too late in the year for any amusement and, as there is nothing to admire in the buildings themselves, the remarkable situation of the town, the principal street almost hurrying into the water, the walk to the Cobb, skirting round the pleasant little bay, which in the season is animated with bathing machines and company, the Cobb itself, its old wonders and new improvements, with the very beautiful line of cliffs stretching out to the east of the town, are what a stranger's eye will seek; and a very strange stranger it must be, who does not see charms in the immediate environs of Lyme, to make him wish to know it better. The scenes of its neighbourhood, Charmouth, with its high grounds and extensive sweeps of country, and still more its sweet retired bay, backed by dark cliffs, where fragments of low rock among the sands make it the happiest spot for watching the flow of the tide, for sitting in unwearied contemplation; – the woody varieties of the village of Up Lyme, and, above all, Pinny, with its green chasms between romantic rocks, where the scattered forest trees and orchards of luxuriant growth declare that many a generation must have passed away since the first partial falling of the cliff prepared the ground for such a state, where a scene so wonderful and so lovely is exhibited, as may more than equal any of the resembling scenes of the far-famed Isle of Wight: these places must be visited, and visited again, to make the worth of Lyme understood.'

appearance of a particular view. But even in her own day, the work of Capability Brown and then Humphrey Repton, whose work as a landscape designer she mentions in *Mansfield Park,* were reshaping the countryside to create a new kind of English landscape.

With a little imagination the modern visitor may still be able to visualize a scene as it was in Jane Austen's time. What will be much more difficult to capture is the close familiarity and sense of place which she would have experienced. She would not have been able to make a spur-of-the-moment visit to the seaside or to Godmersham. It would have taken three days to reach Kent from Chawton or Steventon. A trip was a considerable undertaking and a visit would consequently be of some duration. This would have enabled Jane, not only to gain intimate knowledge of a town and its environs, but to make the acquaintance of many of her host's neighbours.

There were regular coach services across the length and breadth of the country but it was also possible to hire a private post-chaise should you be without a carriage of your own. Whether by stagecoach or post-chaise, a long journey would have required frequent changes of horses to allow the journey to continue with the minimum of interruption. The Royal Mail stagecoach service was very precisely timed. From Glasgow in Scotland south to London took two-and-a-half days. There were some scheduled stops to allow passengers half an hour for a meal and some others of 15 minutes duration where there was a great deal of post-office business to be undertaken: but in most places horses were waiting ready and a mere five minutes were allowed to get four horses changed and off again. Passengers would either have to sleep in the coach or book their travel

TOP
Lyme Regis from the Cobb. Lyme gained its royal title when Edward I used its harbour during his wars against France in the 13th century. Later the Cobb was erected to provide it with more shelter. Parliamentary forces were besieged here during the Civil War, bombarded from the sea by Royalist cannon. In 1685, the Duke of Monmouth landed here to lead the rebellion against James II. In the 18th century Lyme became a holiday resort and it was a favourite place with Jane Austen who first visited in November 1803.

BOTTOM LEFT
The Cobb at Lyme Regis, a massive stone wall curving out into the sea to protect ships in the harbour from the prevailing south-westerly winds and waves.

BOTTOM RIGHT
Granny's Teeth, the steps on the Cobb from which Louise Musgrove falls in *Persuasion.*
There was too much wind to make the high part of the new Cobb pleasant for the ladies, and they agreed to get down the steps to the lower, and all were contented to pass quietly and carefully down the steep flight, excepting Louisa; she must be jumped down them by Captain Wentworth. In all their walks, he had had to jump her from the stiles; the sensation was delightful to her. The hardness of the pavement to her feet, made him less willing upon the present occasion; he did it, however; she was safely down, and instantly, to shew her enjoyment, ran up the steps to be jumped down again. He advised her against it, thought the jar too great; but no, he reasoned and talked in vain; she smiled and said, 'I am determined I will': he put out his hands; she was too precipitate by half a second, she fell on the pavement of the Lower Cobb, and was taken up lifeless!'
Persuasion

Godmersham Park, the estate where Edward Austen was brought up after his adoption by his relation Thomas Knight. The property, which he later inherited, consists of rich parkland in the valley of the Stour, its watermeadows studded with enormous oak trees. Godmersham House provided Jane Austen with first-hand experience of living in the kind of mansion which she describes in *Mansfield Park* and *Pride and Prejudice* whose Pemberley is described in a very similar setting of rising ground above a river with woody hills behind. A handsome early 18th-century building designed as a central structure with two wings, it was altered over the years but the later additions were largely removed in a reconstruction of about 1835 which restored its original appearance as Jane Austen would have known it.

in stages. Private travellers would be able to make an overnight halt but would still need fresh horses at other stages. To travel with your own horses would mean proceeding at a much slower pace to allow them time to rest.

In *Sense and Sensibility* Willoughby, thinking that Marianne is dying and desperate to reach her, makes the journey of about 210 kilometres (130 miles) from London to Clevedon (near Bristol) in his chaise in only 12 hours, taking a ten-minute break at Marlborough to obtain some luncheon – but he must have had a change of horses. A more usual pace was just over eleven kilometres (seven miles) an hour with even less in hilly country.

There were a variety of different types of coaches and carriages in private use ranging from the four-wheeled

coach which could take six passengers to the chariot with accommodation for three passengers plus a box for driver and additional passenger. There were open, hooded and fully closed landaus, and light phaetons which often required only two horses. Two-wheeled vehicles included two-horse curricles and gigs, pulled by a single horse, which were the easiest to manage as well as the least expensive.

Mr. Austen kept a carriage at Steventon but this was given up when they moved to Bath but shortage of money meant that there was no question of his family having one after his death. But friends and relations would often send their carriages to pick Jane up when she was going to a ball and even send a carriage across country to collect the Austen ladies for a visit.

A view from Box Hill, Surrey, which Jane visited from Great Bookham and where she set a key scene in *Emma.*

BELOW
St. Lawrence's Church, Godmersham, beside the River Stour outside the walls of Godmersham Park, dates from 824 and has a Norman tower with its own eastern apse, once a chapel separate from the rest of the church.

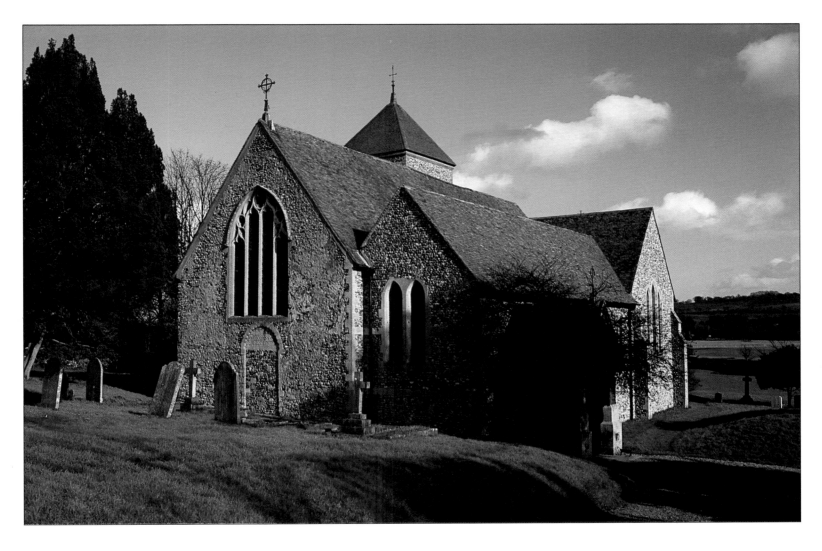

Canterbury Cathedral. Jane Austen would have known Canterbury well. Mrs. Knight's home, on the site of the White Friars priory, disappeared long ago and although Canterbury was heavily bombed in the Second World War, the magnificent cathedral and much of the old city survives. Indeed, bombing helped reveal some Roman features which Jane Austen could never have seen.

James's wife and children were travelling with Jane and since there was not room for all of them in one carriage James went ahead by public coach. It took eleven-and-a-half hours for them to drive down into Kent.

'*At half after seven yesterday morning Henry saw us into our own carriage, and we drove away from the Bath Hotel; which, by-the-bye, had been found most uncomfortable quarters – very dirty, very noisy, and very ill-provided. James began his journey by the coach at five. Our first eight miles were hot; Deptford Hill brought to my mind our hot journey into Kent fourteen years ago; but after Blackheath we suffered nothing, and as the day advanced it grew quite cool. At Dartford, which we reached within the two hours and three-quarters, we went to the Bull, the same inn at which we breakfasted in that said journey, and on the present occasion had about the same bad butter.*

'*At half past ten we were again off,*

and, travelling on without any adventure reached Sittingbourne by three. Daniel was watching for us at the door of the George, and I was acknowledged very kindly by Mr. and Mrs. Marshall, to the latter of whom I devoted my conversation, while Mary went out to buy some gloves. A few minutes, of course, did for Sittingbourne; and so off we drove, drove, drove, and by six o'clock were at Godmersham.

'Our two brothers were walking before the house as we approached, as natural as life. Fanny and Lizzy met us in the Hall with a great deal of pleasant joy; we went for a few minutes into the breakfast parlour, and then proceeded to our rooms. Mary has the Hall chamber. I am in the Yellow Room – very literally – for I am writing in it at this moment. It seems odd to me to have such a great place all to myself, and to be at Godmersham without you is also odd.'
Jane Austen writing to Cassandra, 15 June 1808.

Chilham Castle and the River Stour.
Chilham, a village of old houses clustered around a square with a 15th-century church, is only about three kilometres (two miles) from Godmersham. Chilham Park, where Jane Austen was the guest of James Wilman, an admirer of her niece Fanny, was once the owner of the property whose castle's 12th-century keep forms part of a Jacobean mansion surrounding an hexagonal courtyard.

WINCHESTER

Winchester is only 22 kilometres (14 miles) from Steventon and ten kilometres (just over six miles) from Chawton. It was close enough for James to have gone to Winchester Fair to buy a horse for Steventon and for Edward's sons to have gone to school there. Jane would almost certainly have made excursions from Chawton and would have been familiar with the remains of its Norman castle and its cathedral.

Winchester, county town of Hampshire, was the site of a settlement long before the time of Christ and was the Roman market town of Venta Belgarum. Here Saxons sought protection behind what remained of the Roman fortifications and as Witanceaster it became the capital of Alfred the Great's Wessex kingdom, and not only of Saxon kings but of the Danish Cnut and of William I after the Norman conquest. Here kings were crowned and buried and pilgrims came to the shrine of St. Swithin in the cathedral where he had been bishop in the ninth century. The great hall of the castle was where the Parliaments of England met for more than 400 years.

London eventually replaced Winchester as capital of the kingdom and the coming of the Reformation soon put an end to pilgrimage and swept away the monastic foundations. The ancient castle was largely destroyed in the Civil War and though Charles II began a new palace in 1683 it was unfinished when he died and was converted into barracks. Most of the old town walls were pulled down towards the end of the 18th century.

When Jane Austen moved into lodgings in Winchester in 1817 the town, after years of dependence upon the military and local agricultural trade, was beginning to assume a new character, making a bid to attract more commerce and visitors. Three old churches had recently been demolished to make way for redevelopment, there was a billiard room in Westgate and dances were being held in the ancient hospice of St. John on the north of the Broadway.

Jane saw little of this. On 24 May 1817, she travelled from Chawton in James's carriage with Cassandra and her brother Henry, her nephew William Knight accompanying them on horseback in the rain. She claimed not to find the journey very tiring, and 'had it been a fine day' thought 'she would have felt none', but was concerned about the men getting a soaking.

Their lodgings had been arranged by Elizabeth Heathcote, one of the Bigg sisters from Manydown, married and living in Winchester. They were at Mrs. David's, 8 College Street, behind the houses of the Cathedral Close furthest from the High Street. There was accommodation for herself, Cassandra and a nurse and they had a 'neat little drawing room with a bow-window' that overlooked the garden of the headmaster of Winchester College. Cassandra was not satisfied with the nurse and James's wife Mary came to take her place.

Doctor Lyford appears to have

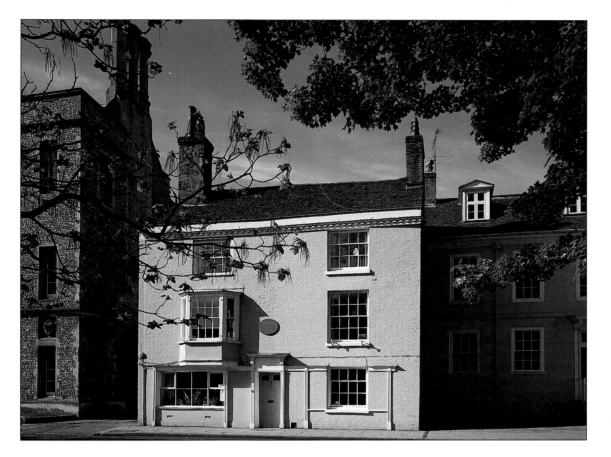

8 College Street, Winchester,
where Jane and Cassandra lodged
and Jane Austen died.

diagnosed a 'wasting disease' which usually meant either cancer or tuberculosis, although there have been other suggestions that she was suffering from a form of Addinson's disease. Though Jane sometimes seemed to be in recovery and relatively free from pain, she may have been well aware that the prognosis was not hopeful. It was with a wry humour that she wrote to her nephew James Edward a few days after her arrival in College Street that 'Mr. Lyford says he will cure me, and if he fails I shall draw up a memorial and lay it before the Dean and Chapter.'

Mrs. Heathcote and her sister Alathea called at College Street every day and though Jane spent most of her time on a sofa, she was able to move from room to room watching the world go by from the windows. On another occasion she was able to take a outing about the town in a sedan chair and she looked forward to more and the use of a wheelchair when the weather was

Winchester Cathedral, the west front. The Cathedral of the Holy Trinity, St. Peter, St. Paul and St. Swithin lies in a hollow and it is only from the Close that its scale is visible from the exterior. A Saxon cathedral was rebuilt in 1079, the eastern part of which was reconstructed in 1202 and the nave and west front were remodelled in the 14th century. There were further embellishments and restorations in later years.

suitable. But her condition worsened. Her brother Charles came to see her on 19 June and feared that he was probably seeing her for the last time. Lyford had no hope and though he told James that 'he saw no signs of immediate dissolution but, with such a pulse – 120 – it was impossible for any person to last long.' Henry and James were now constant visitors and eventually felt it their duty to tell Jane of the seriousness of her decline. She managed to keep her composure and requested they celebrate

Holy Communion and administer the Sacrament to her while she was able to take it in full comprehension. Thus it was duly administered by them, for Henry as well as James were now both clergymen.

On 15 July, St. Swithin's Day, Jane appeared to rally and wrote, or perhaps dictated, a few light verses on the theme of the saint bringing rain to the forthcoming Winchester Race Meeting as punishment for holding them. They were the last thing she wrote. By

evening she was weaker, though she had slept longer in the night and more comfortably. Late in the afternoon of Thursday 17 July, Cassandra returned from an errand in the town, made at Jane's request, to find her sister recovering from an attack. She began to describe the incident in detail when she was again seized with pain. When Cassandra asked if there was anything she wanted Jane answered that she required nothing but death and asked that 'God give me patience. Pray for me, oh Pray for me'. Lyford was called and administered a drug to ease her pain, probably laudanum, and she drifted into unconsciousness. Cassandra sat with her, a pillow on her lap to support Jane's head. After six hours she allowed Mary to relieve her for a few hours before resuming her vigil. Jane died at 4.30 am on 18 July 1817.

The Dean of Winchester had given permission for her to be buried in the Cathedral and early on the following Thursday morning, so as not to conflict

The nave of Winchester Cathedral is the second longest in Europe, second only to that of St. Peter's in Rome. The overall length of the cathedral is 169.5 metres (556 ft).

with regular morning service, a small procession left College Street with the coffin attended by three brothers, Edward, Frank and Henry, together with James Edward in place of his father who was ill. It was usual for men only to attend the obsequies and Cassandra watched from the window. Jane was buried in the north aisle of the cathedral where a dark slab now marks her grave. A few days later, an obituary in *The Courier* made the first public identification of her by name as 'Authoress of *Emma, Mansfield Park,* *Pride and Prejudice* and *Sense and Sensibility*'. Henry Austen arranged for the publication of *Northanger Abbey* (his choice of title) and *Persuasion* at the end of 1817 (though they bear the date 1818). James Edward Austen, who had accompanied his aunt's coffin to its final resting place, published *A Memoir of Jane Austen* in 1870 with a second edition which included some of her early writings and part of the unfinishd *Sanditon*. In the intervening years, all her writings have appeared in print to the everlasting pleasure of her readers.

Jane Austen is buried beneath a dark stone slab in the north aisle of Winchester Cathedral. There is a brass memorial to her on the wall nearby and above it a stained glass window was placed to her memory in 1900.

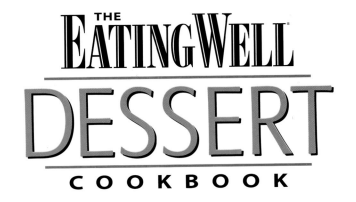

EatingWell BOOKS

A Division of EW Communications L.P.
Box 1001, Ferry Road, Charlotte, Vermont 05445-1001

© 1996 by EW Communications L.P.

EATING WELL: The Magazine of Food & Health®, is a registered trademark of EW Communications L.P.
For subscription information, write to EATING WELL, P.O. Box 52919, Boulder, CO 80322-2919 or call (800) 678-0541.

Library of Congress Cataloging-in-Publication Data
The Eating well dessert cookbook: 150 recipes to bring dessert back into your life, from the magazine of food & health.
p.   cm.
Includes index.
ISBN 1-884943-09-8 (hardcover) — ISBN 1-884943-10-1 (softcover)
1. Desserts.   2. Low-fat diet—Recipes.   I. Eating well.
TX773.E32 1996   96-1772
641.8'6—dc20   CIP

Editorial Director: Scott Mowbray   **Editor:** Susan Stuck   **Managing Editor:** Wendy S. Ruopp
Recipe Editor: Susan Herr   **Test Kitchen Director:** Patsy Jamieson   **Nutrition Editor:** Elizabeth Hiser
Recipe Development & Analysis: Susanne Davis   **Additional Recipe Development:** Lisa Cherkasky   **Recipe Tester:** Beth-Ann Bove
Proofreaders: Euan Bear, Suzanne Seibel, Anne Treadwell   **Permissions:** David Grist

Design Director: Joannah Ralston   **Associate Art Director:** Elise Whittemore-Hill
Photographer: Matthew Klein   **Photography Stylist:** Kemper Hyers   **Food Stylist:** Rick Ellis

Front cover: Key Lime Pie (*recipe on page 38*) **Back cover:** Carrot Cupcakes (*recipe on page 20*),
Cran-Strawberry Ice Pops (*recipe on page 164*), Lemon Squares (*recipe on page 132*)

Distributed by
Artisan, a Division of Workman Publishing
708 Broadway, New York, NY 10003

Printed and bound in Canada by
Metropole Litho Inc., Montreal, Quebec

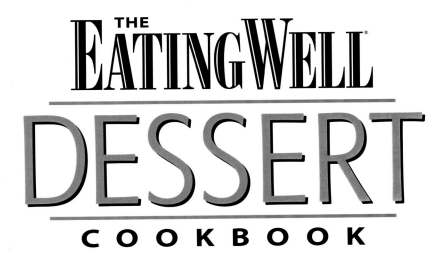

THE EATINGWELL DESSERT COOKBOOK

150 Recipes
To Bring Dessert Back
Into Your Life

from
The Magazine of Food & Health

Raspberry Frozen Yogurt (*page 169*) & Sicilian Fig Cookies (*page 110*)

Chocolate-Cherry Bars (*page 100*)

CONTENTS

INTRODUCTION

It's time to bring dessert back into your life. No longer need dessert be too sweet, too rich or too heavy. The recipes in this diverse collection combine fresh flavors and healthful ingredients in a light, deft style that yields scrumptious results. Here you will find 150 treats that really do keep the EATING WELL mandate: to present our readers with a new approach to healthy cooking that fits the needs of their active lives.

In these pages you will find desserts for every occasion. Looking for a quick conclusion to a weeknight supper? Peach-Melon Frozen Yogurt or Brandied Nectarines can be made in under 15 minutes. Sweet delicacies for celebrations? Bake a Banana Spice Cake for Mom's birthday or a Café au Lait Cheesecake for Dad's. You have a choice of five harvest pies to grace a Thanksgiving table: the Mincemeat Tart has only three grams of fat per serving. Summer refreshments abound, from light and lemony confections to quick frozen fruit pops to nutritious (and portable) bars to pack into picnic baskets.

These desserts are not hard to make. The recipes are straightforward, having more to do with flavor than decoration. Still, skilled bakers will find they cannot wait to experiment with the innovative fat-cutting techniques, such as substituting dates for fat in a chocolate cake. Novice cooks intimidated by the words "pie crust" might want to start out with the easy Cranberry-Granola Blondies or Rum-Raisin Bread Pudding; neither takes more than 20 minutes to assemble. From there, they may feel confident to move on to the Lemon Cream Pie with its easy graham-cracker crust.

Some of these recipes have appeared in EATING WELL Magazine, many others have been developed expressly for this book. All have been tested and re-tested in the EATING WELL Test Kitchen, and that means one thing—these are recipes that work. You will find scores of tips throughout the book that give you a little extra information about a recipe. Some explain particular baking techniques, others help you select ingredients or suggest substitutions or variations.

Like all recipes from EATING WELL, these desserts are part of a diet built around fundamental, widely recognized healthy-eating guidelines: no more than 30 percent of calories in the overall diet should come from fat, and meals should include plenty of grains, vegetables and fruits. We not only pay attention to the amount of fat in a recipe, but also the source of fat, and strive to keep saturated fat to one-third of the total fat. No dessert in this book has more than 10 grams of fat per serving—not even the cheesecake! A nutritional analysis follows every recipe; it includes a breakdown of calories, protein, fat, saturated fat, carbohydrate, sodium and cholesterol for one serving. Nearly half of the recipes in this book are considered very low in fat—three grams or less per serving.

The desserts in this collection help you achieve another goal of healthy eating—to eat a variety of foods. At least 30 different types of fruit are used throughout the book: berries, peaches and plums are highlights of summer desserts; all manner of citrus fruits, apples, pears and dried fruits are part of cold-weather offerings.

So it's time to have a little fun and sit down to luscious desserts with a brightness and a lightness that will allow you and your family to enjoy dessert once again—with no trace of guilt and no end of satisfaction.

—Susan Stuck

♦ *For a list of the fat-free and very-low-fat recipes in this book, please turn to page 190.*

THE HEALTHY DESSERT KITCHEN

At EATING WELL, we have found that by emphasizing fruits (fresh, frozen and dried), whole grains and low-fat or nonfat dairy products, dessert can be healthful and satisfying. Here are some of the provisions and equipment we depend on to achieve delicious low-fat results:

DRY INGREDIENTS

BROWN SUGAR: Today's brown sugar is actually white sugar to which molasses has been added. Brown sugar adds moistness and deepens flavors, a plus for low-fat desserts. Light brown sugar is preferred when a strong molasses flavor is not desirable. Dark brown sugar is particularly good for deepening the flavor of chocolate.

CAKE FLOUR: A finely ground, soft white flour. Low in protein, it develops less gluten during mixing, so baked goods are more tender. An acceptable substitute can be made by replacing 2 tablespoons of flour with corn-starch for each cup of all-purpose white flour.

CORNMEAL: Adds an appealing crunchy texture to baked goods. If the package is labeled "stone-ground," the cornmeal includes the germ and some of the hull, so it is coarser and more nutritious. Store it in the freezer to keep the oils from going rancid.

DUTCH-PROCESS COCOA POWDER: Significantly lower in fat than chocolate, unsweetened cocoa powder is used to replace chocolate in dessert recipes. In Dutch-process cocoa, the natural acid has been neutralized, and the cocoa has a darker color and deeper flavor as a result. It is widely available at supermarkets or specialty-food stores.

INSTANT-DISSOLVING SUGAR: Also called superfine or bar sugar, this white sugar has a very fine granulation. Because it dissolves so quickly, it is excellent for instant frozen yogurts made in a food processor and for uncooked fruit sauces.

SEMOLINA OR SEMOLINA FLOUR: A golden, granular flour milled from the hearts of protein-rich durum wheat berries. Sometimes called pasta flour, because this is how it is most often used, it adds a pleasant grainy texture to desserts. Gourmet stores, Italian markets or large supermarkets will carry it.

WHOLE-WHEAT PASTRY FLOUR: A fine-textured, soft wheat flour that includes the wheat germ, giving it a higher fiber content than white flours. Look for it at health-food stores. Store in the freezer.

FATS & OILS

BUTTER: It is the only ingredient that will make baked goods taste truly buttery, but butter is too high in saturated fat to use in large quantity. The EATING WELL solution is to use a small amount of butter and magnify its flavor by heating until it turns a nutty brown. The recipes in this book were tested with and analyzed using unsalted butter.

CANOLA OIL: Pressed from rapeseed, this neutral-flavored vegetable oil is extremely low in saturated fats and quite high in monounsaturated fats. A must for low-fat cooking.

NONSTICK COOKING SPRAY: A mixture of oil and lecithin, this is a convenient and low-fat way to keep baked goods from sticking to the pan. It is available in aerosol and nonaerosol containers.

NUT OILS: Walnut and hazelnut oils are pressed from

toasted nuts. Buy nut oils in small bottles and store in the refrigerator, as they become rancid more quickly than other oils. When a recipe contains nuts, using a small amount of nut oil heightens the flavor. These oils are high in heart-healthy monounsaturated fats.

DAIRY & EGGS

BUTTERMILK: Tangy buttermilk, made by culturing skim milk with bacteria, is high in acid, helping to tenderize biscuits and cakes and keep them moist. If you don't have buttermilk on hand, substitute a mixture of half nonfat plain yogurt and half skim milk.

EGGS: All of the fat in an egg, about 6 grams, is found in the yolk. To reduce the fat in recipes, we cut back on the yolks and substitute additional egg whites. Because of the risk of salmonella contamination, adding raw meringue to a mousse or a filling is no longer recommended. To avoid that risk, our recipes use cooked meringues. Please note that all the recipes in this book were developed using large eggs.

EVAPORATED SKIM MILK: Made by evaporating nearly half of the water from fresh skim milk, this thick and slightly sweet canned milk product is a good replacement for cream in desserts where strong flavors will mask the slightly cooked flavor.

NONFAT AND LOW-FAT COTTAGE CHEESE: When the excess moisture is pressed out and the remaining curd is pureed in a food processor, this makes a great addition to cream cheese to expand its volume or a replacement for cream cheese in pastry doughs.

NONFAT AND LOW-FAT YOGURT: Like buttermilk, acidic yogurt helps tenderize baked goods and is a good replacement for sour cream. To replace cream cheese, make plain yogurt into yogurt cheese; use a brand without added starch, gum or gelatin and drain it overnight in the refrigerator in a strainer lined with cheesecloth. It will reduce in volume by about two-thirds.

SWEETENED CONDENSED MILK: Now available in both reduced-fat and nonfat forms, this is a canned mixture of sugar and milk from which about 60 percent of the water has been evaporated. It adds creaminess and body to desserts like custards and pie fillings.

FLAVOR ENHANCERS

CRYSTALLIZED GINGER: Also termed "candied," this is fresh ginger that has been cooked in a sugar syrup and dried. It lends a peppery pizzazz to desserts. Buy it at Asian markets or health-food stores, where it will be less expensive.

DRIED TART CHERRIES AND CRANBERRIES: Practically interchangeable, these two colorful fruits are wonderful in any number of desserts, helping to balance sweetness. They should be stored in an airtight container to keep them moist. Steep overly dry fruits in hot water for a few minutes to restore softness. Dried cranberries are widely available, but dried tart cherries may require a trip to a gourmet-food shop.

INSTANT ESPRESSO POWDER: More intense than instant coffee powder, a small amount of this dissolved in water or alcohol gives desserts a strong coffee flavor and intensifies the flavor of chocolate desserts. Find it at a large supermarket or specialty-food store.

SPICES: Because fat enhances flavor, baked goods with relatively small amounts of fat often need greater quantities of spices to prevent them from tasting flat. For best flavor, replace the spices on your shelf yearly.

SPIRITS & LIQUEURS: Alcohol adds a fat-free boost to flavors. Clear spirits distilled from fruits, such as kirsch (from cherries) or eau-de-vie de framboise (from raspberries), are effective in berry desserts. Calvados, an apple brandy from France, is a marvelous addition to apple confections. Liqueurs, such as Amaretto, with its almond flavor (actually made from peach pits), and orange-flavored Grand Marnier, add rich, mellow tones to a variety of recipes. Whenever possible, we have given a nonalcoholic alternative.

VANILLA AND ALMOND EXTRACTS: In low-fat desserts, the quality of extracts becomes even more important, because the flavor is more apparent. Avoid imitation extracts, which taste harsh and artificial, and buy only those labeled "pure."

VANILLA BEANS: They are expensive, but vanilla beans lend a complex flavor and fragrance to simple dishes, such as poached fruit, that cannot be matched by extract. Beans should be supple, not dried out. If the tiny seeds haven't been scraped out of the center, the bean can be reused two or three times.

ZEST: The term for the colored outside layer of a citrus peel. The oils in this layer are intensely flavored, making zest a flavorful addition to many desserts, especially fruit desserts. Use the small holes on a box grater to grate the zest, or a swivel-bladed peeler to remove it in long strips. Avoid the white "pith" just beneath, which is bitter.

BAKING PANS

The correct pan size is important to successful baking, but this can be confusing territory. If you have been baking for years, the size of the pans in your cupboard may be somewhat different from the pan we specify in the recipe or what is available in housewares stores. It is certainly possible to substitute a slightly different pan size, but try to keep the surface area close to the same. For instance, a good substitute for a 7-by-11-inch rectangular pan (with an area of 77 square inches) would be a 9-inch square pan (81 square inches).

Baking pans can be made of metal or glass, but cakes and bars bake slightly faster in glass pans. It is important to check baked goods often toward the end of the baking time, and to rely on directions in the recipe like "until it feels firm when lightly pressed in the center" or "until a skewer inserted in the center comes out clean" to determine when the dish is done.

Heavy baking sheets help prevent cookies from burning on the bottom. If you don't have one, stack two cookie sheets to solve the problem. Nonstick baking sheets are a wise investment.

SPECIAL EQUIPMENT

CHEESECLOTH: A loosely woven cotton cloth useful for fine straining or making pressed cottage cheese or yogurt cheese. Look for it at the supermarket or gourmet shops.

ICE CREAM MAKER: Look for the small countertop variety where you prefreeze the liquid-filled canister. They don't make a lot of ice cream, but are inexpensive and no-fuss.

INSTANT-READ THERMOMETER: Because it registers temperature so quickly, this tool is essential when making a meringue over simmering water, the only reliable way to destroy possible salmonella bacteria in an unbaked meringue.

NUTMEG GRATER OR GRINDER: While ground spices are usually fine if recently purchased, nutmeg is an exception. Always grate nutmeg fresh, as the flavor is quite different and far superior.

PARCHMENT PAPER: A strong paper, useful for lining baking sheets and cake pans to prevent sticking. While less expensive wax paper will often do instead, parchment is essential for cookies that tend to stick, such as meringues. Find it at kitchen-equipment shops.

SKEWERS: Bamboo skewers, the kind used for shish kebab, are indispensable for testing cakes and custards or to loosen cakes from fluted molds.

◆**HELPFUL TIPS**
Throughout the book, notes about ingredients, equipment and techniques are highlighted by the colored diamond.

UNFORGETTABLE CAKES

The gathering of family, friends or colleagues around the table as you cut into a cake—each person protesting that her

slice is much too big—is the high point of many a celebration. Round and high—or even square and squat—cakes are used to mark important events in our lives. The cakes in this chapter are appropriate for occasions as merry as birthdays and as memorable as graduations. You will also find cakes for the more spontaneous celebrations. A superabundance of peaches in July? Celebrate it with a peach upside-

down cake. Like most of these light, delicious cakes, it uses fruits to spark bright, fresh flavors. And all are proof positive that a cake can be both festive and low in fat.

RICOTTA CHEESECAKE

Tart apricots and sweet golden raisins garnish this Italian specialty.
It can be served year-round but it is particularly appropriate at Easter.

CRUST

2½ tablespoons Grape-Nuts *or* Cheerios cereal

1 tablespoon walnuts

1 tablespoon sugar

Pinch of ground cinnamon

FILLING

1 tablespoon pine nuts

⅓ cup golden raisins

⅓ cup dried apricots, diced

⅓ cup dark rum, kirsch *or* fresh orange juice

3 ounces reduced-fat cream cheese (6 tablespoons), softened

¾ cup sugar

16 ounces part-skim ricotta cheese (1¾ cups)

¼ cup nonfat plain yogurt

¼ cup all-purpose white flour

1 large egg

2 large egg whites

1 tablespoon fresh lemon juice

2 teaspoons grated lemon zest

⅛ teaspoon salt

TO MAKE CRUST:

Preheat oven to 325°F. Lightly oil an 8-inch springform pan or coat it with nonstick cooking spray. In a food processor, combine cereal, walnuts, sugar and cinnamon; process until fine crumbs form. Place the crumb mixture in the prepared pan; tilt and rotate the pan to coat the bottom and sides. Tap the pan on the counter to evenly distribute the crumbs. Set aside.

TO MAKE FILLING:

1. In a small dry skillet over low heat, stir pine nuts until lightly toasted, about 3 minutes. Transfer to a plate and set aside to cool.

2. In a small saucepan, combine raisins and apricots with rum, kirsch or juice; warm gently over low heat but do not boil. (*Alternatively, warm in a microwave oven.*) Let plump for about 20 minutes. Drain.

3. In a large mixing bowl, beat cream cheese with an electric mixer until smooth. Add sugar and beat until creamy. Add ricotta, yogurt, flour, egg, egg whites, lemon juice, lemon zest and salt, beating until thoroughly blended. (*Alternatively, mix ingredients in a food processor.*) Stir in the drained plumped fruit.

4. Transfer the batter to the prepared pan. Sprinkle with reserved pine nuts and bake for about 55 minutes, or until puffed at the edges but still slightly wobbly in the center. Turn off the oven and leave the cheesecake inside with the door closed for 30 minutes longer. Remove the cheesecake from the oven and let it cool completely on a wire rack. Remove the outer ring of the pan. Serve at room temperature or refrigerate, covered, for up to 2 days.

Serves 8.

270 calories per serving: 11 grams protein, 8 grams fat (5 grams saturated fat), 36 grams carbohydrate; 194 mg sodium; 47 mg cholesterol.

PEACH-BOURBON UPSIDE-DOWN CAKE

Bake this Southern-inspired, moist and fruity cake when peaches are plentiful—from late June through July.

1. Preheat oven to 350°F. Lightly oil a 9-inch round cake pan or coat it with nonstick cooking spray.

2. In a bowl, toss peaches with brown sugar, 1 tablespoon of the bourbon, if using, and cornstarch. Spoon the fruit into the prepared pan, arranging it in an even layer; set aside.

3. Spread pecans in a pie pan and bake for about 5 minutes, or until fragrant; let cool slightly. In a food processor, combine the pecans, flour, baking powder and salt; process until the pecans are ground to a fine meal.

4. In a mixing bowl, beat the 2 egg whites with an electric mixer until soft peaks form. Gradually beat in ⅓ cup of the sugar, continuing to beat until the egg whites are stiff and glossy; set aside. In a separate mixing bowl, beat the whole eggs with the remaining ⅓ cup sugar until thick and pale, about 5 minutes. Beat in the remaining 1 tablespoon of bourbon, if using, and vanilla. Whisk one-fourth of the reserved beaten egg whites into the whole-egg mixture. Sprinkle half of the flour mixture over the top and fold in with a rubber spatula just until blended. Fold in the remaining beaten whites, then the remaining flour mixture.

5. Spread the batter over the fruit in the pan. Bake for 35 to 45 minutes, or until the top springs back when lightly touched and a skewer inserted in the center comes out clean. Let cool in the pan for 5 minutes, then invert onto a serving plate, rearranging any stray fruit. Serve warm or at room temperature.

Serves 10.

180 calories per serving: 3 grams protein, 5 grams fat (1 gram saturated fat), 31 grams carbohydrate; 111 mg sodium; 43 mg cholesterol.

4	cups peeled and sliced fresh peaches (about 6 peaches)
2	tablespoons brown sugar
2	tablespoons bourbon (optional)
1	tablespoon cornstarch
½	cup pecan halves
⅔	cup sifted cake flour
1	teaspoon baking powder
¼	teaspoon salt
2	large egg whites
⅔	cup sugar
2	large eggs
1½	teaspoons pure vanilla extract

◆ **PEELING PEACHES**

To remove the fuzzy skin from peaches, submerge them in boiling water for 20 seconds or so. Remove, dunk them in cold water, then slip off the skin.

A BOWL-OF-FRUIT CAKE

Celebrate summer's bounty with a simple cake ring that is filled to overflowing with seasonal fruits. The fruits listed here are suggestions; use what looks best at the market.

SPONGE CAKE RING

- 1 cup less 2 tablespoons unsifted cake flour
- 1 teaspoon baking soda
- 2 large eggs
- 2 large egg whites
- 1 cup sugar
- 2 teaspoons fresh lemon juice
- 2 teaspoons pure vanilla extract
- ⅓ cup skim milk, heated to about 150°F

FRUIT FILLING & GLAZE

- ½ cup sugar
- ¼ cup apricot brandy *or* fresh orange juice
- 2 teaspoons unsalted butter
- 4 cups pitted and sliced fresh nectarines (about 1½ pounds)
- 3 cups seedless green grapes (about 1 pound)
- 2 cups sweet cherries, pitted and halved (about 1 pound)

TO MAKE SPONGE CAKE RING:

1. Preheat oven to 350°F. Lightly oil an ovenproof ring mold with a 6- to 7-cup capacity or coat it with nonstick cooking spray. Dust the mold with flour, shaking out the excess.

2. Sift cake flour and baking powder into a bowl; set aside. In a mixing bowl, beat eggs and egg whites together with an electric mixer. Add sugar and beat on medium speed for 3 minutes, or until the mixture is pale and fluffy. On low speed, beat in lemon juice, vanilla and the reserved flour mixture just until the flour is incorporated. Beat in the hot milk.

3. Transfer the batter to the prepared mold. Bake for 22 to 25 minutes, or until a cake tester inserted in the cake comes out clean. Let cool in the pan for 5 minutes. Run a knife around the pan sides to loosen the cake. Invert onto a wire rack to cool while you prepare the filling and glaze.

TO PREPARE FRUIT FILLING AND GLAZE:

1. In a small saucepan, stir sugar and 1 cup water over medium-low heat until the sugar dissolves. Remove from the heat and stir in apricot brandy or orange juice. Pour half of the syrup into a small bowl, cover and set aside to cool.

2. Add butter to the syrup remaining in the saucepan, stirring until the butter has melted. Brush some of this glaze over the bottom and sides of the cake. Invert the cake onto a serving platter and brush the top of the cake with the remaining glaze. Cover and leave at room temperature until serving time.

◆**SPECIAL EQUIPMENT**

A ring mold is a deep, circular mold with a rounded bottom and a large center hole. You may use a 9-inch tube pan instead, but you will need to serve some of the fruit salad in a bowl alongside.

3. In a large bowl, combine fruit and the reserved cooled syrup. Cover and refrigerate for at least 1 hour or up to 3 hours. Just before serving, fill the center of the cake with the fruit filling. Spoon any syrup remaining in the bowl over the fruit.

Serves 10.

290 calories per serving: 5 grams protein, 3 grams fat (1 gram saturated fat), 62 grams carbohydrate; 120 mg sodium; 45 mg cholesterol.

A Bowl-of-Fruit Cake

BLUEBERRY TORTE

EATING WELL's *Test Kitchen Director Patsy Jamieson makes a trek to a cabin on the Maine coast every summer. She developed this cheesecake-like torte to celebrate the abundance of blueberries she finds there.*

1½ cups all-purpose white flour

½ cup sugar

1½ teaspoons baking powder

½ teaspoon ground cinnamon

¼ teaspoon salt

¼ cup canola oil

2 large egg whites, lightly beaten

1 tablespoon melted butter

2 teaspoons pure vanilla extract

1 large egg

⅔ cup nonfat sweetened condensed milk

2 tablespoons cornstarch

1½ cups nonfat plain yogurt

Grated zest of 1 lemon

3 cups fresh *or* frozen unsweetened (*not* thawed) blueberries

Confectioners' sugar for dusting

1. Preheat oven to 300°F. Lightly oil a 9-inch springform pan or an 8-inch square cake pan or coat it with nonstick cooking spray.

2. In a mixing bowl, stir together flour, sugar, baking powder, cinnamon and salt with a fork. Add oil, egg whites, butter and 1 teaspoon of the vanilla; mix with a fork or your fingertips until well blended. Press into the bottom of the prepared pan.

3. In a mixing bowl, whisk together whole egg, condensed milk and cornstarch until smooth. Add yogurt and whisk until smooth. Blend in lemon zest and the remaining 1 teaspoon vanilla. Pour over the crust. Sprinkle blueberries evenly over the top.

4. Bake the torte for 1¼ to 1½ hours, or until the top is just set. (The center will quiver slightly when the pan is gently shaken.) Let cool in the pan on a wire rack. Run a knife around the inside of the pan to loosen the torte, then remove the outer ring of the pan. Serve warm or chilled, dusted with confectioners' sugar.

Serves 12.

240 calories per serving: 6 grams protein, 6 grams fat (1 gram saturated fat), 40 grams carbohydrate; 152 mg sodium; 23 mg cholesterol.

BLACKBERRY SKILLET CAKE

Enjoy a summer's day with an easy cake. Any blackberry variety is suitable here, from loganberries to marionberries to wild blackberries. Huckleberries are good too.

TO PREPARE FRUIT:

Lightly oil a 10-inch ovenproof skillet or coat it with nonstick cooking spray. Pour apple-juice concentrate into the skillet and add berries, distributing them evenly. To prevent the berries from floating to the top of the batter during baking, place the skillet and berries in the freezer while mixing the cake batter.

TO MAKE CAKE:

1. Preheat oven to 350°F. In a small bowl, stir together flour, baking powder and salt. In a mixing bowl, beat egg whites with an electric mixer at high speed until soft peaks form. Gradually add apple-juice concentrate, beating until stiff peaks form. Reduce the mixer speed to low and add milk, oil and vanilla, beating until well blended. With a rubber spatula, gently fold in the dry ingredients. Remove the skillet from the freezer and pour the batter over the berries.

2. Bake for 35 to 40 minutes, or until the top is golden and a skewer inserted in the center comes out clean. Let cool in the skillet on a wire rack for 10 to 15 minutes. Run a knife around the inside of the pan to loosen the cake and invert onto a serving plate. Let sit for a few minutes before removing the skillet, so the cake can absorb all the juices. Serve warm or at room temperature.

Serves 8.

265 calories per serving: 6 grams protein, 10 grams fat (1 gram saturated fat), 40 grams carbohydrate; 258 mg sodium; 0 mg cholesterol.

FRUIT

⅓ cup frozen apple-juice concentrate, thawed

3 cups blackberries, fresh or frozen

CAKE

1½ cups whole-wheat pastry flour (*see page 8*)

2 teaspoons baking powder

½ teaspoon salt

3 large egg whites

¾ cup frozen apple-juice concentrate, thawed

⅔ cup skim milk

⅓ cup canola oil

2 teaspoons pure vanilla extract

PLUM CAKE

A lightly spiced cake with a dramatic topping of glistening plums—it's perfect for a September birthday.

1 cup plus 2 tablespoons sugar

1½ pounds purple plums (about 8 medium plums)

1½ cups sifted cake flour

⅔ cup whole-wheat pastry flour (*see page 8*)

1½ teaspoons baking powder

½ teaspoon baking soda

1½ teaspoons ground cinnamon

½ teaspoon freshly grated nutmeg

½ teaspoon salt

⅔ cup nonfat plain yogurt

¼ cup canola oil

1 large egg

1 large egg white

1 teaspoon pure vanilla extract

½ cup red currant jelly

1. Preheat oven to 350°F. Line a 9-inch springform pan with foil, smoothing out the wrinkles. Lightly oil the foil or coat it with nonstick cooking spray. Sprinkle 2 tablespoons of the sugar in the bottom of the pan and set aside.

2. Halve plums lengthwise and remove the pits. Cut each half lengthwise into thin slices. Arrange circular rows of overlapping slices in the prepared pan; place any remaining slices in an even layer on top.

3. In a mixing bowl, stir together cake flour and whole-wheat flour, the remaining 1 cup sugar, baking powder, baking soda, cinnamon, nutmeg and salt. In another bowl, whisk together yogurt, oil, egg, egg white and vanilla until well combined. Stir the yogurt mixture into the dry ingredients with a rubber spatula just until blended.

4. Gently spoon the batter onto the plums, smoothing the top. Bake for 40 to 50 minutes, or until a skewer inserted in the center of the cake comes out clean.

5. Remove the outer ring of the springform pan, fold back the foil, and invert the cake onto a cake plate. Remove the pan bottom and foil.

6. In a small saucepan, whisk jelly over low heat until melted. Brush over the top of the warm cake. Serve warm or at room temperature.

Serves 10.

320 calories per serving: 5 grams protein, 7 grams fat (1 gram saturated fat), 62 grams carbohydrate; 223 mg sodium; 22 mg cholesterol.

◆**PICKING PLUMS**
Select slightly underripe plums for this cake—they hold their shape better while baking.

BANANA SPICE CAKE

As this bakes, it fills the whole house with a warm, spicy aroma that is particularly nice around the holidays. Delicious with Tropical Fruit Compote (page 59).

1. Preheat oven to 350°F. Lightly oil a large (12-cup) Bundt pan or coat it with nonstick cooking spray. Set aside.

2. Sift flour, baking powder, baking soda, cinnamon, nutmeg, allspice, ginger, cloves and salt together into a bowl; set aside.

3. In a small saucepan, melt butter over low heat. Cook, swirling the pan, until the butter turns a nutty brown, about 1 minute. Pour the butter into a small bowl and let cool slightly.

4. In a clean mixing bowl, beat egg whites with an electric mixer on low speed just until frothy. Add cream of tartar, increase the speed to medium and beat until soft peaks form. Gradually beat in ¾ cup of the sugar, 2 tablespoons at a time, just until firm peaks form; set meringue aside.

5. In a large mixing bowl, combine mashed bananas, oil, orange zest, vanilla, egg yolk, the reserved melted butter and the remaining 1 cup sugar; beat to combine. With the mixer on low speed, add the buttermilk and dry ingredients alternately in two additions each; beat just until blended. Add a heaping spoonful of the meringue and beat for just a few seconds to lighten the batter. By hand, fold the remaining meringue into the batter.

6. Pour the batter into the prepared pan and bake for 50 to 60 minutes, or until a skewer inserted in the center comes out clean. Cool in the pan on a wire rack for 10 minutes, then turn out onto the rack to cool completely. Before serving, dust the cake with confectioners' sugar and transfer to a cake plate.

Serves 16.

210 calories per serving: 3 grams protein, 6 grams fat (1 gram saturated fat), 39 grams carbohydrate; 249 mg sodium; 18 mg cholesterol.

2½	cups unsifted cake flour
2	teaspoons baking powder
2	teaspoons baking soda
2	teaspoons ground cinnamon
1	teaspoon freshly grated nutmeg
½	teaspoon ground allspice
½	teaspoon ground ginger
½	teaspoon ground cloves
½	teaspoon salt
2	tablespoons butter
3	large egg whites
¼	teaspoon cream of tartar
1¾	cups sugar
1	cup mashed very ripe bananas (2 large)
¼	cup canola oil
1	tablespoon grated orange zest
1½	teaspoons pure vanilla extract
1	large egg yolk
¾	cup buttermilk
	Confectioners' sugar for dusting

◆ **BROWNING BUTTER**

Heating butter until it becomes fragrant and brown magically magnifies its flavor. Pour the browned butter immediately into a small bowl so it won't continue to darken from the heat of the pan.

CARROT CUPCAKES

Perfect for children's parties or office gatherings at any time of the year.

CUPCAKES

½ cup pitted prunes

1 8-ounce can crushed pineapple

1¼ cups sifted cake flour

1 teaspoon ground cinnamon

1 teaspoon baking powder

½ teaspoon baking soda

½ teaspoon salt

1 large egg

1 large egg white

¾ cup sugar

¼ cup canola oil

1 cup grated carrots

TO MAKE CUPCAKES:

1. Preheat oven to 325°F. Line 12 muffin cups with paper liners or lightly oil or coat the cups with nonstick cooking spray.

2. In a food processor, combine prunes with ¼ cup hot water and process until smooth; set aside. Drain pineapple in a strainer set over a small bowl, pressing firmly to extract most of the juice. Set the pineapple aside and reserve the juice for another use.

3. In a bowl, whisk together flour, cinnamon, baking powder, baking soda and salt. In a mixing bowl, whisk together egg, egg white, sugar, oil and the reserved prune puree. Add the dry ingredients to the egg mixture and stir with a rubber spatula until blended. Stir in carrots and the reserved pineapple.

4. Divide the batter among the prepared muffin cups, filling them about two-thirds full. Bake the cupcakes for 25 to 30 minutes, or until they spring back when lightly pressed in the center. Let the cupcakes sit in the pan for about 2 minutes, then transfer to a wire rack to cool before frosting.

Carrot Cupcakes

TO MAKE CREAM CHEESE FROSTING:

In a bowl, beat cream cheese, marshmallow creme and lemon juice with an electric mixer until smooth and creamy. Spread each cupcake with frosting and sprinkle with pecans, if using.

Makes 1 dozen cupcakes.

195 calories each: 3 grams protein, 7 grams fat (2 grams saturated fat), 31 grams carbohydrate; 206 mg sodium; 24 mg cholesterol.

CREAM CHEESE FROSTING

- 4 ounces reduced-fat cream cheese
- ½ cup marshmallow creme, such as Fluff
- ½ teaspoon fresh lemon juice
- 2 tablespoons chopped toasted pecans (optional)

GLAZED POPPY-SEED CAKE

A perennial favorite that looks dressy—with very little fuss.

TO MAKE CAKE:

1. Preheat oven to 375°F. Lightly oil a 6-cup or larger Bundt or tube pan or coat it with nonstick cooking spray. Sprinkle the pan with 2 or 3 spoonfuls of sugar, tapping out the excess.

2. In a mixing bowl, whisk together flour, poppy seeds, baking powder, baking soda and salt; set aside. In another bowl, whisk egg until frothy. Add sugar, sour cream, buttermilk, oil, lemon zest and vanilla and whisk until well combined. Stir in the dry ingredients just until moistened. Transfer the batter to the prepared pan, smoothing the top.

3. Bake for 20 to 30 minutes, or until the top springs back when lightly touched and a skewer inserted in the center comes out clean. Run a knife around the inside of the pan and turn the cake out onto a wire rack to cool completely.

TO MAKE GLAZE:

In a bowl, whisk together confectioners' sugar and enough of the lemon juice to make a smooth, thick glaze. Drizzle the glaze over the cake and let stand for a few minutes until set.

Serves 12.

260 calories per serving: 4 grams protein, 7 grams fat (2 grams saturated fat), 48 grams carbohydrate; 252 mg sodium; 24 mg cholesterol.

CAKE

- 2 cups all-purpose white flour
- 2 tablespoons poppy seeds
- 1½ teaspoons baking powder
- 1½ teaspoons baking soda
- ½ teaspoon salt
- 1 large egg
- 1¼ cups sugar
- ¾ cup reduced-fat sour cream
- ⅓ cup buttermilk
- 3 tablespoons canola oil
- 2 teaspoons grated lemon zest
- 1 teaspoon pure vanilla extract

GLAZE

- 1¼ cups confectioners' sugar
- 1½-2 tablespoons fresh lemon juice

GINGER-LEMON STACK CAKE

Three layers of an airy gingerbread with a tart lemon filling in between, this is a dependable, all-occasion cake.

LEMON FILLING

- ½ cup sugar
- 2 large eggs
- 2 large egg whites
- ⅓ cup fresh lemon juice
- 1 tablespoon grated lemon zest
- 2 tablespoons butter

GINGERBREAD LAYERS

- 1¾ cups sifted cake flour, plus extra for dusting pan
- ¾ cup sugar
- 1 teaspoon baking powder
- ½ teaspoon baking soda
- ½ teaspoon salt
- 1 tablespoon ground ginger
- 1 tablespoon ground cinnamon
- 1 teaspoon ground allspice
- ½ teaspoon freshly grated nutmeg
- ¾ cup buttermilk
- ½ cup dark molasses
- 3 large egg whites
- 3 tablespoons canola oil
  Lemon slices for garnish

TO MAKE LEMON FILLING:

Have a small bowl ready. In a heavy saucepan, thoroughly whisk together sugar, eggs, egg whites, lemon juice and lemon zest. Add butter and cook over low heat, whisking constantly, until the mixture has thickened and bubbled several times, about 5 minutes. (The lemon filling must be thoroughly thickened but not allowed to scramble.) Immediately transfer to the bowl. Place a piece of wax paper or plastic wrap directly on the surface to prevent a skin from forming and refrigerate until completely chilled.

TO MAKE GINGERBREAD LAYERS:

1. Preheat oven to 350°F. Lightly oil three nonstick 9-inch round cake pans or coat them with nonstick cooking spray; dust them with flour, tapping out the excess. (If the pans are not nonstick, line the bottoms with circles of parchment or wax paper and lightly oil or spray.)

2. Into a mixing bowl, sift flour, sugar, baking powder, baking soda, salt, ginger, cinnamon, allspice and nutmeg. In another bowl, whisk together buttermilk, molasses, egg whites and oil; whisk this mixture into the dry ingredients just until blended. Divide the batter among the three prepared pans, spreading it in thin, even layers.

3. Place the pans on the middle oven rack. (If they will not all fit, place one on the rack below, switching it with another pan midway through baking.) Bake for 12 to 15 minutes, or until the top springs back when lightly touched in the center; do not overbake. Let the cake layers cool in the pans for 3 minutes. Turn them out onto wire racks to cool completely, right-side up (removing the paper, if used).

TO ASSEMBLE CAKE:

Place a cake layer on a serving plate. Spread with half of the lemon filling. Repeat with a second cake layer and the remaining lemon filling. Top with the third cake layer. Garnish the top with lemon slices. (*The cake can be made up to 1 day in advance and stored in the refrigerator, covered with plastic wrap. Garnish just before serving.*)

Serves 12.

200 calories per serving: 4 grams protein, 7 grams fat (2 grams saturated fat), 33 grams carbohydrate; 222 mg sodium; 41 mg cholesterol.

BUTTERMILK POUND CAKE

Keep a cake in the freezer, to be thawed and dressed up with fresh fruit or sorbet for a last-minute celebration.

1. Preheat oven to 325°F. In a food processor or blender, puree drained pears. Transfer to a 9-by-13-inch or similar shallow baking dish and bake for 40 to 45 minutes, stirring occasionally, or until the puree is thick and reduced to 1 cup. (*Alternatively, stir the puree in a saucepan over medium-low heat until reduced to 1 cup, 10 to 15 minutes. This method is faster but messier and requires more attention.*) Transfer the puree to a mixing bowl and let cool completely.

2. Preheat oven to 350°F. Lightly oil a 10-inch tube pan or coat it with nonstick cooking spray.

3. In a small saucepan, melt butter over low heat. Cook, swirling the pan, until the butter turns a nutty brown, about 1 minute. Pour into a small bowl, stir in oil and set aside.

4. Sift cake flour, salt, baking powder and baking soda into a bowl and set aside. To the reserved pear puree, add 1½ cups of the sugar, buttermilk, vanilla, lemon zest, egg yolks and the butter-oil mixture and whisk until smooth. Add the dry ingredients in two additions, folding with a whisk just until blended.

5. In a clean mixing bowl, with clean beaters, beat the 4 egg whites until soft peaks form. While continuing to beat, slowly add the remaining ¼ cup sugar and beat until stiff, but not dry, peaks form.

6. With a rubber spatula, gently fold the beaten whites into the batter. Transfer the batter to the prepared pan. Bake for 40 to 45 minutes, or until a skewer inserted in the center comes out clean. Let cool in the pan for 5 minutes, then turn out onto a wire rack to cool, right-side up. (*The cake can be made in advance and stored in the freezer for up to 1 month.*)

Serves 16.

230 calories per serving: 4 grams protein, 4 grams fat (1 gram saturated fat), 45 grams carbohydrate; 227 mg sodium; 31 mg cholesterol.

2	16-ounce cans pears in light syrup, drained
2	tablespoons butter
2	tablespoons canola oil
3½	cups sifted cake flour
1	teaspoon salt
1	teaspoon baking powder
½	teaspoon baking soda
1¾	cups sugar
1	cup buttermilk
1	tablespoon pure vanilla extract
1	tablespoon grated lemon zest
2	large eggs, separated
2	large egg whites

◆**LOW-FAT BAKING TIP**
Fruit purees can fill in for fat in baking, but prune puree or apple butter is too assertive for some desserts. The delicate flavor of canned pears works beautifully in this pound cake; baking the puree in a shallow dish is a spatter-free way to thicken it.

ORANGE CHIFFON CAKE

This recipe makes a large cake, ideal for large gatherings. Serve it with sorbet or fresh figs and orange slices, as pictured below.

2¼ cups sifted cake flour

1½ cups sugar

1 tablespoon baking powder

¼ teaspoon salt

1 tablespoon grated orange zest

½ cup fresh orange juice

¼ cup fresh lemon juice

½ cup canola oil

¼ cup frozen orange-juice concentrate, thawed

2 teaspoons pure vanilla extract

2 large eggs

5 large egg whites

¼ teaspoon cream of tartar

1. Preheat oven to 325°F. Have ready a 10-inch angel food cake pan, preferably with a removable bottom, and a long-necked bottle.

2. Into a mixing bowl, sift flour, 1¼ cups of the sugar, baking powder and salt. Stir until well blended. Make a well in the center of the dry ingredients and add orange zest, orange juice, lemon juice, oil, orange-juice concentrate and vanilla; do not mix. Set aside.

3. Separate the two whole eggs, adding the yolks to the well of dry ingredients and putting the whites in another large bowl. Add the remaining 5 egg whites and cream of tartar to the second bowl. Beat the whites with an electric mixer on high speed until they form soft peaks; gradually beat in the remaining ¼ cup sugar and continue to beat until stiff, but not dry, peaks form.

4. Without washing the beaters, beat the reserved bowl of dry and wet ingredients together just until blended. With a rubber spatula, fold this mixture into the egg whites in three additions. Pour the batter into the ungreased pan, smoothing the top.

5. Bake for 60 to 70 minutes, or until the top springs back when

Orange Chiffon Cake

lightly touched in the center. Immediately invert the pan over a long-necked bottle to cool completely upside down.

6. Once the cake has cooled, set it upright. Run a knife around the inside of the pan and slip off the outer ring of the pan. Run a knife under the bottom of the cake to release it. Invert the cake, remove the pan bottom and set the cake on a serving plate.

Serves 16.

210 calories per serving: 3 grams protein, 8 grams fat (1 gram saturated fat), 33 grams carbohydrate; 121 mg sodium; 27 mg cholesterol.

◆ *Chiffon cakes cool upside down to keep them high and delicate, so have a bottle ready over which to invert the pan.*

DATE & WALNUT CAKE

Like many Greek and Middle Eastern sweets, this cake is infused with a honey syrup. The cake is made with semolina flour, which makes it moist and dense.

TO MAKE CAKE:

1. Preheat oven to 325°F. Lightly oil an 8-by-12-inch or 7-by-11-inch baking pan or coat it with nonstick cooking spray.

2. In a mixing bowl, stir together sugar and yogurt. Add semolina, dates, walnuts, orange zest and baking soda; stir until well combined. Spread the batter evenly in the prepared pan. Bake for 30 to 40 minutes, or until the top is golden and the cake is set in the center.

TO MAKE HONEY SYRUP AND FINISH CAKE:

While the cake is baking, combine sugar, orange juice, honey, lemon juice and cinnamon in a saucepan; bring to a simmer and cook over low heat for 4 minutes. When the cake comes out of the oven, cut it into 15 pieces. Spoon the hot syrup evenly over the top, getting some around the edges and into the cuts. Let the cake cool in the pan on a wire rack. Serve warm or at room temperature.

Serves 15.

170 calories per serving: 3 grams protein, 2 grams fat (0 grams saturated fat), 37 grams carbohydrate; 65 mg sodium; 0 mg cholesterol.

CAKE

¾ cup sugar

¾ cup nonfat plain yogurt

1½ cups semolina flour (*see page 8*)

¾ cup chopped dates

½ cup chopped walnuts

2 teaspoons grated orange zest

1 teaspoon baking soda

HONEY SYRUP

⅓ cup sugar

⅓ cup fresh orange juice

⅓ cup honey

1 tablespoon fresh lemon juice

¼ teaspoon ground cinnamon

TRIPLE GINGERBREAD

Fresh, candied and ground ginger make this the most gingery gingerbread ever. It is the perfect warmup after a wintry day's activities.

GINGERBREAD

1½	cups all-purpose white flour
½	cup packed light brown sugar
1¼	teaspoons baking soda
1	teaspoon ground ginger
1	teaspoon ground cinnamon
½	teaspoon ground mace
¼	teaspoon ground cloves
⅛	teaspoon salt
½	cup dark molasses
½	cup fresh orange juice
1	large egg
2	large egg whites
3	tablespoons canola oil
2	tablespoons finely chopped crystallized ginger (*see page 9*)
1	tablespoon grated fresh ginger
1	teaspoon pure vanilla extract

WARM CITRUS SAUCE

½	cup white sugar
1	tablespoon cornstarch
¾	cup fresh orange juice
¼	cup fresh lemon juice
1	teaspoon grated orange zest
1	teaspoon grated lemon zest
2	tablespoons dark rum (optional)
1½	teaspoons unsalted butter

TO MAKE GINGERBREAD:

1. Preheat oven to 350°F. Lightly oil an 8-inch square baking pan or coat it with nonstick cooking spray. Set aside.

2. In a mixing bowl, whisk together flour, brown sugar, baking soda, ground ginger, cinnamon, mace, cloves and salt. Break up any sugar clumps with your fingers.

3. In another mixing bowl, beat together molasses, orange juice, egg, egg whites, oil, crystallized and fresh gingers, and vanilla with an electric mixer on medium speed until smooth. Add the dry ingredients and mix on low speed just until blended. Transfer the batter to the prepared pan.

4. Bake for 30 minutes, or until a skewer inserted in the center comes out clean. Let cool in the pan on a wire rack for about 15 minutes.

TO MAKE SAUCE:

1. While the gingerbread is baking, whisk together white sugar and cornstarch in a saucepan. Whisk in citrus juices and zests. Cook over medium heat, whisking constantly, until the sauce thickens and boils. Cook, stirring, for 1 minute. Strain the sauce through a fine sieve into a bowl and whisk in rum, if using, and butter. (*The sauce can be made several days ahead and gently reheated at serving time.*)

2. To serve, remove the warm cake from the pan and cut into 9 squares. Serve warm with the sauce.

Serves 9.

295 calories per serving: 4 grams protein, 6 grams fat (1 gram saturated fat), 56 grams carbohydrate; 178 mg sodium; 25 mg cholesterol.

SWEDISH ALMOND CAKE

In Sweden this buttery cake is called Toska Tårta *and is served with afternoon coffee.*

TO MAKE CAKE:

1. Preheat oven to 350°F. Lightly oil a 9-inch round cake pan or coat it with nonstick cooking spray; set aside. Sift together flour, baking powder, baking soda and salt into a bowl; set aside.

2. In a food processor or blender, puree pears until smooth. Measure out ½ cup of the puree; keep the remainder for another use. In a mixing bowl, combine ½ cup of the sugar, butter, oil, vanilla, almond extract and the ½ cup pear puree. Whisk until well combined; set aside.

3. In a clean mixing bowl, beat egg whites with an electric mixer on low speed until frothy. Add cream of tartar and beat on medium-high speed until soft peaks form. Gradually add the remaining ¾ cup sugar and beat until firm peaks form. Set the meringue aside.

4. Add ¼ cup of the buttermilk to the reserved wet ingredients and beat with the mixer on low speed. Add half of the dry ingredients and beat on low speed until just combined. Repeat with the remaining buttermilk and flour. (Be careful not to overmix or the cake will be tough.)

5. With a rubber spatula, fold in the reserved meringue. Transfer the batter to the prepared cake pan. Bake for 25 to 30 minutes, or until a skewer inserted in the center comes out clean. Let the cake cool in the pan on a wire rack for 10 minutes.

TO MAKE CARAMEL-ALMOND TOPPING:

1. In a small saucepan, combine sugar with ¼ cup water. Bring to a simmer over low heat, stirring to dissolve the sugar. Increase the heat to medium and cook, without stirring, until the syrup turns a deep caramel, 4 to 7 minutes. Remove the pan from the heat and slowly add buttermilk. (The caramel will harden.) Return the caramel to low heat and simmer, stirring constantly, until the caramel dissolves. Stir in almonds and almond extract.

2. Place the cake, upside-down, on a serving platter. With a thin skewer, poke holes all over the top. Spoon the topping over the cake, spreading the almonds evenly and letting the caramel drip down the sides. Let the cake stand for about 1 hour before serving, to absorb the syrup.

Serves 12.

255 calories per serving: 4 grams protein, 7 grams fat (2 grams saturated fat), 47 grams carbohydrate; 237 mg sodium; 6 mg cholesterol.

1½ cups unsifted cake flour
1 teaspoon baking powder
1 teaspoon baking soda
½ teaspoon salt
1 16-ounce can pears in light syrup, drained
1¼ cups sugar
2 tablespoons butter, melted
2 tablespoons canola oil
1 teaspoon pure vanilla extract
½ teaspoon pure almond extract
3 large egg whites
¼ teaspoon cream of tartar
½ cup buttermilk

CARAMEL-ALMOND TOPPING

¾ cup sugar
⅓ cup buttermilk
½ cup sliced almonds
1 teaspoon pure almond extract

Italian Cornmeal Cake

ITALIAN CORNMEAL CAKE

Called polenta dolce in Italian, this cake is not overly sweet. It is quite wonderful when served with fresh fruit.

1. Preheat oven to 350°F. Lightly oil an 8-inch springform pan or deep 8-inch round cake pan or coat it with nonstick cooking spray. Dust it with flour, tapping out the excess.

2. In a small bowl, stir together flour and cornmeal; set aside. Separate egg yolks and whites into two mixing bowls. Beat the yolks with an electric mixer on low speed until blended; gradually beat in ½ cup of the sugar and continue beating on high speed until the yolks are thick and pale, about 3 minutes. Beat in lemon and orange zests and vanilla.

3. With clean beaters, beat the egg whites on low speed just until foamy; increase speed to high. When the whites begin to form soft peaks, gradually add the remaining ¼ cup sugar, beating until the whites are stiff and glossy. With a large rubber spatula, gently fold the whites into the beaten yolks. Then gently fold in the reserved dry ingredients just until combined. Transfer the batter to the prepared pan, smoothing the top.

4. Bake for 25 to 30 minutes, or until the center is puffed and springs back when lightly pressed. Loosen the edges and unmold the cake onto a wire rack; let cool completely.

5. With a long serrated knife, cut the cake horizontally into two layers. Set the bottom layer on a serving plate and spread with orange marmalade. Replace the top layer and dust with confectioners' sugar.

Serves 8.

220 calories per serving: 5 grams protein, 3 grams fat (1 gram saturated fat), 44 grams carbohydrate; 35 mg sodium; 107 mg cholesterol.

¾ cup all-purpose white flour

¼ cup yellow cornmeal, preferably stone-ground

4 large eggs, at room temperature

¾ cup sugar

1 teaspoon grated lemon zest

1 teaspoon grated orange zest

1 teaspoon pure vanilla extract

½ cup orange marmalade
   Confectioners' sugar for dusting

◆**ZESTING**

The zest is the colored outside layer of a citrus peel. The oils in this layer are intensely flavored. When grating or peeling the zest, avoid the white pith just beneath, which is bitter.

CAFÉ AU LAIT CHEESECAKE

With its light coffee flavor and silken texture, this remarkable cheesecake is a perfect dinner-party finale—elegant, satisfying and (though no one will guess) low in fat.

CRUST

3	tablespoons Grape-Nuts *or* Shredded Wheat cereal
1	tablespoon walnuts
1	tablespoon sugar

FILLING

2½	tablespoons instant espresso coffee powder
2½	tablespoons coffee liqueur, such as Kahlúa *or* water
16	ounces nonfat cottage cheese (2 cups)
12	ounces reduced-fat sour cream (1⅓ cups)
12	ounces reduced-fat cream cheese (1½ cups), softened
1¼	cups granulated sugar
6	tablespoons all-purpose white flour
2	large eggs
2	large egg whites
1½	tablespoons unsweetened cocoa powder
¼	teaspoon salt
⅛	teaspoon ground cinnamon

TO MAKE CRUST:

Preheat oven to 300°F. Lightly oil a 9-inch springform pan or coat it with nonstick cooking spray. In a food processor, combine cereal, walnuts and sugar; process until fine crumbs form. Place the crumb mixture in the prepared pan; tilt and rotate the pan to coat the bottom and sides with crumbs. Tap the pan on the counter to evenly distribute the crumbs. Set aside.

TO MAKE FILLING:

1. In a small bowl, dissolve instant coffee powder in coffee liqueur or water and set aside. Place cottage cheese in a double layer of cheesecloth and gather the corners at the top; squeeze out as much liquid as possible. Place the pressed cottage cheese in a food processor and process until very smooth, about 2 minutes. Add sour cream, cream cheese, sugar, flour, eggs, egg whites, cocoa, salt, cinnamon and the coffee liqueur mixture; process until smooth.

2. Transfer the batter to the prepared pan and bake for about 1 hour, or until firm around the edges but still wobbly in the center. Turn off the oven and leave the cheesecake inside with the door closed for 30 minutes longer. Remove the cheesecake from the oven and let it cool completely on a wire rack. Remove the outer ring of the pan. Cover the cheesecake with plastic wrap that has been lightly sprayed with nonstick cooking spray. Refrigerate for at least 4 hours or up to 2 days.

Serves 16.

195 calories per serving: 8 grams protein, 8 grams fat (5 grams saturated fat), 22 grams carbohydrate; 159 mg sodium; 51 mg cholesterol.

◆**LOW-FAT BAKING TIP**

Nonfat cottage cheese can replace a lot of the usual high-fat cream cheese in a cheesecake, but it needs to have some of the water removed.

HEAVENLY PIES

W hen the crust is tender and the filling is fresh and
sweet, a pie can be a little slice of paradise. But
pie-baking seems to intimidate many cooks, which
is a shame because, in the words of accomplished pie baker
and cookbook author Lisa Cherkasky, "As long as a pie is
homemade, it is good. Even if it doesn't come out picture
perfect, people still love it."

Pies present a particular challenge for the low-fat baker,
because a tender crust requires a certain amount of fat, and
a two-crust pie, even if made with EATING WELL's reduced-
fat crust, is a little too rich in fat for us. But an easy solution
is to bake a one-crust pie, leaving it plain and unadorned or
perhaps adding a streusel or meringue topping.

RHUBARB CUSTARD PIE

For the prettiest pie, choose rhubarb that has a deep fuchsia-red color.

CRUST

1 cup all-purpose white flour
1 tablespoon sugar
⅛ teaspoon salt
1 tablespoon butter
3 tablespoons canola oil

FILLING

¾ cup sugar
1 tablespoon butter, softened
1 large egg
2 large egg whites
¼ cup skim milk
1 teaspoon pure vanilla extract
1½ pounds rhubarb, trimmed and cut into ¼-inch pieces (5 cups)
2 tablespoons all-purpose white flour

MERINGUE

3 large egg whites
¼ teaspoon cream of tartar
½ cup sugar

♦**WORKING WITH A LOW-FAT CRUST**

Because there is so little fat in EATING WELL's *pie crust, it would get too dry if it were rolled out on a floured surface. Instead, roll the dough between sheets of plastic wrap.*

TO MAKE CRUST:

1. Position oven rack at the lowest level; preheat to 375°F. Lightly oil a 9-inch glass pie pan or coat it with nonstick cooking spray.

2. In a bowl, stir together flour, sugar and salt. In a small saucepan, melt butter over low heat, swirling the pan, until the butter turns a nutty brown, about 30 seconds. Pour into a small bowl and let cool. Stir in oil. Using a fork, slowly stir the butter-oil mixture into the dry ingredients until the mixture is crumbly. Gradually stir in enough ice water (1 to 2 tablespoons) so that the dough will hold together. Press the dough into a flattened disk.

3. Place two sheets of plastic wrap on the work surface, overlapping them by 2 inches. Place the pastry in the center and cover with two more overlapping sheets of plastic wrap. With a rolling pin, roll the dough into a circle about 12 inches in diameter. Remove the top sheets and invert the dough over the prepared pie pan. Carefully peel away the remaining plastic wrap. Fold the edges under at the rim and crimp. Chill the pastry while you prepare the filling.

TO MAKE FILLING:

In a mixing bowl, beat together sugar and butter until fluffy. Beat in egg, egg whites, milk and vanilla until well blended. In another bowl, toss rhubarb with flour. Stir the rhubarb into the egg mixture. Turn the filling into the crust-lined pan, spreading evenly. Bake for about 1¼ hours, or until the filling is firm. Let cool to room temperature before topping with meringue.

TO MAKE MERINGUE:

1. Preheat oven to 375°F. In a large mixing bowl, beat egg whites with an electric mixer on medium speed until frothy. Add cream of tartar and beat on high speed just until soft peaks form. While continuing to beat egg whites, gradually add sugar. Beat until stiff and glossy.

2. Spread the meringue over the cooled pie, making sure it touches the edge of the crust all the way around. Bake for 12 to 15 minutes, or until the top is lightly browned. Let cool for 1 hour before serving.

Serves 8.

295 calories per serving: 6 grams protein, 9 grams fat (2.5 grams saturated fat), 50 grams carbohydrate; 113 mg sodium; 34 mg cholesterol.

TWO-BERRY PIE

Raspberries and blueberries unite in a chilled pie. The berry filling is quite nice on its own, served in parfait glasses. The crust is an easy graham-cracker crust that is pressed into the pie pan.

TO MAKE CRUST:

1. Preheat oven to 350°F. Lightly oil a 9-inch pie pan or coat it with nonstick cooking spray.

2. In a mixing bowl, whisk egg white until frothy. Add graham cracker crumbs, butter and oil and blend with a fork or your fingertips until thoroughly combined. Press the mixture in an even layer on the bottom and sides of the pie pan.

3. Bake for 10 minutes, or until lightly browned. (Do not be concerned if there are small cracks.) Cool on a wire rack.

TO MAKE FILLING:

1. In a 1½-quart saucepan, combine 1 cup of the blueberries, 1 cup of the raspberries, sugar, wine and lemon juice. Cook over low heat, mashing with the back of a spoon, for about 5 minutes, or until the sugar is dissolved. Remove from the heat.

2. In a small saucepan, sprinkle gelatin over ¼ cup water; let soften for about 3 minutes. Heat over low heat for 1 to 2 minutes, or until the gelatin is dissolved. Stir into the berry mixture. Gently stir in the remaining 1 cup blueberries, 1 cup raspberries and liqueur, if using. Pour into a heat-proof bowl and set it over a larger pan of ice water. Stir gently for about 5 minutes, or until the mixture thickens slightly. Pour into the prepared crust, cover and refrigerate until set, at least 5 hours or overnight.

Serves 10.

160 calories per serving: 2 grams protein, 5 grams fat (1 gram saturated fat), 27 grams carbohydrate, 1 gram alcohol; 66 mg sodium; 5 mg cholesterol.

CRUST

1	large egg white
1½	cups graham cracker crumbs (12 whole crackers) (*see tip on page 140*)
1½	tablespoons butter, melted
1½	tablespoons canola oil

FILLING

2	cups fresh *or* frozen unsweetened blueberries
2	cups fresh *or* frozen unsweetened raspberries
⅔	cup sugar
¼	cup dry white wine
2½	tablespoons fresh lemon juice
1	envelope unflavored gelatin (2 teaspoons)
2	tablespoons crème de cassis *or* Chambord liqueur (optional)

◆**INGREDIENT NOTE**

Look for "I.Q.F." berries, meaning individually quick-frozen, which can be measured out as needed.

Raspberry Angel Tartlets

RASPBERRY ANGEL TARTLETS

Individual meringue shells hold a tart lemon filling and a cloud of fresh berries.

TO MAKE MERINGUE SHELLS:

1. Preheat oven to 275°F. Lightly coat eight large (10-ounce) custard cups with nonstick cooking spray.

2. In a large bowl, beat egg whites and cream of tartar with an electric mixer on high speed until soft peaks form. Gradually beat in sugar and continue beating until the whites are thick and glossy, about 5 minutes. Beat in vanilla just until combined. Spread the meringue over the bottoms and slightly up the sides of the prepared cups. (The meringue will rise farther up the sides of the cups during baking, and sink in the center when refrigerated.) Bake for 45 minutes. Use a knife to loosen the shells but do not remove the shells from the cups. Refrigerate immediately.

TO MAKE LEMON FILLING:

Have a medium bowl ready. In a heavy saucepan, whisk sugar, eggs, egg whites, lemon juice and lemon zest until well combined. Add butter and cook over low heat, whisking constantly, until the mixture has thickened and bubbled several times, about 5 minutes (the filling must be thoroughly thickened but not allowed to scramble). Immediately transfer the filling to the bowl. Place a piece of plastic wrap directly on the surface to prevent a skin from forming and refrigerate until completely chilled, about 1 hour. (*The shells and filling can be made up to 1 day ahead and refrigerated separately until just before serving.*)

TO ASSEMBLE TARTLETS:

Spoon the chilled lemon filling into the tartlet shells and fill the centers with fresh raspberries. Dust lightly with confectioners' sugar.

Serves 8.

225 calories per serving: 5 grams protein, 4 grams fat (2 grams saturated fat), 45 grams carbohydrate; 87 mg sodium; 61 mg cholesterol.

MERINGUE SHELLS

- 4 large egg whites
- ¼ teaspoon cream of tartar
- 1 cup sugar
- 1 teaspoon pure vanilla extract

LEMON FILLING

- ½ cup sugar
- 2 large eggs
- 2 large egg whites
- 6 tablespoons fresh lemon juice
- 2 teaspoons grated lemon zest
- 2 tablespoons butter
- 4 cups fresh raspberries
  Confectioners' sugar for garnish

◆ **BEATING EGG WHITES**

Always start with a very clean glass or metal bowl when beating egg whites, because even the tiniest bit of fat will significantly reduce their volume.

BUTTERMILK CUSTARD PIE

A Southern favorite, this pie is smooth, tangy and delicious.

CRUST

1	cup all-purpose white flour
1	tablespoon sugar
⅛	teaspoon salt
1	tablespoon butter
3	tablespoons canola oil

FILLING

¾	cup sugar
¼	cup all-purpose white flour
1	teaspoon cornstarch
½	teaspoon salt
2	large eggs
1	large egg white
2½	cups buttermilk
1	tablespoon fresh lemon juice
1	teaspoon pure vanilla extract
	Freshly grated nutmeg for sprinkling on top
1	cup fresh berries, such as blackberries, raspberries *or* sliced strawberries (optional)

◆ **STRETCHING BUTTER**

To achieve a buttery taste in a reduced-fat pie crust, "stretch" a small amount of butter by cooking it until it turns light brown (not black) and gives off a nutty aroma.

TO MAKE CRUST:

1. In a medium bowl, stir together flour, sugar and salt. In a small saucepan, melt butter over low heat. Cook, swirling the pan, until the butter turns a nutty brown, about 30 seconds. Pour into a small bowl and let cool. Stir in oil. Using a fork, slowly stir the butter-oil mixture into the flour until the mixture is crumbly. Gradually stir in enough ice water (1 to 2 tablespoons) so that the dough will hold together. Press the dough into a flattened disk.

2. Place two overlapping lengths of plastic wrap on the work surface. Set the dough in the center and cover with two more sheets of plastic wrap. With a rolling pin, roll the dough into a circle about 12 inches in diameter. Remove the top sheets and invert the dough into a 9-inch pie pan. Remove the remaining wrap. Fold the edges under at the rim and crimp. Cover loosely with plastic wrap and refrigerate for 15 minutes.

3. Preheat oven to 375°F. Line the pastry shell with a piece of aluminum foil or parchment paper and fill with pie weights or dried beans. Bake for 15 minutes, remove weights and foil or paper and bake for 8 to 10 minutes longer, or until the crust is golden. Reduce oven temperature to 350°F. Cool the pie crust on a wire rack while you make the filling.

TO MAKE FILLING:

1. In a mixing bowl, whisk together sugar, flour, cornstarch and salt. In another bowl, whisk together eggs and egg white until frothy. Whisk in buttermilk, lemon juice and vanilla. Gradually whisk the liquids into the dry ingredients. Pour into the crust and sprinkle the top with grated nutmeg.

2. Cover the edges of the crust with aluminum foil and bake for 30 to 40 minutes, or until the pie is no longer wobbly in the center (do not use a knife to check for doneness or a crack will result). Cool on a wire rack for 15 minutes, and then in the refrigerator until completely cool, about 2 hours. Just before serving, arrange fresh berries around the edge of the pie, if desired.

Serves 8.

255 calories per serving: 7 grams protein, 9 grams fat (2 grams saturated fat), 39 grams carbohydrate; 285 mg sodium; 60 mg cholesterol.

BLUEBERRY STREUSEL PIE

A crunchy, lemony topping crowns this appealing summer dessert.

TO MAKE CRUST:

1. In a medium bowl, stir together flour, sugar and salt. In a small saucepan, melt butter over low heat. Cook, swirling the pan, until the butter turns a nutty brown, about 30 seconds. Pour into a small bowl and let cool. Stir in oil. Using a fork, slowly stir the butter-oil mixture into the flour until the mixture is crumbly. Gradually stir in enough ice water (1 to 2 tablespoons) so that the dough will hold together. Press the dough into a flattened disk.

2. Place two overlapping lengths of plastic wrap on the work surface. Set the dough in the center and cover with two more sheets of plastic wrap. With a rolling pin, roll the dough into a circle about 12 inches in diameter. Remove the top sheets and invert the dough into a 9-inch pie pan. Gently press the dough into the bottom of the pie pan. Remove the remaining wrap. Fold the edges under and crimp. Cover loosely with plastic wrap and refrigerate while you prepare the streusel topping and filling.

TO MAKE STREUSEL TOPPING:

Preheat oven to 375°F. In a bowl, stir together flour, sugar and lemon zest. Add butter, oil and lemon juice and work in with your fingertips until the mixture forms small crumbs; set aside.

TO MAKE FILLING AND BAKE PIE:

In a mixing bowl, stir together sugar and tapioca. Stir in lemon zest and juice. Add blueberries and stir gently to mix. Spoon the filling into the prepared crust. Cover loosely with foil and set in the middle of the oven, with a baking sheet placed on the rack below to catch any drips. Bake for 55 to 65 minutes, or until the berries are juicy and bubbling. (Frozen berries will take about 10 minutes longer.) Uncover the pie, sprinkle evenly with the reserved streusel topping and bake for 12 to 15 minutes longer, or until the streusel is golden. Cool on a wire rack for 30 minutes, then cool completely in the refrigerator, about 2 hours.

Serves 8.

315 calories per serving: 3 grams protein, 10 grams fat (2 grams saturated fat), 55 grams carbohydrate; 68 mg sodium; 8 mg cholesterol.

CRUST

- 1 cup all-purpose white flour
- 1 tablespoon sugar
- ⅛ teaspoon salt
- 1 tablespoon butter
- 3 tablespoons canola oil

STREUSEL TOPPING

- ¾ cup all-purpose white flour
- ¼ cup sugar
- 1 teaspoon grated lemon zest
- 1 tablespoon butter
- 1 tablespoon canola oil
- 1 tablespoon fresh lemon juice

FILLING

- ½ cup sugar
- 1½ tablespoons "minute" tapioca
- 1 teaspoon grated lemon zest
- 1 tablespoon fresh lemon juice
- 5 cups fresh *or* frozen unsweetened blueberries

Key Lime Pie

KEY LIME PIE

*The availability of nonfat sweetened condensed milk and nonfat yogurt have made it quite easy
to transform a high-fat classic into a low-fat delight.*

CRUST

1	large egg white
1½	cups graham cracker crumbs (12 whole crackers) (*see tip on page 140*)
1½	tablespoons butter, melted
1½	tablespoons canola oil

FILLING

1	14-ounce can nonfat sweetened condensed milk
⅔	cup nonfat plain yogurt
2	teaspoons grated lime zest
½	cup fresh lime juice, preferably from Key limes

TO MAKE CRUST:

1. Preheat oven to 350°F. Lightly oil a 9-inch pie pan or coat it with nonstick cooking spray.

2. In a mixing bowl, whisk egg white until frothy. Add graham cracker crumbs, butter and oil and blend with a fork or your fingertips until thoroughly combined. Press the mixture in an even layer on the bottom and sides of the pie pan.

3. Bake for 10 minutes, or until lightly browned. (Do not be concerned if there are small cracks.) Cool on a wire rack.

TO MAKE FILLING:

In a metal mixing bowl, whisk together sweetened condensed milk, yogurt, lime zest and juice. (The metal bowl will allow the filling to cool quickly over ice.) In a small bowl, sprinkle gelatin over 2 tablespoons cold water; let soften for 1 minute, then set the bowl in a skillet of simmering water and stir until the gelatin dissolves completely. Whisk the gelatin into the lime filling. Set the mixing bowl in a larger bowl of ice cubes, stirring occasionally, until it begins to thicken, 15 to 20 minutes. Spread in the pie shell, cover with plastic wrap and refrigerate until firm, about 1 hour.

TO MAKE MERINGUE:

1. Preheat broiler. Bring about 1 inch of water to a simmer in a large saucepan. Put sugar, egg whites, cream of tartar and 2 tablespoons of water in a metal bowl that will fit over the saucepan. Set the bowl over the simmering water and beat with an electric mixer on low speed, moving the beaters around the bowl constantly, until an instant-read thermometer registers 140°F. (This will take 3 to 5 minutes.)

2. Increase the mixer speed to high and continue beating over the heat for 3½ minutes. Remove the bowl from the heat and beat the meringue until cool, about 4 minutes. Beat in vanilla.

3. Top the chilled pie with the meringue, spreading it all the way to the edges and swirling it into peaks. Broil until the meringue is lightly browned, about 2 minutes. Chill the pie for 30 minutes before serving. Garnish with lime slices, if desired.

Serves 8.

295 calories per serving: 8 grams protein, 5 grams fat (2 grams saturated fat), 53 grams carbohydrate; 158 mg sodium; 13 mg cholesterol.

1 envelope plain gelatin (2 teaspoons)

MERINGUE

½ cup sugar

2 large egg whites

¼ teaspoon cream of tartar

1 teaspoon pure vanilla extract

   Thin slices fresh lime for garnish (optional)

◆**KEY LIMES VS. PERSIAN LIMES**

Key limes are rather small, yellow-to-green fruit with a very pungent flavor. The more familiar Persian limes are larger and darker green. For ½ cup juice, you will need 6 to 8 Key limes or 4 to 5 Persian limes.

Upside-Down Apple Pie

UPSIDE-DOWN APPLE PIE

Similar to the classic French Tarte Tatin—with the exception of the crust. Instead of high-fat puff pastry, the tart is baked under a layer of bread, which contributes almost no fat and bakes to a toasty golden brown.

TO PREPARE CARAMELIZED APPLES:

1. Preheat oven to 375°F. Lightly oil a 9-inch round cake pan or coat it with nonstick cooking spray. Melt butter in a heavy skillet over medium heat. Stir in sugar and cook over medium heat, without stirring, until the sugar caramelizes, 5 to 7 minutes. Add orange juice carefully; the mixture will sputter.

2. Peel, halve and core the apples; cut each half into 3 wedges. Add the apple wedges to the skillet, cover and cook until they release their juices, 4 to 5 minutes. Increase the heat to high, uncover and cook until the juices have been reduced to a thick glaze, 2 to 4 minutes. Remove from the heat. Push the apples to one side of the skillet. Spoon out as much caramel as possible from the skillet into the prepared cake pan. Set the apple wedges, rounded sides down, in a circular pattern in the caramel.

TO PREPARE CRUST AND BAKE TART:

1. Trim the crusts from the bread and cut each slice diagonally into 2 triangles. Arrange the triangles over the apples to form a single layer, cutting small pieces of bread as necessary to fill in the gaps. In a small bowl, stir together cider, oil and melted butter; brush lightly over the bread.

2. Bake for 25 minutes, or until the bread is crisp and golden brown. Cool the tart in the pan on a wire rack for about 10 minutes. Set a serving plate on top of the tart and quickly invert it. Reposition any apple pieces that stick to the pan, and drizzle any excess caramel over the top. Serve warm.

Serves 8.

180 calories per serving: 1 gram protein, 4 grams fat (1 gram saturated fat), 36 grams carbohydrate; 76 mg sodium; 4 mg cholesterol.

CARAMELIZED APPLES

2 teaspoons butter

⅔ cup sugar

½ cup fresh orange juice (1 orange)

1½ pounds cooking apples, such as Golden Delicious, Rome Beauty *or* Newtown Pippin (about 4)

BREAD CRUST

8 slices thin-sliced firm white bread (such as Pepperidge Farm)

2 tablespoons apple cider

1 tablespoon canola oil

½ tablespoon melted butter

GINGERY KUMQUAT & CRANBERRY TART

A rather wild and wonderful finish to a holiday meal. Kumquats, with their sweet, orange-flavored rind and tangy flesh, are a lively match for puckery cranberries.

FILLING

16   **kumquats, thinly sliced and seeded,** *or* **1 unpeeled orange, thinly sliced then chopped**

2   **cups fresh** *or* **frozen cranberries**

½   **cup sugar**

⅓   **cup currants**

2   **tablespoons chopped crystallized ginger** (*see page 9*)

CRUST

1¾   **cups all-purpose white flour**

½   **teaspoon baking powder**

½   **teaspoon baking soda**

½   **teaspoon salt**

1   **cup sugar**

2   **tablespoons butter, softened**

2   **tablespoons canola oil**

1   **large egg**

2   **teaspoons grated lemon zest**

4-5   **teaspoons fresh lemon juice**

  Confectioners' sugar for dusting

◆ **CHOOSING KUMQUATS**

A curious fruit in that the rind is often sweeter than the flesh. Look for firm, unblemished kumquats in the produce section in late fall and winter.

TO MAKE FILLING:

In a saucepan, combine kumquats or chopped orange, cranberries, sugar, currants and ginger with ⅔ cup water and bring to a simmer. Cook over low heat until the fruit is tender and the mixture is thick, 3 to 5 minutes. Set aside and let cool to room temperature.

TO MAKE CRUST AND BAKE TART:

1. Place rack in lower third of oven; preheat to 350°F. Lightly oil an 11-inch tart pan, preferably with a removable bottom, or coat it with nonstick cooking spray.

2. In a small bowl, stir together flour, baking powder, baking soda and salt. In a large bowl, beat together sugar, butter, oil, egg, lemon zest and 4 teaspoons lemon juice with an electric mixer until smooth. Beat in the dry ingredients until completely blended. (Dough should be moist. Add a bit more lemon juice if it does not press together easily.) Turn the dough out onto a work surface and knead four or five times.

3. Divide the dough in half. Working through a piece of plastic wrap so the dough doesn't stick to your hand, evenly press half of the dough into the bottom and up the sides of the tart pan. Spoon in the reserved kumquat-cranberry filling and spread evenly.

4. On a floured work surface, roll out the remaining dough into an 11-inch circle. Cut the circle into ½-inch-wide strips. Run a long spatula under the strips to loosen them. Lay half of the strips about ¾ inch apart on top of the filling. (Do not worry if the strips break—simply piece them end-to-end. If the strips are extremely fragile, gather them up, knead them briefly, then reroll.) Lay the remaining strips diagonally across the first strips. Press the ends of the strips into the edge of the crust, removing any excess.

5. Bake the tart for 30 to 40 minutes, or until the pastry is well-browned. Let the tart cool in the pan on a wire rack, covered with a clean towel to soften the top crust slightly. Dust the top lightly with confectioners' sugar.

Serves 10.

290 calories per serving: 3 grams protein, 6 grams fat (2 grams saturated fat), 58 grams carbohydrate; 198 mg sodium; 27 mg cholesterol.

NEW ENGLAND APPLE PIE

Apple butter adds to the mellow fruitiness of this harvest pie.

TO MAKE CRUST:

1. In a medium bowl, stir together flour, sugar and salt. In a small saucepan, melt butter over low heat. Cook, swirling the pan, until the butter turns a nutty brown, about 30 seconds. Pour into a small bowl and let cool. Stir in oil. Using a fork, slowly stir the butter-oil mixture into the flour until the mixture is crumbly. Gradually stir in enough ice water (1 to 2 tablespoons) so that the dough will hold together. Press the dough into a flattened disk.

2. Place two overlapping lengths of plastic wrap on the work surface. Set the dough in the center and cover with two more sheets of plastic wrap. With a rolling pin, roll the dough into a circle about 12 inches in diameter. Remove the top sheets and invert the dough into a 9-inch pie pan. Gently press the dough into the bottom of the pie pan. Remove the remaining wrap. Fold the edges under and crimp. Cover loosely with plastic wrap and refrigerate while you prepare the filling and topping.

TO MAKE FILLING AND TOPPING:

1. Preheat oven to 375°F. Place currants and cranberries in a steamer over simmering water; cover the pan and steam the fruit for 5 minutes, or until softened. Transfer to a mixing bowl and stir in apples, apple butter and cinnamon until well mixed. Spoon the filling into the prepared pie crust. Cover the pie loosely with foil and set in the middle of the oven, with a baking sheet placed on the rack below to catch any drips. Bake for 50 to 60 minutes, or until the filling is bubbling on the edges and the apples are tender.

2. Meanwhile, in a small bowl, work together oats, flour and brown sugar with a fork or your fingertips until there are no large lumps of brown sugar. Drizzle oil and ½ tablespoon water over the top and work together until the mixture forms small crumbs.

3. Uncover the pie and distribute the topping evenly over the apples. Bake, uncovered, for 10 to 15 minutes longer, or until the topping is golden. Serve warm or cooled.

Serves 8.

355 calories per serving: 4 grams protein, 10 grams fat (2 grams saturated fat), 65 grams carbohydrate; 52 mg sodium; 4 mg cholesterol.

CRUST

- 1 cup all-purpose white flour
- 1 tablespoon sugar
- ⅛ teaspoon salt
- 1 tablespoon butter
- 3 tablespoons canola oil

FILLING

- ½ cup currants
- ½ cup dried cranberries
- 6 cups thinly sliced peeled cooking apples, such as Cortland, Granny Smith *or* Golden Delicious (about 6 large apples)
- ⅔ cup apple butter
- ½ teaspoon ground cinnamon

TOPPING

- ⅓ cup "quick" *or* regular rolled oats
- ⅓ cup all-purpose white flour
- ⅓ cup packed light brown sugar
- 1½ tablespoons canola oil

MINCEMEAT TART

The filling for this Thanksgiving standard is rich, dark and spicy, yet it has a fresher flavor than mincemeat from a jar.

FILLING

- 2 juicy apples, such as McIntosh, peeled, cored and diced
- 2 ripe pears, peeled, cored and diced
- ½ unpeeled navel orange, scrubbed and chopped
- ½ cup raisins
- ½ cup chopped dried figs
- ½ cup chopped dried tart cherries
- ½ cup packed dark brown sugar
- 2 tablespoons fresh lemon juice
- ½ teaspoon ground cinnamon
- ¼ teaspoon ground allspice
- ⅛ teaspoon ground cloves
  Pinch of salt
- 3 tablespoons brandy *or* fresh orange juice
- 1 tablespoon butter

DOUGH

- 1¼ cups all-purpose white flour
- 1 tablespoon plus 1 teaspoon sugar
- 1 teaspoon active dry yeast
- 1 tablespoon canola oil
- ¼ teaspoon salt
- 1 egg, lightly beaten with 2 teaspoons water, for glazing

TO MAKE FILLING:

In a large saucepan, combine apples, pears, chopped orange, raisins, figs, cherries, brown sugar, lemon juice, cinnamon, allspice, cloves and salt. Pour in 1½ cups water, bring to a simmer, cover the pan and cook over low heat, stirring occasionally, for 60 to 70 minutes, or until the fruits are very tender. Uncover the pan and continue cooking until the mincemeat is very thick and the juices have evaporated, about 10 minutes longer. Stir in brandy or orange juice and butter and let cool to room temperature.

TO MAKE DOUGH:

Meanwhile, in a mixing bowl, stir together ½ cup of the flour, 1 tablespoon of the sugar, yeast and ½ cup warm water; let stand until the yeast starts to bubble, about 5 minutes. Stir in oil and salt. Stir in the remaining flour, ¼ cup at a time, until the dough becomes too difficult to stir. Turn the dough out onto a lightly floured work surface and knead, adding additional flour if necessary, until the dough is firm and satiny but not dry, about 5 minutes. (Be careful not to add too much flour.) Place the dough in an oiled bowl, cover with plastic wrap, and let rise until doubled in bulk, about 45 minutes to 1 hour.

TO ASSEMBLE AND BAKE TART:

1. Place rack in lower third of oven and preheat to 375°F. Lightly oil an 11-inch tart pan, preferably with a removable bottom, or coat it with nonstick cooking spray.

2. Set one-fourth of the dough aside. On a lightly floured surface, roll out the remaining dough into a 15-inch circle. Fit the dough into the prepared tart pan, letting the dough hang over the edges of the pan. Spread the mincemeat filling in the pan. Fold the edges of the dough in over the filling.

3. Roll out the reserved dough on the floured surface. With a paring knife, cut out leaf shapes and set

them on top of the mincemeat. Lightly brush the leaves and border of the dough with egg glaze and sprinkle with the remaining 1 teaspoon sugar. Bake for 30 to 40 minutes, or until the crust is golden on top and browned on the bottom. If the top of the tart is browning too quickly, cover it loosely with aluminum foil.

4. Place the tart on a wire rack to cool slightly. Remove the rim of the pan and serve the tart warm or at room temperature.

Serves 12.

195 calories per serving: 2 grams protein, 3 grams fat (1 gram saturated fat), 42 grams carbohydrate; 59 mg sodium; 3 mg cholesterol.

◆**NUTRITION NOTE**
Our tart is low in fat and high in vitamins and minerals from the rich complement of fruits.

Mincemeat Tart

PROVENÇAL PEAR TART

A rustic confection that is traditional on Christmas Eve in Provence. The tart is best when served within two hours of baking.

FILLING

1½	pounds ripe pears, such as Bosc *or* Anjou, peeled, cored and coarsely chopped (4-5 pears)
1	tablespoon brown sugar
¼	teaspoon aniseed

DOUGH

1¼	cups all-purpose white flour
2	teaspoons sugar
1	teaspoon active dry yeast
1	tablespoon canola oil
½	teaspoon salt
1	egg, lightly beaten with 2 teaspoons water, for glazing

TO MAKE FILLING:

In a heavy saucepan, combine pears and brown sugar. Add ¼ cup water and bring to a boil over medium-high heat. Reduce the heat to low and cook, covered, stirring occasionally, for 30 minutes. Mash to a chunky puree with a potato masher. Continue to simmer, uncovered, stirring often, until very thick, about 20 minutes. Stir in aniseed and cool to room temperature. (*The filling can be made up to 2 days in advance and stored, covered, in the refrigerator. Bring to room temperature before proceeding.*)

TO MAKE DOUGH:

Meanwhile, in a mixing bowl, stir together ½ cup of the flour, sugar, yeast and ½ cup warm water; let stand 5 minutes. Stir in oil and salt. Stir in the remaining flour, ¼ cup at a time, until the dough becomes too difficult to stir. Turn the dough out onto a lightly floured work surface and knead, adding additional flour if necessary, until the dough is firm and satiny but not dry, about 5 minutes. Place the dough in an oiled bowl, cover with plastic wrap, and let rise until doubled in bulk, about 45 minutes to 1 hour.

TO ASSEMBLE AND BAKE TART:

1. Position rack in lower third of oven and preheat to 375°F. Lightly oil an 11-inch tart pan, preferably with a removable bottom, or coat it with nonstick cooking spray.

2. Set one-third of the dough aside. On a lightly floured surface, roll out the remaining dough into a 14-inch circle. Fit the dough into the prepared tart pan, letting the dough hang slightly over the edges of the pan. Roll out the remaining dough into a 10½-inch circle and cut it into 16 strips ¼ inch wide.

3. Spread the filling in the pan. Lay 8 of the strips across the filling, pressing the ends into the edge. Lay the remaining strips on top at an angle to create a crisscross pattern. Fold the edge of the dough over the ends. Lightly brush the dough with egg glaze.

4. Bake for 30 to 40 minutes, or until the crust is golden. If the tart browns too quickly, cover loosely with foil. Cool on a wire rack.

Serves 8.

150 calories per serving: 3 grams protein, 2 grams fat (0 grams saturated fat), 31 grams carbohydrate; 134 mg sodium; 0 mg cholesterol.

LEMON CREAM PIE

A refreshing finish to a meal at any time of the year.

TO MAKE CRUST:

Preheat oven to 350°F. Lightly oil a 9-inch pie pan or coat it with nonstick cooking spray. In a medium bowl, whisk egg white until frothy. Add graham cracker crumbs, butter and oil and blend with a fork or your fingertips until thoroughly combined. Press the mixture in an even layer on the bottom and sides of the pie pan. Bake for 10 minutes, or until lightly browned. (Do not be concerned if there are small cracks.) Cool on a wire rack.

TO MAKE FILLING:

1. Line a colander or strainer with cheesecloth or coffee filters and set over a bowl. Spoon in yogurt and let drain in the refrigerator until it measures 1½ cups, 45 minutes to 1 hour.

2. Meanwhile, in a heavy nonreactive saucepan, stir together sugar and lemon juice. Bring to a boil and cook over medium-low heat until the syrup reaches 239°F on a candy thermometer (soft-ball stage), about 3 minutes. To be sure the syrup has reached the proper temperature, spoon a few drops into a glass of ice water; it should form a soft ball on the bottom of the glass. Remove the syrup from the heat and pour it into a mixing bowl.

3. In a small bowl, sprinkle gelatin over ⅓ cup cold water. Let soften for 5 minutes, then whisk into the lemon syrup until completely dissolved. Set the syrup aside to cool for 1 hour. (*Alternatively, set the bowl of syrup into a larger bowl of ice and stir occasionally until cool.*)

4. Whisk the drained yogurt and lemon zest into the cooled syrup. Refrigerate until very cool, stirring occasionally, about 1 hour. (*Or, again, stir over ice.*) To enhance the color, add about 2 drops of yellow food coloring, if desired.

5. In a chilled bowl, whip cream until moderately stiff; fold into the yogurt mixture. Spoon the filling into the crust and refrigerate until firm, about 2 hours. Just before serving, garnish with lemon slices and mint sprigs. (*The pie can be made up to 1 day ahead.*)

Serves 8.

280 calories per serving: 6 grams protein, 10 grams fat (5 grams saturated fat), 44 grams carbohydrate; 128 mg sodium; 23 mg cholesterol.

CRUST

- 1 large egg white
- 1½ cups graham cracker crumbs (12 whole crackers) (*see tip on page 140*)
- 1½ tablespoons butter, melted
- 1½ tablespoons canola oil

FILLING

- 2 cups nonfat vanilla yogurt
- 1¼ cups sugar
- ½ cup fresh lemon juice
- 1 envelope plain gelatin (2 teaspoons)
- 1 teaspoon grated lemon zest
  Yellow food coloring (optional)
- ½ cup whipping cream
  Lemon slices and mint leaves for garnish

◆**DRAINING YOGURT**
Avoid yogurts with added starch, gums or gelatin, as these will not drain and thicken properly.

Banana-Chocolate Dream Pie

BANANA-CHOCOLATE DREAM PIE

Creamy, dark and delectable, this is a grownup version of a childhood pleasure.

CRUST

  1   cup all-purpose white flour
  1   tablespoon sugar
  ⅛ teaspoon salt
  1   tablespoon butter
  3   tablespoons canola oil

TO MAKE CRUST:

1. Coat a 9-inch pie pan with nonstick cooking spray. In a medium bowl, stir together flour, sugar and salt. In a small saucepan, melt butter over low heat. Cook, swirling the pan, until the butter turns a nutty brown, about 30 seconds. Pour into a small bowl and stir in oil. Using a fork, slowly stir the butter-oil mixture into the flour until the mixture is crumbly. Gradually stir in enough ice water (1 to 2 tablespoons) so that the dough will hold together. Press the dough into a flattened disk.

2. Place two overlapping lengths of plastic wrap on the work surface. Set the dough in the center and cover with two more sheets of plastic wrap. With a rolling pin, roll the dough into a circle about 12 inches in diameter. Remove the top sheets and invert the dough over the prepared pie pan. Gently press the dough into the bottom of the pie pan. Remove the remaining wrap. Fold the edges under and crimp. Prick the bottom with a fork. Cover and place in the freezer for 10 minutes. Meanwhile, preheat oven to 400°F.

3. Line the pastry shell with a piece of foil or parchment paper and fill with pie weights or dried beans. Bake for 10 minutes. Remove paper and weights. Protect the edges with strips of aluminum foil. Bake for 10 to 12 minutes longer, or until the crust is golden. Cool on a wire rack. Reduce oven temperature to 350°F.

TO MAKE FILLING:

1. In a mixing bowl, whisk together ¼ cup of the evaporated skim milk, egg, brown sugar, cocoa and cornstarch. In a heavy saucepan, heat the remaining 1 cup evaporated skim milk over medium heat until steaming. Whisk the hot milk into the egg mixture. Return the mixture to the pan and cook over medium heat, whisking constantly, until the mixture bubbles and thickens, about 2 minutes. Remove from the heat and add chocolate, stirring until it has melted. Stir in coffee liqueur and vanilla.

2. Peel and thinly slice bananas, arranging in the bottom of the baked pie shell. Spoon in the chocolate filling, spreading evenly. Set aside while you make the meringue.

TO MAKE MERINGUE:

In a large bowl, beat egg whites with an electric mixer until frothy. Add cream of tartar and beat until soft peaks form. Slowly add sugar, beating until the mixture holds stiff, shiny peaks. Blend in vanilla. Spread the meringue over the filling, sealing to the edge of the crust. With a metal spatula or the back of a spoon, make attractive peaks. Bake for 15 minutes at 350°F; the top should be beautifully browned. Cool the pie on a wire rack for about 2 hours before serving.

Serves 8.

305 calories per serving: 7 grams protein, 9 grams fat (2 grams saturated fat), 50 grams carbohydrate; 126 mg sodium; 32 mg cholesterol.

FILLING

- 1¼ cups evaporated skim milk
- 1 large egg
- ⅓ cup packed light brown sugar
- 3 tablespoons unsweetened cocoa powder, preferably Dutch-process
- 1 tablespoon cornstarch
- 1 ounce bittersweet (*not* unsweetened) chocolate, coarsely chopped
- 1 tablespoon Kahlúa *or* other coffee-flavored liqueur
- 1 teaspoon pure vanilla extract
- 2 large *or* 3 small ripe, but firm, bananas

MERINGUE

- 3 large egg whites
- ¼ teaspoon cream of tartar
- ½ cup granulated sugar
- 1 teaspoon pure vanilla extract

♦**INGREDIENT NOTE**
Cream of tartar improves stability and volume in beaten egg whites.

PUMPKIN PIE WITH RUM

Dark molasses and dark rum put this pumpkin pie a cut above all the rest. If you do not have a 9-inch deep-dish pie pan, use a standard 9-inch pie pan and bake the extra filling in a custard cup.

CRUST

- ¾ cup all-purpose white flour
- ¼ cup whole-wheat flour
- 1 tablespoon sugar
- ⅛ teaspoon salt
- 1 tablespoon butter
- 3 tablespoons canola oil

FILLING

- 2 large eggs, lightly beaten
- 1 15- *or* 16-ounce can plain pumpkin puree (1½ cups)
- 1 12-ounce can evaporated skim milk
- ¼ cup dark molasses
- 3 tablespoons dark rum *or* 1 tablespoon vanilla
- ½ cup packed dark brown sugar
- 1 tablespoon cornstarch
- 1 teaspoon ground cinnamon
- 1 teaspoon ground ginger
- ¼ teaspoon freshly grated nutmeg
- ¼ teaspoon salt

TO MAKE CRUST:

1. In a medium bowl, stir together white and whole-wheat flours, sugar and salt. In a small saucepan, melt butter over low heat. Cook, swirling the pan, until the butter turns a nutty brown, about 30 seconds. Pour into a small bowl and let cool. Stir in oil. Using a fork, slowly stir the butter-oil mixture into the flour until the mixture is crumbly. Gradually stir in enough ice water (1 to 2 tablespoons) so that the dough will hold together. Press the dough into a flattened disk.

2. Place two overlapping lengths of plastic wrap on the work surface. Set the dough in the center and cover with two more sheets of plastic wrap. With a rolling pin, roll the dough into a circle about 13 inches in diameter. Remove the top sheets and invert the dough into a 9-inch deep-dish pie pan. Remove the remaining wrap. Fold the edges under at the rim and crimp. Cover loosely with plastic wrap and refrigerate while you prepare the filling.

TO MAKE FILLING:

1. Position rack in lower third of oven; preheat to 350°F. In a mixing bowl, lightly whisk eggs. Add pumpkin, evaporated milk, molasses and rum or vanilla. In a small bowl, combine brown sugar, cornstarch, cinnamon, ginger, nutmeg and salt. Rub through a sieve into the pumpkin mixture and whisk until incorporated.

2. Pour the filling into the prepared crust and bake for 40 to 50 minutes, or until the filling has set and a skewer inserted in the center comes out clean. During baking, cover the edges with foil if they are browning too quickly. Cool on a wire rack.

Serves 8.

270 calories per serving: 7 grams protein, 8 grams fat (2 grams saturated fat), 44 grams carbohydrate; 188 mg sodium; 59 mg cholesterol.

◆**CHECK THE LABEL**

Don't use pumpkin-pie mix—buy canned pumpkin without added spices.

FRUITY
FLOURISHES

The USDA Food Guide Pyramid counsels Americans to eat two to four servings of fruit every day. An excellent idea, but how many days go by when you haven't even had an apple? Simple fruit desserts are a deliciously effective way of getting the fruit you need.

It takes but a few moments to hull some strawberries or to cut up a melon; add a squeeze of lemon and a whisper of sugar, and you have a universally pleasing finish to a meal. Throughout this chapter, subtle embellishments—a spoonful of honey or a well-chosen spice or a splash of liqueur—are used to bring out fruit's inherent goodness.

MIXED-BERRY CHAMPAGNE AMBROSIA

Any combination of berries or cherries (or nectarines or peaches, for that matter) can be used. Several colors make the prettiest presentation, but single-berry ambrosia is delicious too.

¼ cup honey, preferably berry-blossom honey

2 tablespoons fresh lime juice (1 lime)

2 large sprigs fresh mint plus 6 smaller sprigs for garnish

5 cups mixed fresh berries, such as raspberries, blueberries, tiny strawberries, blackberries *or* pitted Bing cherries

2 cups chilled Champagne *or* other sparkling white wine

1. In a small saucepan, combine honey, lime juice and large mint sprigs; warm over low heat just until the honey melts. Remove from the heat and let steep for 5 minutes; discard the mint. Place the fruit in a large bowl, pour the honey mixture over and stir gently to combine. Divide the berry mixture among 6 individual goblets or dessert dishes and refrigerate until ready to serve, up to 1 hour.

2. Just before serving, pour Champagne over the fruit. Garnish each serving with a sprig of mint and serve.

Serves 6.

145 calories per serving: 1 gram protein, 0 grams fat, 23 grams carbohydrate, 7 grams alcohol; 4 mg sodium; 0 mg cholesterol.

◆**FRESH BERRY ADVICE**

Summer berries are fragile, susceptible to mold and have a short storage life.

If possible, buy fruit at fruit stands, where minimal handling means fruit is in its prime.

Look for perfect, unblemished berries in dry, unstained containers.

Wash fresh berries just before using them to prevent moisture absorption.

Mixed-Berry Champagne Ambrosia

PEAR FRANGIPANE

Whole eggs, butter and almonds are essential ingredients in a high-fat frangipane. This low-fat interpretation maintains the richness of the almonds and cuts back on the fat by omitting the yolks and using only a bit of butter for flavor.

3   firm but ripe pears, such as Bosc, Comice *or* Anjou

2   teaspoons fresh lemon juice

2   teaspoons butter, melted

¼   cup whole-wheat pastry flour (*see page 8*)

¼   teaspoon baking powder

2   large egg whites

⅓   cup frozen apple-juice concentrate, thawed

¼   teaspoon pure vanilla extract

⅓   cup ground almonds

¼   cup skim milk

1. Preheat oven to 350°F. Lightly oil a 10-inch pie pan or quiche pan or coat it with nonstick cooking spray. Peel, halve and core pears. Set the pear halves flat-side-down on a cutting board. Cut crosswise into ½-inch-thick slices: keep the pear halves intact, not separating the slices. Brush the surface with lemon juice, then with melted butter.

2. In a small bowl, stir together flour and baking powder. In a mixing bowl, beat egg whites with an electric mixer until soft peaks form. Gradually add apple-juice concentrate and vanilla, beating until stiff peaks form. Fold in the dry ingredients and almonds. Gently stir in milk. (The batter will decrease in volume.) Turn the batter into the prepared pan.

3. To assemble the dessert, slide a metal spatula under a sliced pear half, pressing gently to fan it slightly, and set it stem-end-to-the-center on the batter. Repeat with remaining pear halves. Bake for 25 to 35 minutes, or until golden. Serve warm.

Serves 6.

150 calories per serving: 4 grams protein, 5 grams fat (1 gram saturated fat), 23 grams carbohydrate; 56 mg sodium; 4 mg cholesterol.

◆**GRINDING ALMONDS**

If you have whole, not ground, almonds, grind them in the food processor with a teaspoon of sugar. Do not overwork them or they will get oily.

SLICED ORANGES WITH WARM RASPBERRIES

Warming the berries enhances their flavor and makes a pleasing contrast to the cool orange slices. Fresh pineapple can stand in for the oranges.

1. With a sharp knife, remove and discard the skin and white pith from oranges; slice the oranges crosswise and arrange on 4 dessert plates.

2. In a small saucepan, combine sugar, lemon juice and cinnamon; stir over low heat until bubbling. Add raspberries and stir gently until the berries are warmed through or just thawed. Spoon over the orange slices and serve immediately.

Serves 4.

115 calories per serving: 2 grams protein, 1 gram fat (0 grams saturated fat), 29 grams carbohydrate; 0 mg sodium; 0 mg cholesterol.

4   seedless oranges, such as navel oranges

2   tablespoons sugar

1   tablespoon fresh lemon juice

¼   teaspoon ground cinnamon

2   cups fresh *or* frozen unsweetened raspberries (*not* thawed)

ROASTED PINEAPPLE

The natural sweetness of pineapple comes through particularly well when the fruit is roasted. Pepper adds an unexpected lively accent.

Preheat oven to 500°F. Slice off the top and bottom of pineapple and cut it into 8 slices, each about 1 inch thick. Rub the slices lightly with oil, sprinkle with pepper and place in a single layer on a baking sheet. Roast for 15 minutes, flip slices over and roast for an additional 10 minutes. The pineapple should be lightly browned on both sides. Remove from the oven and immediately sprinkle with brown sugar. (*The pineapple can be roasted up to 2 hours ahead of time; let it cool and then cover loosely with plastic wrap and leave at room temperature.*) Cut into wedges and serve with lime quarters for squeezing.

Serves 6.

80 calories per serving: 1 gram protein, 2 grams fat (0 grams saturated fat), 26 grams carbohydrate; 2 mg sodium; 0 mg cholesterol.

1   large ripe pineapple

2   teaspoons canola oil
    Freshly ground black pepper to taste

2   tablespoons brown sugar

2   limes, quartered

◆**FRESH PINEAPPLE**

A perfectly ripe pineapple will have a fruity aroma and a slight "give" when pressed. Keep it in the refrigerator to prevent further ripening.

Brandied Nectarines

BRANDIED NECTARINES

Perfumed with vanilla and brandy, these nectarines are elegant in their simplicity. Use only perfectly ripe, juicy fruit.

½ cup brandy, preferably
    Cognac
2   tablespoons sugar
    1-inch piece of vanilla
    bean
4   medium nectarines, halved
    and pitted

1. In a skillet large enough to hold the nectarines in a single layer, stir together brandy and sugar. Add vanilla bean. Place nectarines cut-side down in the skillet and bring to a simmer over low heat. (Be careful working over a gas burner, as the warm brandy is quite flammable.) Cover the pan and simmer the nectarines for 10 to 15 minutes, or until just tender when pierced with a skewer. Check occasionally to be sure the nectarines are not sticking to the bottom of the skillet.

2. Remove the pan from the heat, uncover and let cool briefly; slip off and discard the nectarine skins if they come away easily. Transfer the nectarines cut-side up to a serving dish and spoon the syrup over the top. Serve warm.

Serves 4.

90 calories per serving: 1 gram protein, 0 grams fat, 22 grams carbohydrate; 0 mg sodium; 0 mg cholesterol.

SCALLOPED BANANAS

Eating Well Test Kitchen Director Patsy Jamieson developed this recipe for an April Fool's Day feature. The banana pieces resemble fried scallops and the Vanilla Cream looks like tartar sauce.

1. Preheat oven to 450°F. Line a baking sheet with aluminum foil. Set a rack on top and coat it with nonstick cooking spray.

2. In a shallow dish, combine gingersnap crumbs, oil and butter. Mix with your fingertips until well blended; set aside. In a medium bowl, whisk together egg white, brown sugar and lemon juice; set aside.

3. Peel bananas and trim pointed tips. Cut bananas crosswise into ¾-inch pieces. Dip about 6 pieces into the egg-white mixture, then, with 2 forks, transfer them to the crumb mixture. With 2 clean forks, roll the banana pieces in the crumbs until evenly coated. Place on the prepared rack. Repeat with the remaining banana pieces.

4. Bake until crisp, golden and heated through, about 8 to 12 minutes. Arrange the hot bananas on dessert plates, garnish with lemon wedges and mint sprigs and pass the Vanilla Cream separately, if using.

Serves 4.

255 calories per serving: 3 grams protein, 6 grams fat (1 gram saturated fat), 49 grams carbohydrate; 236 mg sodium; 3 mg cholesterol.

1	cup gingersnap crumbs (about 16 cookies)
2	teaspoons canola oil
1	teaspoon butter, melted
1	large egg white
2	tablespoons dark brown sugar
1	teaspoon fresh lemon juice
3	large ripe, but firm bananas
	Lemon wedges and mint sprigs for garnish
½	cup Vanilla Cream (*page 182*), optional

◆**INGREDIENT NOTE**

For this recipe and others in this book, use commercial "old-fashioned" gingersnaps—the small, flat ones sold in a box. They are quite flavorful and very low in fat. Turn cookies into crumbs in a food processor, or place them between two sheets of wax paper and roll them with a rolling pin.

MELON BALLS IN PORT

A traditional pairing updated with a little lime juice.

⅓	cup tawny port
1	tablespoon honey
1	tablespoon fresh lime juice
½	teaspoon grated lime zest
5	crushed mint leaves
1½	cups cantaloupe balls
1½	cups honeydew melon balls
	Fresh mint for garnish

In a bowl, stir together port, honey, lime juice, lime zest and mint leaves until the honey is dissolved. Add cantaloupe and honeydew melon balls and stir gently to coat them. Cover with plastic wrap and chill in the refrigerator for 30 minutes, stirring every 10 minutes or so. Serve garnished with fresh mint leaves.

Serves 4.

95 calories per serving: 1 gram protein, 0 grams fat, 17 grams carbohydrate, 5 grams alcohol; 13 mg sodium; 0 mg cholesterol.

CHERRY AMARETTI GRATIN

Sweet amaretti crumbs make a quick, low-fat topping that is a perfect foil for tart cherries.

4	cups tart cherries (about 1½ pounds), pitted
1	tablespoon fresh lemon juice
1	tablespoon Amaretto *or* other almond liqueur (optional)
1	tablespoon cornstarch
1	cup coarsely crushed amaretti crumbs (about 18 amaretti)
1	tablespoon brown sugar
	Confectioners' sugar for dusting

1. Preheat oven to 400°F. In a bowl, toss cherries with lemon juice, Amaretto, if using, and cornstarch. Spoon the fruit into a 1-quart gratin dish or pie pan or into 4 individual ovenproof dishes.

2. In a small bowl, stir together amaretti crumbs and brown sugar. Sprinkle evenly over the cherry mixture. Bake for 20 to 30 minutes, or until the cherries are bubbling and the topping is golden. Let cool for 15 minutes. Dust with confectioners' sugar and serve.

Serves 4.

170 calories per serving: 2 grams protein, 1 gram fat (0 grams saturated fat), 41 grams carbohydrate; 153 mg sodium; 0 mg cholesterol.

◆ **SPECIAL EQUIPMENT**
Invest in a cherry pitter.
This handy tool makes the pitting go much more quickly.

TROPICAL FRUIT COMPOTE

Whole spices will infuse poaching liquids with subtle but distinct flavors. Here fruit is not cooked in the syrup, but simply macerated so that the tastes remain fresh and distinct. The spiced syrup is also a wonderful sweetener for hot tea or a base for a light punch.

1. In a small saucepan, combine sugar, pineapple juice, lime juice and zest. Tie the cardamom pods, allspice berries, peppercorns, cloves and cinnamon sticks in a square of cheesecloth and add to the saucepan. Bring the liquid to a boil, stirring to dissolve the sugar. Cover the pan, reduce the heat to low and simmer gently for 10 minutes. Remove from the heat and let cool. Stir in orange liqueur or vanilla. Cover and refrigerate for at least 30 minutes or up to 24 hours.

2. Toss the fruit in a serving bowl. Add the syrup and stir gently. Refrigerate for 30 minutes. Remove the spices and serve.

Makes about 4 cups, serves 6.

210 calories per serving: 2 grams protein, 1 gram fat (0 grams saturated fat), 52 grams carbohydrate, 2 grams alcohol; 6 mg sodium; 0 mg cholesterol.

½	cup sugar
½	cup unsweetened pineapple juice
¼	cup fresh lime juice (2 limes)
1	teaspoon grated lime zest
10	whole cardamom pods, lightly crushed
8	whole allspice berries
8	whole black peppercorns
8	whole cloves
2	cinnamon sticks, broken in half
2	tablespoons Curaçao *or* other orange liqueur *or* 1 teaspoon pure vanilla extract
3	kiwi fruit, peeled and sliced
2	mangoes *or* papayas, peeled, seeded and cut into chunks
2	seedless tangerines *or* small oranges, peeled and sliced
2	carambolas (star fruit), thinly sliced
1	cup fresh pineapple chunks
1	banana, sliced

◆**PEELING MANGOES**

The easy way to cut up a mango is to stand it up and slice the skin and fruit from each side as a single piece, just clearing the long, flat seed. Score the flesh in small cubes through to the skin, press the skin so the cut side pops out like a hand grenade, and slice the cubes off the skin.

BAKED FIGS WITH RASPBERRIES & YOGURT CREAM

Figs warm from the oven, cool yogurt cream and juicy fresh raspberries make a sublime trio.

1	cup nonfat plain yogurt
⅓	cup light whipping cream
3	tablespoons confectioners' sugar
1	teaspoon eau-de-vie de framboise *or* kirsch (optional)
8	ripe fresh figs, quartered lengthwise
1	tablespoon granulated sugar
1	tablespoon fresh lemon juice
1	cup fresh raspberries

1. Line a small strainer with cheesecloth or a paper coffee filter and set it over a bowl. Spoon in yogurt and let it drain in the refrigerator until reduced to ½ cup, about 2 hours.

2. In a chilled mixing bowl, beat cream to soft peaks. Add the drained yogurt, confectioners' sugar and framboise or kirsch; fold in with a rubber spatula. (*The yogurt cream may be used immediately or refrigerated, covered, for up to 8 hours.*)

3. Preheat oven to 450°F. In a shallow ovenproof baking dish, arrange figs in a single layer, cut-side up. Sprinkle with granulated sugar and lemon juice. Bake for 15 minutes, or until the figs are heated through and the sugar has melted.

4. Spoon the yogurt cream into 4 dessert dishes. Set the warm figs on top and garnish with raspberries. Serve immediately.

Serves 4.

210 calories per serving: 5 grams protein, 7 grams fat (4 grams saturated fat), 36 grams carbohydrate; 51 mg sodium; 23 mg cholesterol.

♦**SELECTING FRESH FIGS**
Fresh figs have fragile skin and bruise easily; choose blemish-free fruit.
When ripe they are slightly soft and have a mild, sweet scent.
There are green and purple varieties; either will work in this recipe.

Baked Figs with Raspberries & Yogurt Cream

STONE-FRUIT SOUP

A colorful and unusual finale to dinner, and great for breakfast as well.

½ cup dried apricots, thinly sliced

½ cup dried peaches, diced

2 tablespoons sugar

2 cinnamon sticks

1 vanilla bean, split lengthwise

1½ teaspoons cornstarch

½ cup dried tart cherries

2 tablespoons fresh lemon juice

1. In a saucepan, combine apricots, peaches, sugar, cinnamon sticks, vanilla bean and 6 cups water. Bring to a boil, reduce the heat and simmer until the fruit is tender, about 15 minutes.

2. In a small dish, stir together cornstarch and 2 tablespoons cold water. Add the cornstarch mixture to the simmering soup, stirring constantly, until the soup thickens slightly. Remove from the heat and stir in cherries and lemon juice. Cover the pan and let the cherries plump for about 15 minutes. Remove the cinnamon sticks and vanilla bean before serving.

Makes about 6 cups, serves 6.

105 calories per serving: 1 gram protein, 0 grams fat, 27 grams carbohydrate; 3 mg sodium; 0 mg cholesterol.

APPLES POACHED IN WHITE WINE

If you haven't cooked with a real vanilla bean, this simple dessert is a lovely way to experience its exquisite flavor.

2 cups dry white wine

½ cup sugar

4 Golden Delicious apples, peeled, quartered and cored

1 3-inch-long piece vanilla bean

1 3-inch-long strip lemon zest

1. In a large saucepan, heat wine and sugar over medium heat, stirring until the sugar dissolves. Add apples, vanilla bean and lemon zest and bring to a simmer. Reduce the heat to low, cover and cook until the apples are just tender when pierced with a skewer, 8 to 10 minutes. With a slotted spoon, transfer the apples to a serving bowl.

2. Rapidly boil the remaining poaching liquid over high heat until it is reduced to a syrup, about 15 minutes; spoon over the apples and refrigerate until chilled.

Serves 4.

250 calories per serving: 0 grams protein, 0 grams fat, 46 grams carbohydrate; 7 mg sodium; 0 mg cholesterol.

SPICED WINE & FRUIT

This recipe suggests a combination of plums and raspberries, but the spiced-wine syrup can be used with any seasonal fruits.

1. In a saucepan, combine wine, sugar and ¼ cup water. Bring to a boil. Tie vanilla bean, ginger and cinnamon stick in cheesecloth and add to the wine mixture. Reduce the heat to low and simmer for 3 minutes.

2. Add plums, cover and simmer gently for 5 to 7 minutes, turning once or twice, or until tender. Remove the pan from the heat and gently stir in raspberries and lemon juice. Let stand for 20 minutes. Discard the spices. (*The fruit can be prepared ahead and stored, covered, in the refrigerator for up to 2 days.*) Serve warm or cool, with yogurt, if desired.

Serves 4.

180 calories per serving: 0 grams protein, 0 grams fat, 49 grams carbohydrate; 3 mg sodium; 0 mg cholesterol.

1	cup white wine, preferably a slightly sweet Rhine *or* Mosel
½	cup sugar
½	vanilla bean, split lengthwise
4	thin slices peeled fresh ginger
½	cinnamon stick
1	pound prune plums (12-16), halved and pitted
1	cup fresh raspberries
1	tablespoon fresh lemon juice
1	cup nonfat vanilla yogurt (optional)

DRIED FRUIT COMPOTE

An easy winter dessert; leftovers are good at breakfast.

In a large saucepan, combine fruits, sugar, clove and cinnamon stick with 6 cups water. Bring to a simmer over medium heat. Cover the pan, reduce the heat to low and simmer until tender, 30 to 45 minutes. Remove the lemons, clove and cinnamon stick before serving warm or chilled.

Makes about 8 cups, serves 16.

120 calories per serving: 1 gram protein, 0 grams fat, 32 grams carbohydrate; 3 mg sodium; 0 mg cholesterol.

¾	pound pitted prunes
½	pound dried peaches, apples *or* pears
½	cup raisins
1	lemon, quartered
½	cup sugar
1	whole clove
1	cinnamon stick

CRANBERRY BAKED APPLES

Serve these pretty stuffed apples on their own or sitting in a pool of Vanilla Custard Sauce (page 182).

4   large cooking apples, such
      as Golden Delicious,
      Cortland *or* Rome

½   cup dried cranberries *or*
      currants

¼   cup packed light brown
      sugar

2   teaspoons butter

¼   cup apple cider *or* apple
      juice

1. Preheat oven to 450°F. Remove a thin slice from the bottom of each apple so it will stand. Remove a ¾-inch slice from the top. With a melon baller or grapefruit spoon, scoop out the center core of each apple. (Do not cut all the way through the bottom; leave a thick shell on the sides.)

2. In a small bowl, stir together cranberries or currants and brown sugar. Spoon ¼ of the mixture into each apple cavity. Set the apples in a small baking dish. Dot the top of each apple with ½ teaspoon butter. Pour cider or juice around the apples and cover the dish tightly with foil.

3. Bake for 30 minutes, or until the apples are almost tender. Uncover the pan and baste the apples with the pan juices. Bake uncovered for 10 minutes longer, basting once or twice more, or until the apples are tender and the juices are slightly reduced. Spoon the juices into the centers of the apples and serve warm.

Serves 4.

210 calories per serving: 1 gram protein, 2 grams fat (1 gram saturated fat), 50 grams carbohydrate; 26 mg sodium; 5 mg cholesterol.

◆**COOKING APPLES**

Often maligned as bland, a Golden Delicious can be surprisingly juicy and flavorful when eaten straight from the tree. This sweet apple holds its shape very well when cooked.

BAKED PEARS WITH GINGERSNAP CRUMBS

Bathed in honey-lemon syrup, this easy dessert is a comfort on a chilly night.

1. Preheat oven to 425°F. Crush gingersnaps between two pieces of plastic wrap or wax paper with a rolling pin or heavy pan. In a small bowl, whisk together honey, lemon juice and ginger.

2. Place pears, cut-side up, in a shallow 1-quart baking dish. Pour the honey syrup over the pears and sprinkle with the gingersnap crumbs. Bake for 10 minutes, baste with the syrup, then bake for 10 to 15 minutes longer, or until the pears are tender when pierced with a skewer and the syrup has thickened. Serve warm or at room temperature, with the sauce spooned over the pears.

Serves 4.

215 calories per serving: 1 gram protein, 1 gram fat (0 grams saturated fat), 54 grams carbohydrate; 45 mg sodium; 0 mg cholesterol.

4	gingersnaps
¼	cup honey
¼	cup fresh lemon juice (about 2 lemons)
½	teaspoon ground ginger
4	pears, peeled, halved and cored

PEARS ROYALE

Crème de cassis and white wine make up the fruity apéritif known as a kir royale. For this recipe, the black currant liqueur gives the pears a berry richness and a lush mahogany color.

Place oven rack in lower third of oven; preheat to 375°F. Set pear halves, cut-side down, in a baking dish. Pour crème de cassis and lemon juice over the top. Sprinkle with sugar and dot with butter. Bake, uncovered, about 45 minutes, basting occasionally with the pan juices, until the pears are tender and the juices have thickened slightly. Let cool briefly before serving.

Serves 4.

135 calories per serving: 1 gram protein, 2 grams fat (1 gram saturated fat), 36 grams carbohydrate; 156 mg sodium; 4 mg cholesterol.

4	small pears, peeled, halved and cored
⅓	cup crème de cassis
2	tablespoons fresh lemon juice
2	tablespoons sugar
½	tablespoon butter, cut into pieces

Fresh Grapefruit in Honey-Thyme Syrup

FRESH GRAPEFRUIT IN HONEY-THYME SYRUP

Here, the juice of the sectioned grapefruit is simmered down to an herb-scented sauce.

1. With a sharp knife, remove the skin and white pith from grapefruit and discard. Working over a bowl to catch the juice, cut the grapefruit segments from the surrounding membranes, letting them drop into the bowl. Squeeze the juice from the membranes into a small saucepan. Drain any juice from the bowl of segments into the pan as well.

2. With the back of a spoon, crush thyme leaves to release their fragrance. Add them to the saucepan, along with wine and honey. Simmer over medium-low heat until the sauce has reduced to ½ cup, 12 to 15 minutes. Strain the syrup into a bowl and let cool to room temperature.

3. To serve, arrange the grapefruit sections on individual dessert plates and drizzle with syrup. Garnish each plate with a thyme sprig.

Serves 4.

150 calories per serving: 1 gram protein, 0 grams fat, 40 grams carbohydrate; 5 mg sodium; 0 mg cholesterol.

3 **large *or* 4 small grapefruit, preferably pink *or* red**

2 **tablespoons fresh thyme leaves**

½ **cup dry white wine**

¼ **cup honey**

Fresh thyme sprigs for garnish

◆**CHOOSING GRAPEFRUIT**
Grapefruit flesh may be white, pink or ruby red; American consumers prefer pink and red over white, finding them sweeter, although all three varieties contain similar amounts of sugar. New red varieties to watch for include Flame, Star Ruby and Henderson.

CANDIED GRAPEFRUIT PEELS

A great cup of coffee and two or three of these bittersweet confections make a fine conclusion to a winter meal. The peels remain soft and full of flavor because they are made with the entire peel, including the white pith. The same technique works well with navel oranges.

3   **pink grapefruit**
2½ **cups granulated sugar**
2   **teaspoons fresh lemon juice**

1. Thoroughly scrub grapefruit with warm water and rub them dry. Divide the peel of each grapefruit into 4 segments by inserting a sharp knife just down to the flesh, making 4 equidistant longitudinal lines. Carefully peel back the quarters to remove the peel (including the white pith) in one piece. (Reserve the flesh for another use.) Following the contour of the peel, cut each quarter into 6 or 8 lengthwise strips.

2. Put the peels in a large saucepan and cover with cold water. Bring to a boil, blanch for 1 minute and drain. Repeat this step 2 more times.

3. In a large saucepan, combine 1½ cups of the sugar, lemon juice and the blanched peels. Cook over low heat, stirring occasionally, until the sugar dissolves. Simmer, stirring frequently, until nearly all the liquid has evaporated, 30 to 45 minutes. With tongs, transfer the peels to a wire rack and let cool for several hours.

4. Spread the remaining 1 cup sugar in a shallow dish and roll each strip of peel in the sugar, shaking off the excess. (*The peels can be stored in an airtight container, with wax paper between each layer, in a cool, dry place for up to 3 months.*)

Makes 6 to 7 dozen strips of candied peel.

30 calories each: 0 grams protein, 0 grams fat, 7 grams carbohydrate; 0 mg sodium; 0 mg cholesterol.

OLD-FASHIONED COMFORTS

Fools, buckles, cobblers and slumps are quaint names for nearly forgotten desserts. These were creations that cooks made with what was on hand, from the fresh berry confections of summer to the cozy rice puddings of winter. Old-fashioned

desserts have a goodness well worth preserving, except for one aspect. They tend to be high in fat: custards used to call for countless yolks, and full-fat cream was never an issue. Through judicious trimming, these recipes evoke the sweet memories of the past while putting forward a thoroughly enlightened nutrition profile.

RHUBARB & STRAWBERRY CRUMBLE

Serve warm, topped with a scoop of nonfat frozen yogurt.

FILLING

- 1 pound rhubarb, trimmed and cut into ½-inch pieces (4 cups)
- 1 pint strawberries, hulled and quartered
- ½ cup white sugar
- 2 tablespoons all-purpose white flour

CRUMBLE TOPPING

- ½ cup rolled oats
- ½ cup all-purpose white flour
- ½ cup packed light brown sugar
- 1 tablespoon butter, softened
- 1 tablespoon canola oil
- 1 tablespoon cranberry *or* apple juice

TO MAKE FILLING:

Preheat oven to 375°F. In a large bowl, toss together rhubarb, strawberries, white sugar and flour. Transfer the mixture to a shallow 1½-quart baking dish or 9-inch deep-dish pie pan, pressing down on the fruit to form an even layer.

TO MAKE CRUMBLE TOPPING:

1. In a bowl, combine oats, flour, brown sugar, butter and oil; with a fork or your fingers, work the ingredients together until the mixture is crumbly. Stir in the cranberry or apple juice until the mixture is evenly moistened.

2. Distribute the topping mixture evenly over the fruit. Bake for 35 to 40 minutes, or until the fruit is bubbling and the topping is golden.

Serves 6.

270 calories per serving: 3 grams protein, 5 grams fat (1 gram saturated fat), 55 grams carbohydrate; 29 mg sodium; 5 mg cholesterol.

PEACHES & DUMPLINGS

The beauty of this dessert is you don't have to heat up the oven on a hot summer's evening.

1. In a bowl, whisk flour, 1½ teaspoons sugar, baking powder, baking soda and salt. In a small bowl, combine buttermilk, egg yolk and butter. Make a well in the center of the dry ingredients and pour in buttermilk mixture; stir gently to combine.

2. In a clean mixing bowl, beat egg white until soft peaks form. Fold into the batter. Set aside.

3. In a deep skillet or Dutch oven that is at least 10 inches wide, stir together 2½ cups water, the remaining 1 cup sugar and cinnamon. Add peaches and berries. Bring to a boil over medium heat, reduce the heat to low and simmer for 1 to 2 minutes, or just until tender. Do not overcook.

4. Drop the dumpling batter by spoonfuls over the simmering fruit, placing 5 spoonfuls around the outside edge and 1 in the center. Cover and cook for 8 to 10 minutes, or until the dumplings are firm to the touch. Serve warm.

Serves 6.

300 calories per serving: 5 grams protein, 3 grams fat (2 grams saturated fat), 66 grams carbohydrate; 297 mg sodium; 42 mg cholesterol.

1	cup all-purpose white flour
1	cup plus 1½ teaspoons sugar
1½	teaspoons baking powder
½	teaspoon baking soda
¼	teaspoon salt
½	cup plus 2 tablespoons buttermilk
1	large egg, separated
1	tablespoon butter, melted
	Pinch of cinnamon
4	large peaches, peeled (*see tip on page 13*), pitted and sliced (4 cups)
1	cup blackberries *or* blueberries

♦**SUBSTITUTION**

Tangy buttermilk is high in acid, which helps to tenderize cakes, biscuits and dumplings. If you don't have buttermilk in the refrigerator, you can substitute a mixture of half nonfat plain yogurt and half skim milk.

Peach & Tart Cherry Shortcakes

PEACH & TART CHERRY SHORTCAKES

Tender, not-too-sweet biscuits spill over with a luscious mixture of almond-scented fruits.

FRUIT FILLING

1	pound tart cherries, pitted (2 cups)
¼	cup sugar
1	tablespoon fresh lemon juice
1	teaspoon cornstarch
1	tablespoon Amaretto *or* 1 tablespoon water mixed with ⅛ teaspoon almond extract
4	medium peaches (about 1½ pounds), peeled and sliced (*see tip on page 13*)
1	teaspoon grated lemon zest

TO MAKE FRUIT FILLING:

1. In a saucepan, combine cherries, sugar and lemon juice. Heat over low heat, stirring occasionally, until the sugar dissolves. Simmer just until tender, about 5 minutes.

2. In a small bowl, stir together cornstarch and liqueur or water plus extract. Stir the mixture into the cherries and cook just until thickened. Remove from the heat and stir in peaches and lemon zest. Let cool. (*The filling can be made up to 4 hours in advance; cover by placing plastic wrap directly on the surface of the fruit to prevent browning, and refrigerate.*)

TO MAKE BISCUITS:

1. Preheat oven to 425°F. Lightly oil a baking sheet or coat it with nonstick cooking spray; set aside.

2. In a mixing bowl, stir together flour, ⅓ cup of the sugar, baking powder, baking soda and salt. Using a pastry cutter or your fingertips, cut butter into the dry ingredients until crumbly. In a small bowl, combine ¾ cup buttermilk, oil, vanilla and almond extracts. Make a well in the center of the dry ingredients and add the buttermilk mixture. With a fork, stir just until combined, adding additional buttermilk as needed to form a slightly sticky dough. Do not overmix.

3. Place the dough on a lightly floured surface and sprinkle with a little more flour. With your fingertips, gently pat the dough out into a 1-inch-thick round. With a 3- or 3½-inch round cutter, cut out biscuits and transfer them to the prepared baking sheet. Press together the scraps of dough and cut out additional biscuits (you should have 6). Brush the tops with milk. Scatter almonds over the tops and sprinkle with the remaining 1 tablespoon sugar.

4. Bake the biscuits for 10 to 15 minutes, or until golden. Transfer them to a wire rack and let cool slightly. With a serrated knife, split the biscuits. Set the bottoms on dessert plates; spoon on the fruit mixture, top with a scoop of frozen yogurt, if desired, and crown with the biscuit tops. Serve immediately.

Serves 6.

435 calories per serving: 9 grams protein, 10 grams fat (3 grams saturated fat), 79 grams carbohydrate; 359 mg sodium; 12 mg cholesterol.

BISCUITS

2¼	cups all-purpose white flour
⅓	cup sugar, plus 1 tablespoon for sprinkling over biscuits
1½	teaspoons baking powder
1	teaspoon baking soda
¼	teaspoon salt
2	tablespoons cold unsalted butter, cut into small pieces
¾-1	cup buttermilk
1	tablespoon canola oil
½	teaspoon pure vanilla extract
⅛	teaspoon pure almond extract
1	tablespoon skim milk
¼	cup sliced almonds
2	cups nonfat vanilla frozen yogurt (optional)

◆**ABOUT TART CHERRIES**

The season for tart cherries is short and sweet: it peaks in late July. Look for them at farmers' markets. Pitted tart cherries freeze well. You can use sweet cherries in the filling, but reduce the sugar to 2 tablespoons.

BERRY BUCKLE

An old Yankee dessert, a buckle usually includes berries, which are sprinkled over a cake batter and then baked.

TOPPING

⅓	cup rolled oats
⅓	cup all-purpose white flour
⅓	cup packed light brown sugar
1	tablespoon canola oil
1	tablespoon apple *or* cranberry juice
¼	teaspoon ground cinnamon

CAKE

1½	cups all-purpose white flour
½	cup granulated sugar
1	tablespoon baking powder
½	teaspoon salt
1	large egg
1	cup buttermilk
3	tablespoons canola oil
1	tablespoon grated lemon zest
1	teaspoon pure vanilla extract
1	cup fresh *or* frozen unsweetened raspberries, thawed
1	cup fresh *or* frozen unsweetened blackberries, thawed

TO PREPARE TOPPING:

Position oven rack in lower third of oven; preheat to 375°F. In a small bowl, stir together oats, flour, brown sugar, oil, fruit juice and cinnamon; work the mixture together with a fork or your fingers until it is evenly moistened. Set aside.

TO MAKE CAKE:

1. Lightly oil a 9-inch springform pan or coat it with nonstick cooking spray. In a large bowl, stir together flour, sugar, baking powder and salt. In another bowl, whisk together egg, buttermilk, oil, lemon zest and vanilla.

2. Add the egg mixture to the dry ingredients and stir with a rubber spatula just until blended. Spread the batter evenly in the prepared pan. Scatter the berries over the batter, then sprinkle with the reserved topping.

3. Bake for 40 to 45 minutes, or until the top feels firm when lightly pressed in the center. Remove the outer ring of the pan; serve warm or at room temperature.

Serves 10.

240 calories per serving: 4 grams protein, 7 grams fat (1 gram saturated fat), 41 grams carbohydrate; 240 mg sodium; 22 mg cholesterol.

◆**VARIATION**

Blueberries, particularly wild blueberries, would be wonderful too.

HUCKLEBERRY SLUMP

The slump has berries on the bottom and biscuit dough on top.

Preheat oven to 400°F. Lightly oil a 9-inch deep-dish pie pan or coat it with nonstick cooking spray.

TO MAKE FILLING:

Combine huckleberries or blueberries, sugar, cornstarch and lemon juice in a mixing bowl. Transfer to the prepared pan.

TO MAKE BISCUIT DOUGH:

1. In a mixing bowl, whisk together flour, ¼ cup sugar, baking powder, baking soda and salt. Using a pastry cutter or 2 forks, cut butter into the dry ingredients until crumbly. Stir in lemon zest. In a small bowl, whisk together the buttermilk and oil. Make a well in the center of the dry ingredients and pour the buttermilk into the center. With a fork, stir until just combined.

2. Turn the dough out onto a lightly floured surface. Roll or pat into a rough 8-inch circle. Gently lift the dough and set it on the berries. Use your fingers to pinch and patch together. (The dough is supposed to look rough.) Prick the dough in several places with the tines of a fork. Sprinkle the top with the remaining 1 teaspoon sugar.

3. Bake for 25 to 30 minutes, or until the fruit bubbles and the biscuit topping is golden brown. Transfer to a wire rack to cool. Serve warm or at room temperature.

Serves 8.

260 calories per serving: 4 grams protein, 5 grams fat (2 grams saturated fat), 53 grams carbohydrate; 282 mg sodium; 7 mg cholesterol.

FILLING

- 4 cups huckleberries *or* blueberries
- ⅔ cup sugar
- 1 tablespoon cornstarch
- 1 teaspoon fresh lemon juice

BISCUIT DOUGH

- 1½ cups all-purpose white flour
- ¼ cup plus 1 teaspoon sugar
- 1½ teaspoons baking powder
- 1 teaspoon baking soda
- ¼ teaspoon salt
- 1½ tablespoons cold unsalted butter
- 1 teaspoon grated lemon zest
- ¾ cup buttermilk
- 1 tablespoon canola oil

◆**VARIATION**

Blackberries or gooseberries are also excellent here.
Adjust the sugar according to the sweetness of the fruit.

SUMMER PUDDING

Although red currants are classic in summer pudding, they are difficult to come by. Other combinations of berries, such as raspberries or blueberries, can be used. Just be sure that at least half of the berries are red for the pudding to have the nicest color.

2	cups red currants
2	cups blackberries *or* loganberries
⅔	cup sugar
¼	cup pure strawberry jam *or* seedless raspberry jam
1	tablespoon crème de cassis *or* eau-de-vie de framboise (optional)
1	teaspoon fresh lemon juice
7-9	slices firm white sandwich bread, crusts trimmed
1	cup nonfat vanilla yogurt *or* Vanilla Cream (*page 182*)

1. In a large heavy saucepan, combine currants, blackberries or loganberries, sugar and 1 tablespoon water. Bring to a simmer, stirring. Simmer over medium-low heat for 2 minutes. Remove from the heat and stir in jam, liqueur, if using, and lemon juice. Let cool completely.

2. Line a 1-quart pudding basin or soufflé dish with plastic wrap, leaving a 4-inch overhang all around. Cut bread slices in half diagonally, then fit them in the bottom and sides of the dish, trimming further to fit snugly if needed. (You will have extra slices to be used for the top.)

3. Spoon the berry mixture into the bread-lined dish; trim the bread slices level with the top. Use the remaining bread slices to cover the top. Fold the plastic wrap over the pudding, then top with a plate slightly smaller than the diameter of the dish. Weight the plate with a heavy can. Refrigerate for at least 8 hours or up to 24 hours.

4. To serve, remove the weight and plate, then fold back the overlap of plastic wrap. Set a rimmed serving plate over the dish, then invert the pudding onto the plate. Remove the dish and plastic wrap. Carefully cut wedges with a serrated knife and serve each portion with a dollop of yogurt or Vanilla Cream.

Serves 6.

280 calories per serving: 5 grams protein, 1 gram fat (0 grams saturated fat), 63 grams carbohydrate; 183 mg sodium; 1 mg cholesterol.

◆**BERRY PICKING**

Pick berries in the morning, when the temperature of the fruit is not as high. Cool the berries as soon as possible.

Summer Pudding

TIRAMISÙ

This low-fat version of the ultra-high-fat Italian dessert is exceedingly good.

8   ounces ladyfingers (60 ladyfingers)

4   tablespoons brandy

1   tablespoon instant coffee granules, preferably espresso

1   cup plus 2 tablespoons sugar

3   large egg whites

¼   teaspoon cream of tartar

4   ounces mascarpone cheese (½ cup)

4   ounces reduced-fat cream cheese (½ cup), softened

Chocolate shavings (*see tip on page 92*) for garnish

Confectioners' sugar for garnish

◆ **STRETCHING HIGH-FAT INGREDIENTS**
The flavor of rich delights like mascarpone or cream cheese can be stretched by whipping them up with cooked meringue, which is totally fat-free.

1. If ladyfingers are the soft variety, toast them on a baking sheet in a 350°F oven for 6 to 8 minutes.

2. In a small bowl, stir together 3 tablespoons of the brandy, coffee granules and 1 cup water. Brush over the flat side of the ladyfingers. Set aside.

3. Bring about 1 inch of water to a simmer in a large saucepan. In a heatproof mixing bowl large enough to fit over the saucepan, combine sugar, egg whites, cream of tartar and 3 tablespoons of water. Set the bowl over the barely simmering water and beat with an electric mixer at low speed, moving the beaters around the bowl constantly, until an instant-read thermometer registers 140°F. (This will take 3 to 5 minutes.) Increase the mixer speed to high and continue beating over the heat for a full 3½ minutes. Remove the bowl from the heat and beat the meringue until cool, about 4 minutes. Set aside.

4. In a large bowl, beat mascarpone and cream cheese until creamy. Add about 1 cup of the meringue and the remaining 1 tablespoon brandy and beat until smooth, scraping down the sides of the bowl. Fold in the remaining meringue.

5. Line the bottom and sides of a 3-quart trifle bowl or soufflé dish with ladyfingers, the flat sides toward the center. Spoon in one-third of the filling and top with a layer of ladyfingers. Repeat with two more layers of filling and ladyfingers, arranging the final layer of ladyfingers decoratively over the top, trimming to fit, if necessary. Sprinkle with chocolate shavings. Cover and chill for at least 8 hours or overnight. Dust with confectioners' sugar and serve.

Serves 12.

200 calories per serving: 4 grams protein, 6 grams fat (1 gram saturated fat), 31 grams carbohydrate, 2 grams alcohol; 124 mg sodium; 16 mg cholesterol.

CHERRY CLAFOUTIS

Originating in the countryside around the town of Limoges, France, a clafoutis is a baked fruit pudding.

1. Place rack in upper third of oven; preheat to 375°F. Lightly oil a 9-inch glass quiche dish or other small shallow baking dish, or coat it with nonstick cooking spray. Combine cherries and ⅓ cup of the sugar in the prepared dish. Bake for 20 minutes, or until the cherries are tender and very juicy.

2. Meanwhile, in a mixing bowl, whisk eggs, flour, vanilla and the remaining ¼ cup sugar until smooth. Whisk in evaporated skim milk.

3. Drain the juices from the cherries into a small bowl, holding back the fruit with a metal spatula. Reserve the juices. Redistribute the cherries over the bottom of the dish and pour in the egg mixture. Bake for 12 to 15 minutes, or until puffed and set. Dust with confectioners' sugar and serve immediately, with the reserved cherry juices spooned over the top.

Serves 4.

225 calories per serving: 6 grams protein, 3 grams fat (1 gram saturated fat), 46 grams carbohydrate; 57 mg sodium; 107 mg cholesterol.

1	pound tart cherries, pitted
⅓	cup plus ¼ cup sugar
2	large eggs
2	tablespoons all-purpose white flour
1½	teaspoons pure vanilla extract
⅓	cup evaporated skim milk Confectioners' sugar for dusting

◆ **CHERRY STAINS**
If your hands are stained from pitting cherries, a little lemon juice will remove the stains.

Pear-Cranberry Sampler

PEAR-CRANBERRY SAMPLER

Even easier to make than a classic cobbler, this comforting warm fruit dessert uses a French-toast topping.

¼ cup plus 3 tablespoons sugar

1 tablespoon cornstarch

5 ripe pears, cored, peeled and chopped (4 cups)

1 cup fresh *or* frozen cranberries

⅓ cup low-fat milk

2 large eggs

1 teaspoon pure vanilla extract

6 slices firm white bread, crusts trimmed

¼ teaspoon freshly grated nutmeg

1. Preheat oven to 400°F. In an 8-inch square baking dish, stir together ¼ cup of the sugar and cornstarch. Add pears and cranberries and stir until well combined. Place in the oven to bake for 20 minutes, stirring midway, or until the fruit is tender and the juices have begun to thicken.

2. Meanwhile, in a large shallow dish, whisk together milk, eggs and vanilla. Cut each bread slice in half diagonally, and soak in the egg-milk mixture, carefully turning the slices for even soaking.

3. Remove the fruit from the oven and arrange the bread in rows on top of the fruit. Combine nutmeg and the remaining 3 tablespoons sugar; sprinkle evenly over the bread. Bake for 20 minutes more, or until the fruit is bubbling and the bread is golden. Serve immediately.

Serves 6.

260 calories per serving: 5 grams protein, 3 grams fat (1 gram saturated fat), 55 grams carbohydrate; 147 mg sodium; 72 mg cholesterol.

LEMON MOUSSE

This velvety mousse is the perfect answer when a hearty meal needs a light finale.

1. Bring about 1 inch of water to a simmer in a large saucepan. In a heatproof mixing bowl large enough to fit over the saucepan, combine ⅔ cup sugar, egg whites, cream of tartar and 3 tablespoons of water. Set the bowl over the barely simmering water and beat with an electric mixer at low speed, moving the beaters around the bowl constantly, until an instant-read thermometer registers 140°F. (This will take 3 to 5 minutes.) Increase the mixer speed to high and continue beating over the heat for a full 3½ minutes. Remove the bowl from the heat and beat the meringue until cool, about 4 minutes. Set aside.

2. Place 3 tablespoons cold water in a small bowl. If using food coloring, add about 3 drops to the water. Sprinkle in gelatin and let stand for 2 minutes to soften. Dissolve the softened gelatin in the microwave or over the simmering water. Set aside.

3. In another heatproof bowl large enough to fit over the saucepan of simmering water, combine whole eggs, lemon juice, lemon zest and the remaining ¼ cup sugar. Set the bowl over the barely simmering water and whisk slowly and constantly until the mixture thickens and reaches 160°F. Remove the bowl from the heat and whisk in the dissolved gelatin. Let cool for 20 minutes.

4. Beat the whipping cream in a chilled bowl until soft peaks form. Set aside.

5. Whisk about one-fourth of the meringue into the cooled lemon mixture to lighten it. Add the remaining meringue and use a whisk to incorporate it with a folding motion. With a rubber spatula, fold in the whipped cream.

6. Divide the mousse among 6 dessert dishes or stemmed glasses. Cover loosely and refrigerate until set, about 3 hours. (*The mousse can be stored, covered, in the refrigerator for up to 2 days.*) Garnish with lemon slices before serving.

Serves 6.

185 calories per serving: 5 grams protein, 5 grams fat (2 grams saturated fat), 33 grams carbohydrate; 53 mg sodium; 82 mg cholesterol.

⅔ cup plus ¼ cup sugar
3 large egg whites
½ teaspoon cream of tartar
Yellow food coloring (optional)
1 teaspoon unflavored gelatin
2 large eggs
½ cup fresh lemon juice
1 tablespoon grated lemon zest
¼ cup whipping cream
Lemon slices for garnish

◆ **SAFE MERINGUE**

Fluffy meringue is a great tool for adding fat-free lightness to desserts. Although the risk of salmonella contamination in raw egg whites is very low, we do recommend using a cooked meringue.

Egg whites must be heated to 140°F and maintained at that temperature for a full 3½ minutes to destroy any bacteria. You will need an instant-read thermometer to ensure that the proper temperature is reached.

BAKED RICE PUDDING

Plump golden raisins dot these creamy individual puddings.

4½ cups low-fat milk

¾ cup sugar

⅔ cup medium-grain rice, such as arborio

½ cup golden raisins

2 large eggs

1 tablespoon rum, brandy *or* orange juice

1 teaspoon grated orange zest

1 teaspoon pure vanilla extract

1. In a large heavy saucepan, bring milk to a simmer, stirring occasionally to prevent scorching. Add sugar and rice and simmer over low heat, stirring occasionally, until the rice is very tender, about 40 minutes. Stir in raisins and transfer to a bowl to cool; stir occasionally.

2. Preheat oven to 325°F. Lightly coat eight 6-ounce custard cups or ramekins with nonstick cooking spray. In a small bowl, whisk eggs, rum, brandy or orange juice, orange zest and vanilla until well blended; stir into the cooled rice. Spoon into the prepared custard cups.

3. Bake for 25 to 30 minutes, or until the filling is just set. Cool on a wire rack for 10 minutes; run a knife around the insides of the cups and invert onto dessert plates. Serve warm.

Serves 8.

235 calories per serving: 7 grams protein, 3 grams fat (1 gram saturated fat), 45 grams carbohydrate; 86 mg sodium; 59 mg cholesterol.

LEMON PUDDING

A perennial favorite, this version has been lightened by using low-fat milk and fewer egg yolks.

½ cup sugar

1 large egg

1½ tablespoons butter, softened

2 teaspoons grated lemon zest

3 tablespoons all-purpose white flour

1 cup low-fat milk

¼ cup fresh lemon juice

3 large egg whites

Confectioners' sugar for dusting

1. Preheat oven to 350°F. Lightly oil four 6-ounce custard cups or ramekins or coat them with nonstick cooking spray.

2. In a mixing bowl, beat sugar, whole egg, butter and lemon zest with an electric mixer until the mixture is thick and pale, about 3 minutes. Add flour and beat until smooth. Mix in milk and lemon juice.

3. In a clean mixing bowl using clean beaters, beat egg whites until stiff but not dry. Gently fold the whites into the egg-sugar mixture until completely incorporated. Spoon into the prepared cups. Set them in a shallow baking dish and add enough hot water to come two-thirds of the way up the sides. Bake for 30 minutes, or until browned and set. Serve warm or chilled, dusted with confectioners' sugar.

Serves 4.

210 calories per serving: 7 grams protein, 6 grams fat (3 grams saturated fat), 33 grams carbohydrate; 132 mg sodium; 67 mg cholesterol.

CAPPUCCINO BREAD PUDDING

A richly flavored version of an old favorite, drizzled with warm caramel sauce.

1. Lightly oil a 1½- to 2-quart shallow baking dish or coat it with non-stick cooking spray.

2. In a saucepan, simmer coffee over low heat until it is reduced to ½ cup, 7 to 8 minutes; let cool to lukewarm.

3. In a mixing bowl, whisk eggs, brown sugar and cinnamon until smooth. Whisk in evaporated skim milk, then add the lukewarm coffee.

4. Arrange bread cubes in an even layer in the prepared baking dish. Pour the milk mixture evenly over the bread. Let soak for 30 minutes. Meanwhile, preheat oven to 325°F.

5. Sprinkle almonds over the top of the pudding and bake for 25 minutes. Increase oven temperature to 425° and bake for 5 to 8 minutes longer, or until the top is browned and the nuts are toasted. Let stand for 10 minutes.

TO MAKE CARAMEL SAUCE:

1. In a small heavy saucepan, combine sugar, lemon juice and ½ cup water. Bring to a boil over medium-high heat, stirring to dissolve the sugar. Cook, without stirring, until the syrup turns deep amber, 10 to 15 minutes. Remove the caramel from the heat and let cool for 2 minutes. Whisk in butter until it is incorporated, then gradually whisk in evaporated skim milk. Return to low heat and stir until the caramel has dissolved completely. Whisk in vanilla. Let cool slightly before serving.

2. To serve, dust the top of the pudding with confectioners' sugar and pass the warm caramel sauce alongside.

Serves 6.

395 calories per serving: 13 grams protein, 7 grams fat (2 grams saturated fat), 71 grams carbohydrate; 313 mg sodium; 80 mg cholesterol.

1 cup strong brewed coffee, preferably espresso

2 large eggs

⅓ cup packed light brown sugar

½ teaspoon ground cinnamon

1½ cups evaporated skim milk (one 12-ounce can)

4 cups cubed firm white bread, crusts removed (about 8 slices)

¼ cup sliced almonds
Confectioners' sugar for dusting

CARAMEL SAUCE

1 cup white sugar

1 teaspoon lemon juice

1 tablespoon butter

¾ cup evaporated skim milk

½ teaspoon pure vanilla extract

SOUFFLÉED SEMOLINA PUDDING

Unlike many dessert soufflés, this pudding can sit without falling. Old recipes often call for unmolding it after baking, but its golden surface looks so good that you can serve it right from the baking dish.

½ cup raisins

3 tablespoons grappa *or* brandy

2 cups skim milk

½ cup semolina flour (*see page 8*)

2 large eggs, separated

½ cup sugar, plus more for preparing dish

1 tablespoon grated lemon zest

1½ teaspoons pure vanilla extract

1 large egg white
  Pinch of salt

1. Soak raisins in grappa or brandy for 30 to 40 minutes, or until softened, stirring occasionally. Set aside.

2. In a heavy saucepan, bring milk to a boil; reduce the heat to low. Whisking constantly, add semolina in a thin stream. Continue to cook, whisking frequently, for 5 to 8 minutes, or until the mixture is thick and almost moves together as a mass. Remove from the heat and whisk in egg yolks, one at a time. Whisk in ¼ cup of the sugar, lemon zest and vanilla.

3. Transfer to a bowl and cool to lukewarm, whisking occasionally, about 10 minutes. Stir the raisins and their liquid into the semolina mixture.

4. Place rack in lower third of oven; preheat to 350°F. Lightly oil a 1½-quart soufflé dish or coat it with nonstick cooking spray. Sprinkle the dish with sugar, tapping out the excess, and set aside.

5. In a clean mixing bowl, beat the 3 egg whites until frothy, add salt and continue to beat until soft peaks form. Gradually add the remaining ¼ cup sugar and beat until stiff but not dry. Stir one-third of the beaten whites into the semolina mixture. Fold in the remaining whites just until combined. Carefully pour into the soufflé dish.

6. Place the soufflé dish in a baking dish and set on the oven rack. Pour hot water into the baking dish until it reaches 1½ inches up the side of the soufflé dish. Bake for 1 hour and 40 minutes to 1 hour and 50 minutes, or until puffed, golden and set. Carefully remove the dish from the water and cool on a wire rack for 5 minutes before serving.

Serves 6.

210 calories per serving: 7 grams protein, 2 grams fat (1 gram saturated fat), 38 grams carbohydrate; 74 mg sodium; 72 mg cholesterol.

♦**INGREDIENT NOTE**
Grappa is a clear brandy distilled from the skins and stems of grapes.

RUM-RAISIN BREAD PUDDING

Inspired by one of our favorite flavors of ice cream, we developed this very low-fat treat.

1. Preheat oven to 350°F. Put raisins in a small bowl, sprinkle with rum or brandy and set aside to soak for 10 minutes. Lightly oil an 8-inch square baking dish or coat it with nonstick cooking spray. Spread bread in the dish in an even layer.

2. In a mixing bowl, whisk eggs. Add evaporated skim milk, brown sugar, vanilla and nutmeg; whisk until the sugar dissolves. Stir in rum-soaked raisins. Pour the mixture over the bread. With a fork, mix in any unsoaked bread pieces. Let stand for 10 minutes.

3. Bake for 35 to 40 minutes, or until puffed and set in the center. Serve warm, with a scoop of frozen yogurt on top.

Serves 6.

365 calories per serving: 11 grams protein, 3 grams fat (1 gram saturated fat), 72 grams carbohydrate; 272 mg sodium; 73 mg cholesterol.

½   cup raisins

2   tablespoons rum *or* brandy

4   slices whole-wheat bread, torn into small pieces

2   large eggs

1½   cups evaporated skim milk (one 12-ounce can)

¾   cup packed light brown sugar

1   tablespoon pure vanilla extract

½   teaspoon freshly grated nutmeg

3   cups nonfat vanilla frozen yogurt

♦**GRATING NUTMEG**
Use a nutmeg grater or the tiniest holes of a box grater to grate whole nutmeg. (See page 10.)

FLAN

A fairly firm flan with a sublime flavor and silky texture.

½ cup sugar

2 large eggs

3 large egg whites

1 14-ounce can nonfat *or* low-fat sweetened condensed milk

1½ cups skim milk

1 tablespoon pure vanilla extract

1. Preheat oven to 325°F. In a small heavy saucepan, combine sugar with ¼ cup water. Bring to a simmer over low heat, stirring occasionally. Increase the heat to medium-high and cook, without stirring, until the syrup turns a deep amber color, about 5 minutes. (Swirl the pan if the syrup is coloring unevenly.) Immediately pour the syrup into a 1½- or 2-quart soufflé dish or casserole and carefully tilt the dish so that the caramel coats halfway up the side.

2. In a large bowl, whisk together eggs and egg whites. Add condensed milk, skim milk and vanilla, blending well.

3. Pour the mixture through a fine strainer into the caramel-coated dish. Set the dish in a larger shallow pan, such as a roasting pan. Pour enough hot water into the larger pan so it comes halfway up the side of the custard dish. Bake for 60 to 70 minutes, or until the custard is set around the edges but still wobbly in the center.

4. Remove the dish from its water bath to a rack to cool to room temperature. Then cover and refrigerate for at least 4 hours or overnight. To serve, run a knife around the inside of the dish and invert the flan onto a plate.

Serves 6.

310 calories per serving: 11 grams protein, 2 grams fat (1 gram saturated fat), 61 grams carbohydrate; 148 mg sodium; 80 mg cholesterol.

◆**INGREDIENT NOTE**

Sweetened condensed milk was developed in 1853 as a way to keep milk from spoiling. Today, health-conscious cooks use the recently developed low-fat and nonfat versions of the product for puddings and pie fillings—wherever a creamy sweetness is desired.

Flan

APRICOT FOOL

The traditional fruit for a fool is the gooseberry. But tart dried apricots work admirably as well, as does substituting yogurt for most of the usual cream.

1½ cups nonfat plain yogurt

½ pound dried apricots (about 2 cups)

¾ cup granulated sugar

½ cup confectioners' sugar

¼ cup Amaretto *or* ¼ cup fresh orange juice plus ½ teaspoon pure almond extract

1 teaspoon pure vanilla extract

⅓ cup whipping cream

¼ cup sliced almonds

1. Line a sieve with cheesecloth or a coffee filter and set it over a bowl. Spoon in yogurt and let it drain in the refrigerator for 1 hour, or until reduced to 1 cup.

2. Meanwhile, in a heavy saucepan, combine apricots, granulated sugar and 2½ cups water. Bring to a boil over medium heat. Cover and reduce heat to low; simmer until apricots are tender, about 10 minutes. With a slotted spoon, remove 12 apricot halves, chop coarsely and set aside. Transfer the remaining apricots and the cooking liquid to a food processor or blender and puree until smooth. Place in a bowl, cover and refrigerate for 20 to 30 minutes, or until cool but not cold.

3. In a bowl, stir together the cooled apricot puree, drained yogurt, chopped apricots, confectioners' sugar, Amaretto (or orange juice plus almond extract) and vanilla. In a separate bowl, whip cream until stiff. Fold into the apricot mixture. Spoon into a serving bowl or individual dishes or parfait glasses. Cover and refrigerate until chilled, at least 1 hour. (*The recipe can be prepared ahead and stored, covered, in the refrigerator for up to 2 days.*)

4. Preheat oven to 350°F. Spread almonds in a pie pan and toast for 5 to 10 minutes, or until golden. Let cool. Sprinkle the almonds over the fool and serve.

Serves 6.

350 calories per serving: 6 grams protein, 7 grams fat (3 grams saturated fat), 65 grams carbohydrate; 53 mg sodium; 16 mg cholesterol.

APPLE CHARLOTTES

Crisp, golden little versions of the classic French dessert. If you like, serve them with Vanilla Custard Sauce (page 182).

1. Preheat oven to 375°F. Lightly coat four 6-ounce custard cups with nonstick cooking spray. Sprinkle 1 teaspoon sugar in each cup and swirl to coat the inside.

2. Lay 4 slices of bread on a work surface. With a cookie cutter or paring knife, cut out 4 circles of bread, each just large enough to fit in the bottom of a custard cup. Trim the crusts from the 6 remaining slices and cut each slice into 4 squares. Line the inside of each cup with the squares, slightly overlapping them. Set aside.

3. In a large saucepan, toss diced apples with lemon juice. Add raisins, sugar and lemon zest and cook, stirring, over medium-high heat until the mixture comes to a simmer.

4. In a small bowl, whisk flour and 2 tablespoons water until smooth; stir into the apple mixture and cook, stirring, until the mixture thickens. Remove from the heat. Crack the egg into a small bowl and whisk until frothy. Stir some of the hot apples into the egg, then stir the mixture back into the saucepan. Return the pan to the stovetop; stir over low heat until the egg sets and the filling has thickened, about 2 minutes. Remove from the heat and stir in butter and vanilla.

5. Spoon the filling into the bread-lined custard cups. With a rubber spatula, press the filling well down into the cups, smoothing the top. Transfer to a baking sheet and bake for 20 to 25 minutes, or until the bread is golden on the sides and bottom. Run a knife around the insides of the cups and invert onto dessert plates. Serve warm.

Serves 4.

370 calories per serving: 7 grams protein, 5 grams fat (2 grams saturated fat), 78 grams carbohydrate; 279 mg sodium; 58 mg cholesterol.

4	teaspoons sugar
10	slices thin-sliced firm white bread (such as Pepperidge Farm)
2½	cups diced peeled cooking apples, such as Rome Beauty, Cortland, Northern Spy *or* Golden Delicious (about 3 small apples)
2	tablespoons fresh lemon juice
½	cup golden raisins
½	cup sugar
2	teaspoons grated lemon zest
1	tablespoon all-purpose white flour
1	large egg
2	teaspoons butter
½	teaspoon pure vanilla extract

MANGO-CRANBERRY COBBLER

An unlikely combination of fruits in a dessert from Texas chef Stephan Pyles.

4	cups cranberries
1⅓	cups sugar
2	tablespoons grated orange zest
2	tablespoons unsalted butter
2	tablespoons canola oil
1	egg, lightly beaten
1½	cups all-purpose white flour
1	tablespoon baking powder
¾	cup buttermilk
3	ripe mangoes, peeled, pitted and cubed *(see tip on page 59)*

1. Preheat oven to 350°F. Lightly oil an 8-by-12-inch or 7-by-11-inch baking pan or coat it with nonstick cooking spray; set aside.

2. In a food processor, pulse cranberries until coarsely chopped. Place in a large mixing bowl with 1 cup of the sugar and orange zest. Stir to combine. Let stand for 15 minutes, stirring occasionally.

3. In a mixing bowl, beat butter, oil and the remaining ⅓ cup sugar with an electric mixer until light and fluffy. Add egg and mix well. Sift flour and baking powder together and add to the butter mixture alternately with buttermilk.

4. Spread mangoes and the reserved cranberry mixture evenly in the prepared baking pan. Spoon the cobbler dough over the fruit, covering it completely. Bake for 40 to 50 minutes, or until the topping is browned and the fruit mixture is bubbling. Remove from the oven and let stand for 5 to 10 minutes before serving. (*The cobbler can be assembled 1 hour ahead and refrigerated until you are ready to bake it.*)

Serves 8.

360 calories per serving: 5 grams protein, 8 grams fat (2 grams saturated fat), 72 grams carbohydrate; 187 mg sodium; 35 mg cholesterol.

◆**JUDGING MANGOES**

Ripe mangoes are soft, like ripe avocados. The fruit should smell sweet.
Color is not an indication of ripeness. Mangoes are available year-round.

IRRESISTIBLE CHOCOLATE

It's the quintessential indulgence—and an absolute necessity for many of us. But most chocolate desserts are quintessentially rich, because chocolate itself is high in fat and it goes so well with butter, cream and eggs. In the EATING WELL Test Kitchen, chocolate desserts receive special attention: our goal is to create recipes that give this marvelous flavor its full, deep expression, but with a fraction of the fat. Chocolate mousse, fudge cake, chocolate cheesecake and 10 more chocolate classics have been revamped with enticing results.

In many recipes, cocoa powder replaces chocolate: by weight, cocoa has 60 percent less fat than unsweetened chocolate. Many of these recipes specify Dutch-process cocoa, which has a deeper flavor than American-style cocoa and imparts a darker color as well.

CHOCOLATE MOUSSE À L'ORANGE

Enjoy this low-fat mousse spoonful by lovin' spoonful: it is just as luscious as its full-fat cousin.

¾ cup low-fat milk

6 2-inch-long strips of orange zest

1 teaspoon unflavored gelatin

2 tablespoons Grand Marnier *or* other orange liqueur

1 large egg

1 cup packed light brown sugar

⅔ cup unsweetened cocoa powder, preferably Dutch-process

2 ounces bittersweet (*not* unsweetened) chocolate, chopped

2 teaspoons pure vanilla extract

4 large egg whites

½ teaspoon cream of tartar Chocolate shavings (optional)

1. In a small saucepan, heat milk and orange zest until steaming. Remove from the heat and let steep for 10 minutes. Discard the orange zest. In a small bowl, sprinkle gelatin over Grand Marnier; let stand until softened, 1 minute or longer.

2. In another saucepan, whisk together whole egg, ¼ cup of the brown sugar, cocoa and the infused milk until smooth. Cook over low heat, whisking constantly, until thickened, about 5 minutes. Remove from the heat and add the softened gelatin mixture, stirring until the gelatin has dissolved. Then add chocolate and vanilla; stir until the chocolate has melted. Set aside to cool to room temperature, about 30 minutes.

3. Bring about 1 inch of water to a simmer in a wide saucepan. In a heatproof bowl large enough to fit over the saucepan, combine egg whites, cream of tartar, 3 tablespoons water and the remaining ¾ cup brown sugar. Set the bowl over the barely simmering water and beat with an electric mixer at low speed, moving the beaters around constantly, until an instant-read thermometer registers 140°F. (This will take 3 to 5 minutes.) Increase the mixer speed to high and continue beating over the heat for a full 3½ minutes. Remove the bowl from the heat and beat the meringue until cool, 4 to 5 minutes longer.

4. Whisk one-fourth of the meringue into the chocolate mixture until smooth. With a rubber spatula, fold the chocolate mixture back into the remaining meringue until completely incorporated. Spoon the mousse into 6 dessert glasses and chill until set, about 3 hours. (*The mousse can be stored, covered, in the refrigerator for up to 2 days.*) Garnish each mousse with chocolate shavings, if using, and serve.

Serves 6.

250 calories per serving: 6 grams protein, 4 grams fat (0 grams saturated fat), 45 grams carbohydrate; 75 mg sodium; 37 mg cholesterol.

◆**CHOCOLATE SHAVINGS**
Place a block of chocolate (2 ounces or larger) on wax paper and microwave, uncovered, at medium-low (30 percent) power for 15 seconds. Turn chocolate block over and microwave for 10 to 15 seconds longer, or just until the chocolate has softened slightly but has not started to melt. Use a vegetable peeler to shave off curls. (If the chocolate is too hard to shave easily, warm it again.)

Chocolate Mousse à l'Orange

CHOCOLATE SOUFFLÉ

One word describes this soufflé: superb. The deep chocolate flavor comes from cocoa, with a small amount of unsweetened chocolate to intensify it. The result is surprisingly low in fat. Serve with Brandied Cherry Sauce (page 179) or simply on its own.

⅔ cup unsweetened cocoa powder, preferably Dutch-process

¾ cup sugar, plus extra for preparing soufflé dish(es)

4 teaspoons cornstarch

⅛ teaspoon ground cinnamon

1 cup skim milk

2 teaspoons pure vanilla extract

7 large egg whites, at room temperature

¼ teaspoon cream of tartar

Pinch of salt

½ ounce unsweetened chocolate, grated

Confectioners' sugar for dusting

1. In a small heavy saucepan, blend cocoa, ¼ cup of the sugar, cornstarch and cinnamon. Whisk in milk. Bring to a boil over medium heat, whisking constantly. Continue stirring and cook for 1 minute, or until thickened. Remove from the heat and stir in vanilla. Let cool to room temperature.

2. Position rack in the lower third of the oven; preheat to 350°F. Lightly oil a 2-quart soufflé dish or six 1½-cup individual soufflé dishes or coat them with nonstick cooking spray. Sprinkle with a little sugar and tap out the excess.

3. In a large, grease-free mixing bowl, beat egg whites with an electric mixer on medium speed until foamy and opaque. Add cream of tartar and salt; gradually increase speed to high and beat until soft peaks form. Gradually add the remaining ½ cup sugar and beat until stiff, but not dry, peaks form.

4. Stir the cocoa mixture well. Whisk about one-fourth of the beaten egg whites into the cocoa mixture to lighten it. Sprinkle in the grated chocolate and, using a rubber spatula, fold the cocoa mixture back into the remaining whites. Turn into the prepared dish or dishes and smooth the top with the spatula.

5. Place in a deep baking dish or roasting pan. Fill the pan with hot water to come one-third of the way up the side of the dish or dishes. Bake until puffed and the top feels firm to the touch, about 25 minutes for individual soufflés or about 40 minutes for a large soufflé. Dust with confectioners' sugar and serve immediately.

Serves 6.

155 calories per serving: 6 grams protein, 2 grams fat (0 grams saturated fat), 30 grams carbohydrate; 86 mg sodium; 1 mg cholesterol.

CHOCOLATE SHORTCAKES

Delicate chocolate shortcakes are a perfect pairing with early summer's strawberries. The biscuit dough for these shortcakes is especially quick because it doesn't need to be patted or rolled.

TO MAKE FILLING:

Line a sieve with cheesecloth or a coffee filter and set it over a bowl. Spoon in yogurt and let it drain in the refrigerator for 30 to 60 minutes. In a bowl, toss strawberries with sugar. Let stand at room temperature for 20 to 30 minutes, stirring occasionally, until the strawberries have begun to give off juice.

TO MAKE BISCUITS:

1. Preheat oven to 400°F. Line a baking sheet with parchment paper or coat it with nonstick cooking spray.

2. In a mixing bowl, whisk together flour, cocoa, sugar, baking powder, baking soda and salt. Using a pastry cutter or your fingertips, cut butter and cream cheese into the dry ingredients until crumbly. Make a well in the center and add buttermilk, stirring with a fork until evenly moistened. Drop 4 mounds of batter, about 2 inches apart, onto the prepared baking sheet. Shape the mounds into 3-inch circles and bake for 10 to 12 minutes, or until the tops spring back when touched lightly. Transfer the biscuits to a wire rack and let cool slightly.

TO ASSEMBLE SHORTCAKES:

With a serrated knife, slice the biscuits in half crosswise. Set the bottoms on dessert plates. Spoon the strawberries and their juice over the biscuits and add a dollop of the drained yogurt. Crown with the biscuit tops, dust with confectioners' sugar and serve.

Serves 4.

300 calories per serving: 7 grams protein, 6 grams fat (3 grams saturated fat), 57 grams carbohydrate; 428 mg sodium; 15 mg cholesterol.

FILLING

1 cup low-fat vanilla yogurt

1 pint strawberries, hulled and sliced

3 tablespoons sugar

CHOCOLATE BISCUITS

⅔ cup all-purpose white flour

⅓ cup unsweetened cocoa powder

⅓ cup sugar

1½ teaspoons baking powder

¼ teaspoon baking soda

¼ teaspoon salt

1½ tablespoons butter

1½ tablespoons reduced-fat cream cheese

½ cup buttermilk
Confectioners' sugar for dusting

◆**FAT-CUTTING TIP**
Low-fat or nonfat vanilla yogurt drained briefly through cheesecloth or a coffee filter makes a quick and healthy dessert topping.

Chocolate Madeleines

CHOCOLATE MADELEINES

French novelist and notorious shut-in Marcel Proust was passionate about the plump little cakelike cookies called madeleines.
Perhaps the aroma of this chocolate version baking in the oven would have drawn him out of his room.

1. Preheat oven to 400°F. Brush a madeleine pan with oil or coat it with nonstick cooking spray. Dust with flour, tapping out the excess; set aside. (*Alternatively, if you do not have a madeleine pan, coat and flour 18 small fluted tartlet tins.*)

2. Place whole egg and egg white in a mixing bowl and set the bowl in a larger pan of hot water to warm while you prepare the remaining ingredients. Stir the eggs occasionally.

3. Sift flour, cocoa, baking powder, baking soda and salt into a bowl; set aside. Combine buttermilk and oil and set aside.

4. Take the egg bowl off the water, add sugar and beat with an electric mixer on high speed until the mixture is thickened and pale, about 5 minutes. (The beaters should leave a ribbon trail when lifted.) Blend in vanilla and coffee or orange zest. With a rubber spatula, alternately fold the dry ingredients and the buttermilk mixture into the egg mixture, making 3 additions of dry ingredients and 2 additions of liquid.

5. Drop the batter by tablespoonfuls into the prepared pan, filling each depression about three-fourths full; you will use about half of the batter. Bake for 12 to 15 minutes, or until the tops of the madeleines spring back when touched lightly. Immediately loosen the cakes from the pan and invert onto a wire rack to cool. Clean and prepare the pan as above and repeat with the remaining batter. (*The madeleines are best eaten the day they are baked, but they can be wrapped and frozen for up to 1 month.*)

6. If decorating with chocolate, melt it in a small bowl set over a pan of barely simmering water. Drizzle over the scalloped side of the madeleines. Alternatively, dust the madeleines with confectioners' sugar.

Makes about 2 dozen madeleines.

70 calories per madeleine: 1 gram protein, 2 grams fat (0 grams saturated fat), 11 grams carbohydrate; 70 mg sodium; 9 mg cholesterol.

1	large egg
1	large egg white
1	cup all-purpose white flour
¼	cup unsweetened cocoa powder, preferably Dutch-process
1½	teaspoons baking powder
½	teaspoon baking soda
¼	teaspoon salt
½	cup buttermilk
3	tablespoons canola oil
¾	cup sugar
1	teaspoon pure vanilla extract
1	teaspoon instant coffee granules *or* 2 teaspoons grated orange zest
1	ounce bittersweet (*not* unsweetened) chocolate *or* confectioners' sugar for decoration

◆**CHOCOLATE TIMESAVER**
An easy way to decorate with thin lines of chocolate is to melt the chocolate in a plastic bag in the microwave. Then snip a small hole in one corner of the bag and quickly squeeze out lines of chocolate over the dessert.

COCOA ROULADE WITH RASPBERRY CREAM

This light sponge cake is rolled around a luxurious raspberry meringue. Serve drizzled with Raspberry-Chocolate Sauce (page 178), if desired, and a scattering of additional berries.

CAKE

⅓ cup unsweetened cocoa powder, plus additional for dusting the pan and cake

⅓ cup sifted cake flour

1 teaspoon baking powder

¼ teaspoon salt

2 large eggs

½ cup sugar

1½ teaspoons pure vanilla extract

3 large egg whites

TO MAKE CAKE:

1. Preheat oven to 350°F. Lightly oil a 10-by-15-inch baking sheet with sides; line the bottom with parchment or wax paper and oil or spray it again. Dust the paper with cocoa, tapping off the excess. Set aside.

2. In a bowl, whisk together cocoa, flour, baking powder and salt. In a mixing bowl, beat whole eggs and ¼ cup of the sugar with an electric mixer until thickened and pale, about 5 minutes. Beat in vanilla.

3. In a large clean bowl with clean beaters, beat egg whites until soft peaks form. Gradually beat in the remaining ¼ cup sugar, beating until stiff and glossy. Whisk one-fourth of the beaten whites into the whole-egg mixture. Sprinkle half of the cocoa mixture over the top and fold in with a rubber spatula just until blended. Fold in the remaining beaten whites, then the remaining cocoa mixture.

4. Spoon the batter into the prepared pan, spreading it to the edges. Bake for 10 to 15 minutes, or until the top springs back when lightly touched. (Do not overbake or the cake will crack when rolled.) While the cake is baking, place a clean kitchen towel on the work surface. Cover it with parchment or wax paper, spray the paper with nonstick cooking spray and dust lightly with cocoa.

5. Once the cake is done, loosen the edges and invert the cake onto the cocoa-dusted paper. Peel the paper from the top of the cake. Using a serrated knife, trim the edges of the cake, then quickly roll up the cake in the paper-lined towel, starting at a short end. Set the rolled cake, seam-side down, on a rack to cool.

TO MAKE FILLING:

1. Bring about 1 inch of water to a simmer in a large saucepan. Put egg whites, sugar, cream of tartar and 2 tablespoons water in a heatproof bowl that will fit over the pan. Set the bowl over the simmering water and beat with an electric mixer at low speed, moving the beaters around the bowl constantly, until an instant-read thermometer registers 140°F, 3 to 5 minutes. Increase the mixer speed to high and continue beating for a full 3½ minutes. Remove the bowl from the heat and beat the meringue until cool, about 4 minutes.

2. In a small saucepan, sprinkle gelatin over framboise or juice. Let soften for about 3 minutes, then swirl over very low heat just until the gelatin is dissolved. Let cool to room temperature.

3. In a medium bowl, whip cream to firm peaks. Whisk in the gelatin mixture. With a rubber spatula, fold this cream mixture into the cooled meringue, then fold in 1½ cups of the raspberries. Cover and refrigerate until firm and well chilled, about 1 hour.

TO ASSEMBLE CAKE:

Unroll the cooled cake, remove the paper and spread with the raspberry filling. Gently roll it up again and place it on a serving platter, seam-side down. Refrigerate for at least 1 hour or overnight. Dust lightly with additional cocoa just before serving. Serve with Raspberry-Chocolate Sauce, if you like, and garnish with the remaining ½ cup raspberries.

Serves 12.

135 calories per serving: 3 grams protein, 3 grams fat (2 grams saturated fat), 21 grams carbohydrate, 1 gram alcohol; 108 mg sodium; 43 mg cholesterol.

FILLING

2	large egg whites
½	cup sugar
¼	teaspoon cream of tartar
1¼	teaspoons unflavored gelatin
3	tablespoons eau-de-vie de framboise *or* cran-raspberry juice
⅓	cup chilled whipping cream
2	cups fresh raspberries

◆**INGREDIENT NOTE**

Eau-de-vie de framboise is a clear alcohol made from raspberries. It has an intense fruity aroma and flavor.

Chocolate-Cherry Bars

CHOCOLATE-CHERRY BARS

Dramatically dark in color, these chewy bars are studded with dried tart cherries.

2	large eggs
1	large egg white
¾	cup sugar
2	teaspoons pure vanilla extract
¼	teaspoon salt
2	cups chocolate wafer crumbs (about 40 wafers)
1	cup chopped dried tart cherries
¼	cup chopped walnuts

1. Preheat oven to 325°F. Lightly oil an 8-by-12-inch or 7-by-11-inch baking pan or coat it with nonstick cooking spray; set aside.

2. In a large bowl, beat together eggs, egg white, sugar, vanilla and salt with an electric mixer on high speed until the eggs are thick and pale, about 2 minutes. With a rubber spatula, gently fold in chocolate wafer crumbs and cherries just until combined. Transfer the batter to the prepared baking pan; smooth the top. Sprinkle with walnuts. Bake for 30 to 35 minutes, or until a skewer inserted in the center comes out clean.

3. Let cool in the baking pan on a wire rack. Cut into bars. (*Store at room temperature in an airtight container.*)

Makes 15 bars.

150 calories per bar: 3 grams protein, 4 grams fat (0 grams saturated fat), 27 grams carbohydrate; 157 mg sodium; 31 mg cholesterol.

CHOCOLATE CHEESECAKE

The chocolate flavor in this rich and glossy cheesecake is deepened by the addition of coffee.

TO MAKE CRUST:

Preheat oven to 325°F. Lightly oil a 9-inch springform pan or coat it with nonstick cooking spray. Place chocolate wafers, Grape-Nuts, cocoa and sugar in a food processor; pulse until you have fine crumbs. Add oil and 3 tablespoons water; process until the crumbs are moistened. Press the crumb mixture into the bottom and about 1½ inches up the sides of the prepared pan. Set aside.

TO MAKE FILLING:

1. Melt chocolate in the top of a double boiler over hot, not boiling, water or in a microwave oven at medium (50 percent) power. Let cool slightly. Dissolve instant coffee in 1 tablespoon boiling water and set aside.

2. Place cottage cheese in a strainer lined with a double thickness of cheesecloth. Gather up the cheesecloth and squeeze out the moisture from the cottage cheese. Put the pressed cottage-cheese solids in a food processor and blend until completely smooth, about 2 minutes. Add cream cheese, sugar, egg, egg whites, sour cream, cocoa, cornstarch, salt, vanilla, the melted chocolate and the dissolved coffee; process until smooth. Pour into the crumb-lined pan.

3. Bake for about 1 hour, or until firm around the edge but still shiny and slightly soft in the center. Run a knife around the pan to loosen the edges. Let cool in the pan on a wire rack. Cover and refrigerate until well chilled, at least 8 hours or for up to 2 days. Remove the outer ring of the pan. To facilitate cutting, dip a sharp knife in hot water and wipe dry before cutting each slice.

Serves 16.

280 calories per serving: 12 grams protein, 10 grams fat (4 grams saturated fat), 36 grams carbohydrate; 424 mg sodium; 33 mg cholesterol.

CRUST

- 4 ounces chocolate wafers (18 wafers)
- 1 cup Grape-Nuts cereal
- 2 tablespoons unsweetened cocoa powder, preferably Dutch-process
- 2 tablespoons sugar
- 3 tablespoons canola oil

FILLING

- 2 ounces semisweet chocolate
- 2 tablespoons instant coffee powder
- 32 ounces nonfat cottage cheese (4 cups)
- 8 ounces reduced-fat cream cheese, at room temperature
- 1½ cups sugar
- 1 large egg
- 2 large egg whites
- 1 cup reduced-fat sour cream
- ¾ cup unsweetened cocoa powder, preferably Dutch-process
- 2 tablespoons cornstarch
- ⅛ teaspoon salt
- 1 teaspoon pure vanilla extract

♦**INGREDIENT NOTE**

Commercial chocolate wafers are very low in fat yet pack a rich chocolate flavor. They work well for this crumb crust and for the Chocolate-Cherry Bars on page 100.

CHOCOLATE ANGEL FOOD CAKE

Serve this cake with frozen yogurt and fresh fruit.

¼ cup unsweetened cocoa powder (*not* Dutch-process)

¼ cup hot, strong coffee

1¼ cups sugar

¾ cup sifted cake flour

¼ teaspoon salt

12 large egg whites, at room temperature

1 teaspoon cream of tartar

1. Preheat oven to 350°F. Have ready a 10-inch tube pan and a long-necked bottle or funnel. In a medium bowl, dissolve cocoa in coffee; set aside and let cool to room temperature. In another bowl, combine ½ cup of the sugar, flour and salt; set aside.

2. Place egg whites in a large mixing bowl. Using an electric mixer, beat the egg whites until frothy. Add cream of tartar and continue beating until soft peaks form. Gradually add the remaining ¾ cup sugar and beat just until stiff peaks form. Do not overbeat.

3. Sift the dry ingredients over the beaten egg whites in 3 parts, folding in gently after each sifting. Stir approximately 1 cup of the egg-white mixture into the coffee mixture. Fold it back into the egg-white mixture until thoroughly combined. Pour the batter into the ungreased tube pan. Smooth the top and run a small knife or spatula through the batter to remove any air pockets.

4. Bake for 50 to 60 minutes, or until a skewer comes out clean and the top springs back when touched lightly. Invert the pan over the bottle and let cool completely. Turn the cake right-side up and, with a knife, loosen the edges. Invert the cake onto a serving platter.

Serves 16.

91 calories per serving: 3 grams protein, 0 grams fat, 19 grams carbohydrate; 74 mg sodium; 0 mg cholesterol.

◆**ANGEL FOOD SUCCESS**

Avoid any traces of yolk in the egg whites, which will keep them from whipping.
Also, grease in the tube pan will interfere with the rising of the batter.

CHOCOLATE PUDDING CAKE WITH COFFEE SAUCE

As this fudgy pudding cake bakes, the sauce forms in the bottom of the dish beneath a tender blanket of chocolate cake.

1. Preheat oven to 375°F. Coat six 10-ounce custard cups or ramekins lightly with oil or nonstick cooking spray and set them on a baking sheet.

2. Spread nuts in a pie pan and toast in the oven for 5 to 10 minutes, or until fragrant. In a large bowl, stir together flour, sugar, cocoa, baking powder and salt. In a measuring cup, stir together milk, egg, oil and vanilla. Add to the dry ingredients and stir just until combined. Divide the batter among the prepared custard cups or ramekins. In a measuring cup, stir together hot coffee and brown sugar. Pour about one-sixth of the coffee mixture over each dessert. Sprinkle with the reserved toasted nuts.

3. Bake for 15 to 20 minutes, or until the tops spring back when touched lightly. Cool for 5 minutes. Sprinkle with confectioners' sugar and serve hot or warm.

Serves 6.

305 calories per serving: 5 grams protein, 7 grams fat (1 gram saturated fat), 55 grams carbohydrate; 318 mg sodium; 36 mg cholesterol.

2 tablespoons chopped walnuts *or* pecans

1 cup all-purpose white flour

⅓ cup sugar

¾ cup unsweetened cocoa powder, preferably Dutch-process, sifted

2 teaspoons baking powder

½ teaspoon salt

½ cup skim milk

1 large egg, lightly beaten

2 tablespoons walnut oil *or* canola oil

2 teaspoons pure vanilla extract

1⅓ cups hot brewed coffee *or* 1½ tablespoons instant coffee granules dissolved in 1⅓ cups boiling water

¾ cup light *or* dark brown sugar

Confectioners' sugar for dusting

◆**MAXIMIZING THE FLAVOR OF NUTS**
A small amount of toasted walnuts coupled with walnut oil gives a great deal of flavor to this dessert.

CHOCOLATE-DIPPED APRICOTS

Tart apricots are a vibrant counterpoint to dark chocolate in these moist jewels, perfect with after-dinner coffee.

⅓ cup sugar

2 strips lemon zest

1 cinnamon stick

24 dried apricots
(about ¼ pound)

2 ounces bittersweet (*not unsweetened*) chocolate, melted

1 tablespoon chopped peeled pistachios

1. Line a baking sheet with wax paper and place a wire rack on top; set aside. In a small saucepan, combine sugar, lemon zest, cinnamon stick and 1 cup water; bring to a boil, stirring to dissolve the sugar. Reduce the heat to medium and simmer for 3 minutes. Add apricots and simmer gently just until tender, 6 to 8 minutes. With a slotted spoon, transfer the apricots to the rack. Let cool completely.

2. Dip half of a poached apricot in melted chocolate, letting the excess drip off. Sprinkle some chopped pistachios over the chocolate half and return the apricot to the rack. Repeat with the remaining apricots. (You will have some melted chocolate left over.) Refrigerate until the chocolate has set, about 20 minutes. (*The candies may be stored in an airtight container, with wax paper between each layer, in the refrigerator for up to 1 week.*)

Makes 24 pieces.

30 calories per candy: 0 grams protein, 1 gram fat (0 grams saturated fat), 6 grams carbohydrate; 1 mg sodium; 0 mg cholesterol.

◆**MELTING CHOCOLATE**

Coarsely chop chocolate and melt in a small metal bowl set over a pan of barely simmering water or in a small glass bowl in the microwave on medium-low power (30%) for about 2 minutes, stirring once or twice.

CHOCOLATE-BANANA LUNCHBOX CAKE

To ensure that this cake lasts long enough for at least one week's worth of lunches, wrap individual pieces in plastic wrap and store them in the freezer.

1. Preheat oven to 400°F. Lightly oil an 8-by-12-inch or 7-by-11-inch baking pan or coat it with nonstick cooking spray.

2. In a mixing bowl, whisk flour, cocoa, baking soda and salt. In another bowl, whisk mashed banana, buttermilk, brown sugar, corn syrup, oil and vanilla. Make a well in the center of the dry ingredients and add the banana mixture; mix with a wooden spoon or rubber spatula just until the dry ingredients are moistened.

3. Transfer the batter to the prepared baking pan, smoothing the top. Sprinkle chocolate chips and nuts over the top. Bake for about 20 minutes, or until a skewer inserted in the center comes out clean. Let cool in the pan, dust with confectioners' sugar and cut into squares.

Serves 12.

220 calories per serving: 3 grams protein, 6 grams fat (1 gram saturated fat), 40 grams carbohydrate; 182 mg sodium; 1 mg cholesterol.

2 cups sifted cake flour

2 tablespoons unsweetened cocoa powder (*not* Dutch-process)

1 teaspoon baking soda

½ teaspoon salt

¾ cup mashed very ripe banana (2 small bananas)

¾ cup buttermilk

⅔ cup packed light *or* dark brown sugar

¼ cup dark corn syrup

3 tablespoons canola oil

1 tablespoon pure vanilla extract

⅓ cup chocolate chips

2 tablespoons chopped walnuts *or* pecans

Confectioners' sugar for dusting

◆ **STRETCHING HIGH-FAT INGREDIENTS**
Small amounts of high-fat goodies like nuts or chocolate chips have a lot more impact when sprinkled on top of a dessert, rather than mixed into it.

FUDGE CAKE IN A MERINGUE CHEMISE

A moist, fudgy chocolate cake enclosed in a layer of crunchy pecan meringue, this is worthy of any celebration.

CHOCOLATE GLAZE

⅓ cup sugar

3 tablespoons unsweetened cocoa powder, preferably Dutch-process

½ cup evaporated skim milk

1½ ounces bittersweet (*not* unsweetened) chocolate, coarsely chopped

½ teaspoon pure vanilla extract

CHOCOLATE CAKE & MERINGUE

¾ cup chopped pitted dates

½ cup pecan halves

1 ounce unsweetened chocolate

1½ cups cake flour (unsifted)

⅓ cup unsweetened cocoa powder, preferably Dutch-process

1 teaspoon baking powder

½ teaspoon baking soda

½ teaspoon salt

1 large egg, lightly beaten

1¾ cups sugar

¼ cup canola oil

1 teaspoon pure vanilla extract

1 teaspoon instant coffee granules

1 cup buttermilk

3 large egg whites

TO MAKE CHOCOLATE GLAZE:

In a small heavy saucepan, combine sugar and cocoa. Add ¼ cup of the evaporated skim milk and whisk until you have a smooth paste. Add the remaining evaporated skim milk, place over medium heat and bring to a boil, whisking constantly. Cook at a gentle boil, stirring almost constantly, for 2 minutes. Remove from the heat and add bittersweet chocolate; stir until melted. Stir in vanilla. Pour into a bowl, cover and refrigerate until chilled and thickened, about 2 hours.

TO MAKE CHOCOLATE CAKE & MERINGUE:

1. Preheat oven to 325°F. Lightly oil a 9- or 10-inch tube pan (with flat bottom and unfluted sides) or coat it with nonstick cooking spray. Line the bottom with parchment or wax paper; set aside.

2. In a small saucepan, combine dates with ⅓ cup water; bring to a simmer over medium heat. Cook, stirring frequently, until the dates have softened and absorbed most of the liquid, 2 to 3 minutes. Transfer to a mixing bowl and let cool completely.

3. Spread pecans in a shallow baking pan and bake for 5 to 7 minutes, or until fragrant. Select 16 pecan halves for garnish; set aside. Once the remaining pecans are cool, finely chop them. Grate unsweetened chocolate; set aside.

4. Sift flour, cocoa, baking powder, baking soda and salt into a bowl; set aside.

5. When the dates have cooled, add egg, 1 cup sugar, oil, vanilla and coffee granules; beat with an electric mixer for 1 minute. With a rubber spatula, alternately fold the reserved flour mixture and buttermilk into the date/egg mixture, making 3 additions of dry ingredients and 2 additions of buttermilk. Set the cake batter aside.

6. In a clean mixing bowl, with clean beaters, beat egg whites with an electric mixer until soft peaks form. Gradually add the remaining ¾ cup sugar, beating until stiff, glossy peaks form. With a rubber spatula, fold in the reserved grated chocolate and chopped pecans. Spread the meringue on the bottom of the prepared pan and three-quarters of the way up the sides, as though lining it. Pour the reserved cake batter into the pan. (It should be surrounded on all sides by meringue.)

Fudge Cake in a Meringue Chemise

7. Bake for 60 to 65 minutes, or until the top of the cake springs back when touched lightly and the meringue is crisp. If necessary, trim away any meringue that protrudes above the surface of the cake. Let the cake cool in the pan on a rack for 30 minutes. Carefully separate the meringue from the pan with a metal spatula, then turn the cake out onto a serving plate. Peel off parchment or wax paper and let cool completely.

TO GLAZE CAKE:

Carefully pour the chilled chocolate glaze over the cake, spreading gently so that it drips down the sides. Arrange the reserved pecan halves around the top of the cake.

Serves 16.

210 calories per serving: 3 grams protein, 8 grams fat (1 gram saturated fat), 36 grams carbohydrate; 148 mg sodium; 14 mg cholesterol.

◆**FAT-CUTTING TIP**

Dates are the magic ingredient in this low-fat cake. Using the fruit enabled us to cut the oil in the recipe to a mere ¼ cup.

BROWNIES

The combination of full-flavored Dutch-process cocoa, canola oil and moist brown sugar produces a classic fudgy brownie that is low in fat and free of saturated fat.

1 cup sifted cake flour

½ cup Dutch-process cocoa powder

½ teaspoon salt

1½ cups packed light brown sugar

¼ cup canola oil

¼ cup buttermilk

1 large egg

2 large egg whites

2 teaspoons pure vanilla extract

1. Preheat oven to 350°F. Lightly oil an 8-by-12-inch or 7-by-11-inch baking pan or coat it with nonstick cooking spray. Dust with a little flour, tapping out the excess, and set aside.

2. In a small bowl, whisk together flour, cocoa and salt. In a large bowl, beat together brown sugar, oil, buttermilk, egg, egg whites and vanilla with an electric mixer on high speed until smooth, making sure no lumps of brown sugar remain. Add the dry ingredients and beat on low speed just until blended.

3. Transfer the batter to the prepared baking pan. Bake for 25 to 30 minutes, or just until a skewer inserted in the center comes out clean. Let cool in the baking pan on a rack. Cut into bars. (*Store at room temperature in an airtight container.*)

Makes 15 bars.

155 calories per brownie: 2 grams protein, 4 grams fat (0 grams saturated fat), 29 grams carbohydrate; 95 mg sodium; 14 mg cholesterol.

♦**SUBSTITUTION**

If you don't have Dutch-process cocoa, you can use American-style (nonalkalized) cocoa and add ½ teaspoon of baking soda to the dry ingredients to neutralize the slightly sour taste from the cocoa.

THE WELL-STOCKED COOKIE JAR

Grandma's cookie jar is probably a collector's item today. Remember the wonderful cookies she used to make? First she creamed two sticks of butter and a cup of sugar... Ah, the good old days.

Our initial attempts at creating fat-free versions of Grandma's cookies produced gummy results. We put a little of the fat back in, however, and classics like Peanut Butter Cookies and Brown Sugar Crackles are the chewy, crisp proof of our success. Another tactic was to sample the international cookie repertoire,

where we discovered recipes that are naturally low in fat, such as German lebkuchen and Italian biscotti. Here are some new treats for the old precious cookie jar on your kitchen shelf.

SICILIAN FIG COOKIES

A crisp pastry surrounds the moist filling made of dried figs, apricots, dates and raisins.
These are delicious without the icing as well. A perfect Christmas cookie.

COOKIE DOUGH

- 2½ cups all-purpose white flour
- ⅓ cup sugar
- 1¼ teaspoons baking powder
- ½ teaspoon salt
- 3 tablespoons butter, cut into small pieces
- 1 large egg
- 1 large egg white
- ¼ cup low-fat milk
- 2½ tablespoons canola oil
- 1 teaspoon pure vanilla extract
- ¼ teaspoon pure almond extract

FILLING

- ¼ cup slivered almonds
- ¼ teaspoon aniseed
- 2 cups dried figs, stems removed
- 1 cup dried apricots
- ½ cup chopped dates
- ½ cup golden raisins
- ⅓ cup sugar
- 1½ teaspoons grated lemon zest
- 1½ teaspoons ground cinnamon
- ⅛ teaspoon freshly ground black pepper
- ⅓ cup Marsala *or* fresh orange juice

TO MAKE COOKIE DOUGH:

Combine flour, sugar, baking powder and salt in the food processor. Add butter and pulse until the butter is in very small pieces, about 10 seconds. In a large glass measuring cup, whisk together egg, egg white, milk, oil, vanilla and almond extracts; with the food processor running, pour in the liquid and mix just until a smooth dough forms. Scrape the dough onto wax paper or plastic wrap and flatten into a 1-inch-thick disk. Wrap and refrigerate overnight or for up to 2 days.

TO MAKE FILLING:

1. Preheat oven to 350°F. Spread almonds on a baking sheet or in a pie pan. Toast for 3 minutes; add aniseed and continue to toast until the nuts are pale gold and the aniseed is fragrant, about 3 minutes longer. Set aside to cool.

2. In the food processor, combine figs, apricots, dates, raisins, sugar, lemon zest, cinnamon, pepper and the toasted almonds and aniseed. Pulse until the fruits and nuts are finely chopped. With the machine running, pour Marsala or orange juice through the feed tube and process until just blended. (*Use immediately, or cover with plastic wrap and refrigerate for up to 2 days. Return the filling to room temperature before using.*)

TO BAKE COOKIES:

1. Preheat oven to 350°F. Lightly oil 2 large baking sheets or coat them with nonstick cooking spray. Divide the dough into 6 equal pieces. Working with one piece at a time (keeping the remaining pieces refrigerated), roll out on a lightly floured surface into a 4-by-12-inch rectangle. (Don't worry if the edges are ragged.) Measure a scant ½ cup of the filling and use your hands to spread it in a strip down the center of the dough.

2. Use a wide spatula or pastry scraper to lift the sides of the dough over the filling to form a roll. Use your fingers to press down the seam, which may be a bit ragged and uneven. With a sharp knife, slice the roll on the diagonal into 1-inch-long cookies. Set the cookies on a prepared baking sheet, spacing them about 1 inch apart. Repeat these steps with the remaining dough and filling.

3. Bake the cookies, one sheet at a time, for 15 to 18 minutes, or until the bottoms are pale golden and the tops are lightly colored. Transfer the cookies to a wire rack to cool.

TO MAKE ICING:

In a small bowl, whisk together confectioners' sugar, milk, vanilla and almond extracts until smooth. Place the cookies close together on wax paper. Drizzle the tops of the cookies liberally with icing. (*Store the cookies in an airtight container for up to 4 days.*)

Makes about 5 dozen cookies.

80 calories per cookie: 1 gram protein, 2 grams fat (0 grams saturated fat), 16 grams carbohydrate; 26 mg sodium; 5 mg cholesterol.

ICING

1¼ cups confectioners' sugar

2 tablespoons low-fat milk, plus more as needed

¼ teaspoon pure vanilla extract

¼ teaspoon pure almond extract

PINE NUT COOKIES

These cookies should be made on a dry day so they turn out crisp.

1. Preheat oven to 250°F. Line 2 baking sheets with parchment paper and set aside.

2. In a mixing bowl, beat egg whites and salt with an electric mixer on low speed until foamy; raise the speed to high. When the whites begin to form soft peaks, gradually add sugar, beating until the whites are shiny with no traces of grittiness and form stiff peaks. With a rubber spatula, fold in pine nuts and lemon zest. Drop tablespoonfuls of the batter, about 1 inch apart, on the prepared baking sheets.

3. Bake for 40 minutes, switching the positions of the baking sheets midway; turn off the oven and leave the cookies in the closed oven to dry for 3 more hours. Peel the cookies off the parchment paper. (*Store in an airtight container at room temperature for up to 1 week.*)

Makes 3 dozen cookies.

20 calories per cookie: 1 gram protein, 1 gram fat (0 grams saturated fat), 3 grams carbohydrate; 5 mg sodium; 0 mg cholesterol.

3 large egg whites, at room temperature

Pinch of salt

½ cup sugar

½ cup pine nuts

2 teaspoons grated lemon zest

◆**STORAGE TIP**
Pine nuts should be stored in the freezer.

Brown Sugar Crackles

BROWN SUGAR CRACKLES

These sweet sugar cookies have an appealing crazed top and a chewy middle.

1. Preheat oven to 350°F. Lightly oil 3 baking sheets or coat them with nonstick cooking spray and set aside.

2. In a small bowl, stir together white and whole-wheat flours, baking powder, baking soda and salt. In a mixing bowl, beat together brown sugar, butter, oil, eggs and vanilla with an electric mixer on high speed until smooth, making sure no lumps of brown sugar remain, about 1 minute. Stir in the dry ingredients until completely blended. (The dough will be stiff.)

3. Divide the dough in half and press each half into a flat disk. On a lightly floured surface, roll out one of the disks to a ¼-inch thickness. Cut out cookies with a 2-inch round cookie cutter, placing the cookies 1 inch apart on the prepared baking sheets. Repeat with the remaining dough. Press the scraps together and cut out additional cookies.

4. Bake the cookies, one sheet at a time, for 8 to 10 minutes, or until they are puffed in the middle and browned around the edges. Let stand for about 2 minutes on the baking sheets, then remove to a wire rack to cool completely. (*Store the cookies in an airtight container for up to 3 days.*)

Makes about 4 dozen cookies.

80 calories per cookie: 1 gram protein, 2 grams fat (1 gram saturated fat), 14 grams carbohydrate; 84 mg sodium; 11 mg cholesterol.

2 cups all-purpose white flour

⅔ cup whole-wheat flour

1 teaspoon baking powder

1 teaspoon baking soda

1 teaspoon salt

2 cups packed light brown sugar

¼ cup butter, softened

¼ cup canola oil

2 large eggs

2 teaspoons pure vanilla extract

PEPPERED LEBKUCHEN

These Christmas cookies are great with a cup of coffee at any time of the year.
Lebkuchen get even better after a few days as they mellow to a wonderful deep flavor.

COOKIE DOUGH

2	cups all-purpose white flour
1	teaspoon freshly grated nutmeg
1	teaspoon ground cinnamon
1	teaspoon ground allspice
½	teaspoon ground cloves
½	teaspoon ground ginger
¼	teaspoon ground mace
¼	teaspoon baking soda
¼	teaspoon salt
¼	teaspoon freshly ground black pepper
½	cup honey
½	cup packed dark brown sugar
1	large egg
1½	teaspoons grated lemon zest
1½	teaspoons grated orange zest

GLAZE

¼	cup confectioners' sugar
2	teaspoons fresh lemon juice
1	teaspoon fresh orange juice
½	teaspoon grated lemon zest
½	teaspoon grated orange zest

TO MAKE COOKIE DOUGH:

In a mixing bowl, whisk together flour, nutmeg, cinnamon, allspice, cloves, ginger, mace, baking soda, salt and pepper until thoroughly combined. In another, larger mixing bowl, blend honey, brown sugar, egg and lemon and orange zests. Add the dry ingredients and stir to make a smooth, somewhat soft and sticky dough. Transfer the dough onto wax paper or plastic wrap and shape into a flat, ½-inch-thick disk. Wrap and refrigerate at least 4 hours or overnight.

TO MAKE GLAZE:

In a small bowl, whisk together confectioners' sugar, citrus juices and zests until smooth. Cover and set aside.

TO BAKE COOKIES:

1. Preheat oven to 350°F. Lightly oil 2 large baking sheets or coat them with nonstick cooking spray. Working with half of the dough at a time, roll it out on a lightly floured surface into a large rectangle slightly less than ¼ inch thick. With a pastry wheel or pizza cutter, trim the edges and cut into 1¼-by-2-inch rectangles. Transfer the cookies to the prepared baking sheets, spacing them about 1 inch apart.

2. Bake the cookies, one sheet at a time, for 8 to 10 minutes, or until the edges are lightly colored and the cookies are firm. Immediately transfer to a wire rack. Brush the tops of the warm cookies with the reserved glaze. Let stand until the glaze sets, about 1 hour. (*Store the lebkuchen in an airtight container for up to 3 weeks.*)

Makes about 4 dozen cookies.

45 calories per cookie: 1 gram protein, 0 grams fat, 10 grams carbohydrate; 18 mg sodium; 4 mg cholesterol.

MORAVIAN SPICE COOKIES

The Moravian Settlement in Old Salem, North Carolina, is famous for its tins of crisp, spicy wafers very similar to these.

1. In a small saucepan, melt butter over low heat. Cook, swirling the pan, until the butter turns a nutty brown, about 1 minute. Add molasses, brown sugar and oil, stirring to melt the sugar. Transfer to a mixing bowl and let cool for 5 minutes.

2. Add cinnamon, ginger, cloves, allspice and baking soda to the bowl and beat in with an electric mixer on medium speed. With the mixer on low speed, add flour, ½ cup at a time, beating just until incorporated.

3. Turn the dough out onto a large sheet of plastic wrap; flatten it into a disk and wrap it up. Let the dough rest at room temperature for 1 to 2 hours before rolling. (*Alternatively, the dough can be made up to 3 days in advance and stored in the refrigerator. Bring to room temperature before rolling.*)

4. Preheat oven to 350°F. Lightly oil 2 baking sheets or coat them with nonstick cooking spray. Divide the dough in half and rewrap the unused portion. On a floured surface, roll the dough out as thin as possible, less than ¹⁄₁₆ inch. Cut out cookies with a small (2-inch) cutter and place them about ¼ inch apart on the prepared baking sheets. Bake, one sheet at a time, for 8 to 10 minutes, or until the cookies are crisp and just beginning to brown on the edges. Transfer to a wire rack to cool. Repeat with the remaining dough. (*Store the cookies in an airtight container for up to 2 weeks.*)

Makes about 6 dozen cookies.

30 calories per cookie: 0 grams protein, 1 gram fat (0 grams saturated fat), 5 grams carbohydrate; 6 mg sodium; 1 mg cholesterol.

2 tablespoons butter
½ cup molasses
¼ cup dark brown sugar
2 tablespoons canola oil
1 teaspoon ground cinnamon
½ teaspoon ground ginger
½ teaspoon ground cloves
½ teaspoon ground allspice
½ teaspoon baking soda
2 cups all-purpose white flour

FILLED OATMEAL-DATE COOKIES

These sturdy cookies are just right for the lunchbox.

FILLING

1½	cups chopped pitted dates
⅓	cup packed light brown sugar
2	teaspoons fresh lemon juice
1	teaspoon grated lemon zest

DOUGH

¼	cup pecans *or* walnuts
1½	cups packed light brown sugar
1	large egg
2	large egg whites
¼	cup canola oil
¼	cup apple butter
2	teaspoons pure vanilla extract
2	cups all-purpose white flour
1	teaspoon baking soda
1	teaspoon ground cinnamon
1	teaspoon salt
½	teaspoon baking powder
2	cups rolled oats

TO MAKE FILLING:

In a small saucepan, combine dates, brown sugar, lemon juice, lemon zest and ⅓ cup water. Bring to a simmer over medium heat. Cook, stirring, until thickened, about 30 seconds. Set aside to cool.

TO MAKE DOUGH:

1. Place rack in upper third of oven; preheat to 350°F. Lightly oil 3 baking sheets or coat them with nonstick cooking spray; set aside. Spread nuts in a pie pan and toast in the oven until fragrant and lightly browned, about 5 minutes. Let cool briefly, then finely chop.

2. In a large mixing bowl, combine brown sugar, egg, egg whites, oil, apple butter and vanilla. Beat with an electric mixer until smooth and pale in color, about 2 minutes. Sift flour, baking soda, cinnamon, salt and baking powder into the mixing bowl. Add rolled oats and stir until well combined.

3. Drop the dough by heaping teaspoonfuls onto the prepared baking sheets, spacing cookies about 1½ inches apart. With the back of a teaspoon, dipped in water to prevent sticking, make a depression in the center of each mound. Fill with a scant teaspoon of the reserved date filling. Top with another heaping teaspoon of dough, spreading it to roughly cover the filling. Sprinkle each cookie with a scant ¼ teaspoon of the toasted nuts. Bake, 1 sheet at a time, for 12 to 15 minutes, or until lightly browned on top. Transfer the cookies to wire racks to cool. (*If keeping for longer than 1 day, freeze in an airtight container with wax paper between the layers.*)

Makes about 3 dozen cookies.

130 calories per cookie: 2 grams protein, 3 grams fat (0 grams saturated fat), 25 grams carbohydrate; 95 mg sodium; 6 mg cholesterol.

♦**STORAGE NOTE**
Store reduced-fat cookies in the freezer to help keep their flavor fresh.

RUGELACH

Expect some of the filling to ooze out during baking, but don't worry—there will still be plenty inside the cookie.

TO MAKE DOUGH:

Place cottage cheese on a double thickness of cheesecloth. Gather up the corners of the cheesecloth and firmly squeeze out all the moisture; you should end up with 1 cup of cottage cheese. In a mixing bowl, beat the cottage cheese, cream cheese, sugar, oil, butter and vanilla with an electric mixer until light and fluffy. Mix together flour and salt and add to the cheese mixture; stir with a wooden spoon until just blended. Wrap the dough in wax paper, then in plastic wrap, and chill for at least 2 hours or preferably overnight.

TO MAKE FILLING:

1. Set oven rack in upper third of oven; preheat to 350°F. Spread walnuts on a pie pan and toast in the oven 5 to 10 minutes, until fragrant and lightly browned. Let cool briefly, then chop. Prepare 2 baking sheets by coating with nonstick cooking spray or lining with parchment paper.

2. In a small bowl, stir together brown sugar, Grape-Nuts, cinnamon and the chopped walnuts. Cover and set aside.

TO FORM AND BAKE RUGELACH:

1. Divide the dough into four equal parts. On a lightly floured surface, roll each portion into a 10-inch-diameter circle. (Keep the remaining dough chilled until ready to use.) Sprinkle with one-fourth of the brown-sugar mixture and 2 tablespoons currants, pressing slightly so that the filling adheres. Cut the circle into 8 wedges. Beginning at the widest end, roll up each wedge and curve into a crescent. Place on a prepared baking sheet. Repeat with the remaining dough.

2. Bake for 20 to 25 minutes, or until tops are light brown. Immediately transfer to a wire rack and let cool. (*Store in an airtight container, with wax paper between the layers, for up to 4 days.*)

Makes 32 rugelach.

100 calories per rugelach: 3 grams protein, 3 grams fat (1 gram saturated fat), 17 grams carbohydrate; 66 mg sodium; 4 mg cholesterol.

DOUGH

2 cups nonfat cottage cheese

4 ounces reduced-fat cream cheese (½ cup)

½ cup sugar

2 tablespoons canola oil

2 tablespoons butter, softened

1 teaspoon pure vanilla extract

3 cups sifted cake flour

½ teaspoon salt

FILLING

2 tablespoons walnuts

½ cup packed light brown sugar

2 tablespoons Grape-Nuts cereal

1 teaspoon ground cinnamon

½ cup currants

◆**LOW-FAT BAKING**

Grape-Nuts cereal has a crunch and flavor similar to real nuts, so mixing the two in fillings and crusts is a good fat-reducing trick.

HAZELNUT-ANISE BISCOTTI

Crunchy and dry, these biscotti are perfect for dipping in a glass of sweet wine, coffee or tea.

1	cup hazelnuts (filberts)
2¼	cups all-purpose white flour
4	teaspoons aniseed
1	teaspoon baking powder
½	teaspoon salt
3	large eggs
1	cup sugar
1	teaspoon pure vanilla extract

1. Preheat oven to 325°F. Lightly oil a baking sheet or coat it with nonstick cooking spray and set aside. Spread hazelnuts in a pie pan and bake for 8 to 12 minutes, or until lightly toasted. If the hazelnuts have skins, place them in a clean kitchen towel, fold the towel over and rub off the skins. Let cool.

2. In a mixing bowl, stir together flour, aniseed, baking powder and salt. In another mixing bowl, beat eggs, sugar and vanilla with an electric mixer on high speed until thick and pale, about 3 minutes. With a wooden spoon, stir in the dry ingredients, followed by the hazelnuts (the dough will be very soft and sticky).

3. With two rubber spatulas, form the dough into three 10-inch-long logs on the prepared baking sheet. Smooth the logs with a spatula or moistened hands.

4. Bake for 30 minutes, or until the logs are lightly browned and spring back when lightly pressed in the center. Carefully transfer the logs to a cutting board; slice them crosswise into ½-inch-thick slices. Stand the slices upright on a baking sheet, ½ inch apart. Return the biscotti to the oven to bake for 10 to 15 minutes longer, or until lightly colored and crisp. Transfer the biscotti to a wire rack to cool. *(Store the biscotti in an airtight container for up to 1 month.)*

Makes about 4 dozen biscotti.

60 calories per biscotto: 1 gram protein, 2 grams fat (0 grams saturated fat), 9 grams carbohydrate; 33 mg sodium; 13 mg cholesterol.

◆**INGREDIENT NOTE**
Hazelnuts, also called filberts, are rich in monounsaturated fats. The shelled nuts quickly go rancid at room temperature; store them in the refrigerator or freezer.

Hazelnut-Anise Biscotti (*left*) & Poppy Seed-Orange Biscotti (*page 120*)

POPPY SEED-ORANGE BISCOTTI

The flavor of biscotti actually improves after a few days in an airtight tin, and they keep well for a month or longer. They are wonderful to have on hand to serve with midafternoon tea or postdinner coffee. (Photograph on page 119.)

2 cups all-purpose white flour

1 cup sugar

¼ cup poppy seeds

1 teaspoon baking powder

½ teaspoon baking soda

¼ teaspoon salt

2 large eggs

2 large egg whites

3 tablespoons grated orange zest

1 tablespoon frozen orange-juice concentrate, thawed

1. Preheat oven to 325°F. Lightly oil a baking sheet or coat it with nonstick cooking spray; set aside.

2. In a mixing bowl, combine flour, sugar, poppy seeds, baking powder, baking soda and salt. In another mixing bowl, whisk together eggs, egg whites, orange zest and orange-juice concentrate. Add to the dry ingredients and mix well. The dough will be very soft and sticky.

3. Working on a very well-floured surface, shape the dough into 2 logs, each about 14 inches long and 1½ inches thick. Place the logs on the prepared baking sheet and bake for 20 to 25 minutes, or until firm to the touch. Transfer the logs to a cutting board to cool. Reduce the oven temperature to 300°F.

4. Slice the logs diagonally into ½-inch-thick slices. Stand the slices upright on the baking sheet, ½ inch apart, and bake for 40 minutes. Transfer biscotti to a wire rack to cool. (*Store in an airtight container for up to 1 month.*)

Makes about 4 dozen biscotti.

40 calories per biscotto: 1 gram protein, 1 gram fat (0 grams saturated fat), 8 grams carbohydrate; 32 mg sodium; 9 mg cholesterol.

LEMON THINS

Light and citrusy, this is the perfect cookie to pair with sorbets or summery fruit compotes.

1. Preheat oven to 350°F. Lightly oil 2 baking sheets or coat them with nonstick cooking spray. In a mixing bowl, whisk together flour, cornstarch, baking powder and salt; set aside.

2. In a mixing bowl, cream ½ cup of the sugar, butter and oil with an electric mixer on medium speed until fluffy. Add egg white, lemon zest and vanilla; beat until smooth. Beat in lemon juice. Add the dry ingredients and fold in with a rubber spatula just until combined.

3. Drop the dough by teaspoonfuls, 2 inches apart, onto the prepared baking sheets. Place the remaining ¼ cup sugar in a saucer. Spray the bottom of a wide-bottomed glass with nonstick cooking spray and dip it in the sugar. Flatten the dough with the glass into 2½-inch circles, dipping the glass in the sugar each time.

4. Bake for 8 to 10 minutes, or until the cookies are just starting to brown around the edges. Transfer the cookies to a flat surface (not a rack) to crisp. *(Store in an airtight container for up to 3 days.)*

Makes 2½ dozen cookies.

60 calories per cookie: 1 gram protein, 2 grams fat (1 gram saturated fat), 10 grams carbohydrate; 44 mg sodium; 9 mg cholesterol.

1¼	cups all-purpose white flour
⅓	cup cornstarch
1½	teaspoons baking powder
¼	teaspoon salt
¾	cup sugar
2	tablespoons butter, softened
2	tablespoons canola oil
1	large egg white
1½	teaspoons grated lemon zest
1	teaspoon pure vanilla extract
3	tablespoons fresh lemon juice

◆**INGREDIENT NOTE**
Fresh-squeezed lemon juice has a more lemony punch than reconstituted lemon juice.

PECAN CRISPS

Serve these delicious cookies with coffee-flavored frozen yogurt.

2 tablespoons butter

¼ cup chopped pecans

½ cup sugar

2 large egg whites

⅓ cup all-purpose white flour, sifted

2 teaspoons pure vanilla extract

1. Preheat oven to 300°F. Lightly oil 2 baking sheets or coat them with nonstick cooking spray.

2. In a small saucepan, melt butter over medium heat. Add pecans and stir until the butter is lightly browned and the pecans are toasted, about 1 minute. Transfer to a medium bowl. Whisk in sugar. Add egg whites, flour and vanilla; whisk just until smooth.

3. Drop the batter by rounded teaspoonfuls, 2 inches apart, onto the prepared baking sheets. With the back of a spoon or a small metal spatula, smooth the batter into thin circles 3 inches in diameter. Bake, one sheet at a time, for 10 to 12 minutes, or until golden. Immediately loosen the cookies with a metal spatula.

4. While still hot, remove the cookies from the baking sheet one by one and drape each over a rolling pin. If the cookies become too firm to shape, return them to the oven for about 30 seconds, or until they become pliable. Once the cookies have set, carefully transfer them to a wire rack to finish cooling. (*Store the cookies in an airtight container for up to 3 days. If they lose their crispness, place them in a 350°F oven for about 1 minute, then reshape.*)

Makes about 2 dozen cookies.

40 calories per cookie: 1 gram protein, 2 grams fat (1 gram saturated fat), 6 grams carbohydrate; 15 mg sodium; 3 mg cholesterol.

OATMEAL LACE COOKIES

Thin and elegant, this is a cookie for company.

1. Preheat oven to 400°F. Lightly oil 3 baking sheets or coat them with nonstick cooking spray. Dust them with flour, tapping off the excess.

2. In a bowl, stir together oats, corn syrup and oil. In a small saucepan, melt butter over low heat. Cook, swirling the pan, until the butter turns a nutty brown, about 1 minute. Stir the butter into the oat mixture and set aside.

3. In a mixing bowl, beat egg and sugar with an electric mixer on medium speed until thick and pale, about 5 minutes. Beat in vanilla. In a small bowl, stir together flour, baking powder and salt; fold into the egg mixture. Gently stir in the reserved oat mixture.

4. Drop the batter by teaspoonfuls, about 2 inches apart, onto the prepared baking sheets. Bake, one sheet at a time, for about 5 minutes, or until the cookies are golden and lacy. Let the cookies cool on the baking sheet for about 30 seconds, then carefully transfer them to a flat surface (not a rack) to cool.

5. Place the cookies on a sheet of parchment or wax paper. Pour melted chocolate into a small plastic bag and snip a tiny hole in one corner. Squeeze thin lines of chocolate over the cookies. Let the cookies stand until the chocolate has set, about 1 hour. (*Store in an airtight container with wax paper between the layers for up to 3 days.*)

Makes about 2½ dozen cookies.

50 calories per cookie: 1 gram protein, 2 grams fat (1 gram saturated fat), 7 grams carbohydrate; 41 mg sodium; 9 mg cholesterol.

1 cup rolled oats

⅓ cup light corn syrup

1 tablespoon canola oil

2 tablespoons butter

1 large egg

⅓ cup sugar

1½ teaspoons pure vanilla extract

2 tablespoons all-purpose white flour

1 teaspoon baking powder

¼ teaspoon salt

1 ounce bittersweet (*not unsweetened*) *or* semisweet chocolate, melted

PEANUT BUTTER COOKIES

A healthier version of an old favorite, with much less saturated fat than the original.

2   cups packed light brown sugar

½   cup peanut butter

¼   cup canola oil

2   large eggs

2   teaspoons pure vanilla extract

2   cups all-purpose white flour

⅔   cup whole-wheat flour

1   teaspoon baking powder

1   teaspoon baking soda

½   teaspoon salt

⅓   cup chopped peanuts

1. Preheat oven to 350°F. Lightly oil 3 baking sheets or coat them with nonstick cooking spray.

2. In a mixing bowl, combine brown sugar, peanut butter, oil, eggs and vanilla; add 5 teaspoons water and beat with an electric mixer until smooth. In a small bowl, stir together white and whole-wheat flours, baking powder, baking soda and salt. Stir the dry ingredients into the brown-sugar mixture just until combined.

3. Roll the dough between your palms into 1-inch balls. Place 2 inches apart on the prepared baking sheets. Flatten the cookies with a fork, dipping it into flour if it begins to stick to the dough. Sprinkle with peanuts, pressing them lightly into the dough with your fingers.

4. Bake the cookies, one sheet at a time, for 8 to 10 minutes, or until golden. Transfer to a wire rack to cool. (*Store in an airtight container for up to 3 days.*)

Makes about 4 dozen cookies.

95 calories per cookie: 2 grams protein, 3 grams fat (0 grams saturated fat), 15 grams carbohydrate; 65 mg sodium; 9 mg cholesterol.

◆**SMART SHOPPER**

Choose natural peanut butter because it has no hydrogenated fats.

CHOCOLATE-CHOCOLATE CHIP COOKIES

Soft and chewy, with a deep chocolate flavor.

1. Preheat oven to 350°F. Line 2 or 3 baking sheets with parchment paper. (You may coat the sheets with nonstick cooking spray instead, but the cookies will spread more and have thin and crispy edges.)

2. In a small bowl, stir together flour, cocoa, baking soda and salt; set aside. In a small cup, dissolve coffee powder in vanilla and set aside.

3. Melt butter in a small saucepan over low heat. Cook, swirling the pan, until the butter turns a nutty brown, about 1 minute. Pour into a mixing bowl. Add cream cheese, brown sugar and white sugar. Beat with an electric mixer on low speed until smooth. Add egg and egg white and beat until well incorporated. Add the reserved dry ingredients and dissolved coffee and stir until just combined (the batter will be runny).

4. Drop the batter by slightly rounded tablespoonfuls, 2 inches apart, onto the prepared baking sheets. Sprinkle each cookie with 6 or 7 of the chocolate chips. Bake, one sheet at a time, for 10 to 12 minutes, or until the cookies are puffed and feel "set" when lightly pressed. Slide the parchment paper, with the cookies still attached, onto the counter to cool completely. Gently peel off the paper. (*Store in an airtight container for up to 3 days.*)

Makes about 2½ dozen cookies.

55 calories per cookie: 1 gram protein, 2 grams fat (1 gram saturated fat), 10 grams carbohydrate; 73 mg sodium; 10 mg cholesterol.

¾ cup all-purpose white flour

¼ cup unsweetened cocoa powder, preferably Dutch-process

½ teaspoon baking soda

½ teaspoon salt

1 tablespoon instant coffee powder

2 teaspoons pure vanilla extract

2 tablespoons butter

2 ounces reduced-fat cream cheese (¼ cup)

½ cup packed light brown sugar

⅓ cup white sugar

1 large egg

1 large egg white

½ cup semisweet chocolate chips

MEXICAN MERINGUE COOKIES

These light delights were inspired by Mexican grating chocolate, which is flavored with cinnamon.

½ cup slivered almonds

1 cup sugar

5 tablespoons Dutch-process cocoa powder

3 tablespoons cornstarch

1½ teaspoons ground cinnamon

4 large egg whites

¼ teaspoon cream of tartar

1 teaspoon pure vanilla extract

¼ teaspoon pure almond extract

1½ ounces semisweet *or* bittersweet (*not* unsweetened) chocolate

1. Preheat oven to 350°F. Spread almonds in a pie pan and bake for 5 to 10 minutes, or until lightly toasted. Set aside to cool. Reduce the oven temperature to 200°. Line 2 large baking sheets with parchment paper; set aside.

2. In a food processor, pulse the toasted almonds with ⅓ cup of the sugar until finely chopped. Add cocoa, cornstarch and cinnamon and pulse just until mixed. In a large mixing bowl, beat egg whites with an electric mixer on low speed just until frothy. Add cream of tartar, increase the mixer speed to medium and beat until soft peaks form. Gradually add the remaining ⅔ cup sugar, 2 tablespoons at a time, beating until the whites form firm but still moist peaks. Add vanilla and almond extracts and beat just until blended. In 2 additions, gently fold the cocoa mixture into the beaten whites just until blended. (A few streaks of white may remain.)

3. Drop heaping teaspoonfuls of the batter, 1 inch apart, onto the prepared baking sheets, or pipe the batter through a pastry bag fitted with a ½-inch plain tip. Bake, using both oven racks, for 1½ hours, alternating the positions of the pans halfway through the baking time. Turn off the oven and let the meringues cool in the oven for 1 hour, then peel them off the parchment paper.

4. Melt chocolate in a small bowl set over a pan of almost simmering water or in the microwave. Use a small pastry brush to apply a thin coating of chocolate to the flat side of the meringues. Let the meringues stand, chocolate-side up, until the chocolate has set. (*Store the cookies in an airtight container for up to 5 days.*)

Makes about 4 dozen cookies.

30 calories per cookie: 1 gram protein, 1 gram fat (0 grams saturated fat), 5 grams carbohydrate; 5 mg sodium; 0 mg cholesterol.

Mexican Meringue Cookies

PUMPKIN COOKIES

Moist and cakelike, these gently spiced cookies go well with a glass of milk.

1⅓	cups all-purpose white flour
1	teaspoon baking powder
½	teaspoon baking soda
½	teaspoon salt
1	teaspoon ground cinnamon
½	teaspoon ground ginger
¼	teaspoon ground allspice
¼	teaspoon freshly grated nutmeg
¾	cup canned plain pumpkin puree
¾	cup packed light brown sugar
2	large eggs
¼	cup canola oil
¼	cup dark molasses
1	cup raisins

1. Preheat oven to 350°F. Lightly oil 3 baking sheets or coat them with nonstick cooking spray.

2. In a mixing bowl, whisk together flour, baking powder, baking soda, salt, cinnamon, ginger, allspice and nutmeg. In another bowl, whisk together pumpkin, brown sugar, eggs, oil and molasses until well combined. Stir the wet ingredients and raisins into the dry ingredients until no traces of dry ingredients remain.

3. Drop the batter by level tablespoonfuls onto the prepared baking sheets, spacing the cookies 1½ inches apart. Bake for 10 to 12 minutes, switching the pans midway, or until firm to the touch and lightly golden on top. Transfer the cookies to a wire rack and let cool. (*Store the cookies in an airtight container, with wax paper between the layers, for up to 2 days.*)

Makes about 3 dozen cookies.

70 calories per cookie: 1 gram protein, 2 grams fat (0 grams saturated fat), 13 grams carbohydrate; 56 mg sodium; 12 mg cholesterol.

LUNCHBOX BARS & SQUARES

Bars belong to the no-fuss branch of the baker's repertoire. They can be mixed easily and baked all at once in a single pan. They're sturdy, too, making them ideal for packing into bag lunches or picnic baskets. Mixed with whole grains or studded with dried fruit, these low-fat bars nourish the hungriest student or day hiker, and because they are so low in saturated fat, it's okay to have two.

If you are planning a weekend of outdoor activities, bake a couple of batches on Thursday or Friday night—bars and squares keep well for up to three days in a tightly closed container at room temperature.

RASPBERRIES & CREAM SQUARES

A shortbread base is topped with raspberries swirled with a lemony yogurt "cream."

CRUST

1	cup all-purpose white flour
¼	teaspoon baking powder
¼	teaspoon baking soda
¼	teaspoon salt
½	cup sugar
1	tablespoon butter, softened
1	tablespoon canola oil
1	large egg white
1	teaspoon pure vanilla extract

RASPBERRY LAYER

¼	cup sugar
2	tablespoons cornstarch
12	ounces frozen unsweetened raspberries (3 cups)

"CREAM" LAYER

⅔	cup nonfat sweetened condensed milk
½	cup nonfat plain yogurt
1	large egg
2	tablespoons cornstarch
2	tablespoons fresh lemon juice
1	teaspoon grated lemon zest
1	teaspoon pure vanilla extract

TO MAKE CRUST:

1. Preheat oven to 350°F. Lightly oil an 8-by-12-inch or 7-by-11-inch baking pan or coat it with nonstick cooking spray.

2. In a small bowl, stir together flour, baking powder, baking soda and salt. In a mixing bowl, beat together sugar, butter, oil, egg white and vanilla with an electric mixer until smooth. Stir in the dry ingredients until blended and crumbly.

3. Press the dough into the prepared baking pan in an even layer. Bake the crust for 15 to 20 minutes, or until it is puffed all over and browned around the edges.

TO MAKE RASPBERRY AND CREAM LAYERS:

1. While the bars are baking, stir together sugar and cornstarch in a saucepan. Add raspberries and toss. Stir over medium heat until the mixture is simmering and thickened. When the crust is baked, spread the warm raspberry mixture in an even layer over the crust.

2. In a bowl, whisk together sweetened condensed milk, yogurt, egg, cornstarch, lemon juice, lemon zest and vanilla until smooth; pour over the raspberry layer, tilting the pan to spread it evenly. Drag a fork through the cream layer down into the raspberry layer below to create a marbled effect. Bake for 25 to 30 minutes, or until the filling is puffed and set.

3. Let cool completely in the pan on a wire rack. Cut into squares. (*Store, covered, in the refrigerator for up to 2 days.*)

Makes 20 squares.

115 calories per square: 2 grams protein, 2 grams fat (1 gram saturated fat), 23 grams carbohydrate; 68 mg sodium; 14 mg cholesterol.

TROPICAL FRUIT BARS

Chewy pineapple and papaya, tart lime and sweet coconut combine in an exotic bar.

1. Preheat oven to 350°F. Lightly oil an 8-by-12-inch or 7-by-11-inch baking pan or coat it with nonstick cooking spray

2. In a mixing bowl, whisk together flour, ginger, baking powder, baking soda and salt; set aside. In another bowl, whisk together brown sugar, oil, egg, vanilla and lime zest until no lumps of brown sugar remain. Whisk in lime juice and milk. Add the dry ingredients, pineapple and papaya and stir just until combined.

3. Spread the batter evenly in the prepared pan. Sprinkle coconut over the top. Bake for 20 to 25 minutes, or until golden on top. Let cool completely in the pan on a wire rack. Cut into bars. (*Store at room temperature in an airtight container for up to 3 days.*)

Makes 15 bars.

140 calories per bar: 2 grams protein, 5 grams fat (0 grams saturated fat), 24 grams carbohydrate; 88 mg sodium; 14 mg cholesterol.

1¼ cups sifted cake flour

2 teaspoons ground ginger

½ teaspoon baking powder

½ teaspoon baking soda

¼ teaspoon salt

½ cup packed light brown sugar

¼ cup canola oil

1 large egg

2 teaspoons pure vanilla extract

1 teaspoon grated lime zest

3 tablespoons fresh lime juice

2 tablespoons low-fat milk

¾ cup chopped dried pineapple

¾ cup chopped dried papaya

½ cup flaked sweetened coconut

♦ **SMART SHOPPER**
Health-food stores carry many kinds of dried fruits and the price is usually better than at the supermarket.

LEMON SQUARES

While the world clearly doesn't need another recipe for classic lemon squares,
it does need this reduced-fat update; these have a pleasantly tart filling to balance the sweet crust.

CRUST

1	cup all-purpose white flour
¼	teaspoon baking powder
¼	teaspoon baking soda
¼	teaspoon salt
½	cup sugar
1	tablespoon butter, softened
1	tablespoon canola oil
1	large egg white
1	teaspoon grated lemon zest

FILLING

¾	cup sugar
2	teaspoons grated lemon zest
¼	cup fresh lemon juice
1	large egg
1	large egg white
2	tablespoons all-purpose white flour
¼	teaspoon baking powder
	Confectioners' sugar for dusting

TO MAKE CRUST:

1. Preheat oven to 350°F. Lightly oil an 8-by-12-inch or 7-by-11-inch baking pan or coat it with nonstick cooking spray.

2. In a small bowl, stir together flour, baking powder, baking soda and salt. In a mixing bowl, beat together sugar, butter, oil, egg white and lemon zest with an electric mixer until smooth. Stir in the dry ingredients until blended and crumbly.

3. Press the dough in an even layer in the prepared baking pan. Bake the crust for 15 to 20 minutes, or until it is puffed all over and browned around the edges.

TO MAKE FILLING:

Meanwhile, in a bowl, combine sugar, lemon zest and juice, egg, egg white, flour and baking powder; whisk until smooth. Pour evenly over the hot crust and bake for 15 to 20 minutes longer, or until set. Let cool completely in the pan on a wire rack. Cut into squares and dust with confectioners' sugar. (*Store, covered, in the refrigerator for up to 3 days.*)

Makes 18 squares.

100 calories per square: 2 grams protein, 2 grams fat (0.5 grams saturated fat), 20 grams carbohydrate; 67 mg sodium; 14 mg cholesterol.

Lemon Squares

WHOLE-WHEAT BLUEBERRY BARS

A moist fruit filling with a crunchy topping, which is made with the same dough as the crust.

CRUST

1⅓ cups plus about 3 tablespoons whole-wheat pastry flour

½ teaspoon baking powder

½ teaspoon baking soda

½ teaspoon salt

1 cup packed light brown sugar

2 tablespoons butter, softened

2 tablespoons canola oil

1 large egg

1 teaspoon pure vanilla extract

BLUEBERRY FILLING

½ cup white sugar

2 tablespoons all-purpose white flour

1 teaspoon grated lemon zest

2 cups fresh *or* frozen unsweetened blueberries

1 tablespoon fresh lemon juice

Confectioners' sugar for dusting (optional)

◆ **SMART SHOPPER**

Whole-wheat pastry flour is available at health-food stores and large supermarkets; the bars can also be made with all-purpose white flour.

TO MAKE CRUST:

1. Preheat oven to 350°F. Lightly oil an 8-by-12-inch or 7-by-11-inch baking pan or coat it with nonstick cooking spray; set aside.

2. In a large bowl, whisk together 1⅓ cups of the flour, baking powder, baking soda and salt. In another bowl, beat together brown sugar, butter, oil, egg and vanilla with an electric mixer on high speed until smooth, making sure no lumps of brown sugar remain, about 1 minute. Add the dry ingredients and stir with a wooden spoon until well blended. The dough will be quite firm.

3. Transfer two-thirds of the dough to the prepared baking pan; cover the dough with a piece of plastic wrap and use it to press the dough into the bottom of the pan in an even layer. Remove the plastic wrap. Bake for 15 minutes, or until puffed and golden.

4. Using your fingertips, gradually work enough of the remaining 3 tablespoons flour into the remaining dough until it resembles coarse crumbs; set aside to use as the topping.

TO MAKE FILLING:

1. In a small bowl, stir together the sugar, flour and lemon zest. In a saucepan, combine blueberries and lemon juice; cook, stirring, over medium heat until the berries begin to exude juice. Add the sugar mixture and stir until the filling reaches a simmer and thickens.

2. With a wooden spoon, push down the higher outside edges of the baked crust; pour the hot filling over it and spread all the way to the sides of the pan. Sprinkle the crumb topping over the top. Bake for 15 to 20 minutes longer, or until the topping is golden.

3. Transfer the baking pan to a wire rack and let cool, covered with a kitchen towel to soften the crumbs slightly. Cut into bars. If desired, dust lightly with confectioners' sugar. (*Store, covered, in the refrigerator for up to 3 days.*)

Makes 15 bars.

170 calories per bar: 2 grams protein, 4 grams fat (1 gram saturated fat), 33 grams carbohydrate; 135 mg sodium; 18 mg cholesterol.

CRANBERRY-GRANOLA BLONDIES

Packed with dried fruit and cereal, these firm bars are excellent travelers.

1. Preheat oven to 350°F. Lightly oil a 9-by-13-inch baking pan or coat it with nonstick cooking spray; set aside.

2. In a small bowl, whisk together flour, baking powder and salt. In a large bowl, beat together brown sugar, oil and egg whites with an electric mixer on high speed until smooth, making sure no lumps of brown sugar remain. Add the dry ingredients and beat on low speed just until blended. Stir in granola and dried fruit. (The batter will be quite thick.)

3. Transfer the batter to the prepared baking pan; smooth the top. Bake for 20 to 25 minutes, or until the blondies are golden brown on top and feel "set" when lightly pressed in the center.

4. Let cool in the baking pan on a wire rack. Cut into bars. (*Store at room temperature in an airtight container for up to 3 days.*)

Makes 20 bars.

150 calories per bar: 2 grams protein, 3 grams fat (0 grams saturated fat), 29 grams carbohydrate; 103 mg sodium; 0 mg cholesterol.

1	cup all-purpose white flour
1	teaspoon baking powder
½	teaspoon salt
1¼	cups packed light brown sugar
¼	cup canola oil
3	large egg whites
2	cups low-fat granola cereal with raisins
1	cup dried cranberries *or* chopped dried tart cherries

◆**GETTING AHEAD**

Bake bars in an aluminum-foil pan; cool, then freeze the whole thing. Alternatively, line a glass or metal baking dish with enough foil to come well up over the edges; once the bars have cooled, lift out the entire uncut layer, wrap and freeze for up to 2 months.

CHOCOLATE CHIP BARS

A bar version of the classic cookie, these slightly chewy confections are a delight.

⅔ cup all-purpose white flour

½ teaspoon baking soda

½ teaspoon salt

2 tablespoons butter

2 ounces reduced-fat cream cheese (¼ cup)

½ cup packed light brown sugar

½ cup white sugar

1 large egg

1½ teaspoons pure vanilla extract

½ cup semisweet chocolate chips, coarsely chopped, *or* mini chocolate chips

1. Preheat oven to 375°F. Lightly oil an 8-by-12-inch or 7-by-11-inch baking pan or coat it with nonstick cooking spray. Set aside.

2. In a mixing bowl, stir together flour, baking soda and salt; set aside. Melt butter in a small saucepan over low heat. Cook, swirling the pan, until the butter turns a nutty brown, 30 to 60 seconds. Pour into a large mixing bowl. Add cream cheese, brown sugar and white sugar. Beat with an electric mixer on low speed until smooth. Add egg and vanilla; beat until well incorporated. Add the reserved dry ingredients and chocolate chips and stir just until combined.

3. Pour the batter into the prepared baking pan and bake for 20 to 25 minutes, or until a skewer inserted in the center comes out clean. Let cool completely in the pan on a wire rack. Cut into bars. (*Store at room temperature in an airtight container for up to 3 days.*)

Makes 15 bars.

115 calories per bar: 2 grams protein, 4 grams fat (1.5 grams saturated fat), 21 grams carbohydrate; 142 mg sodium; 20 mg cholesterol.

HERMITS

These moist, spicy favorites keep well (if they get the chance).

1. Preheat oven to 350°F. Lightly oil a 9-by-13-inch baking pan or coat it with nonstick cooking spray; set aside.

2. In a small bowl, whisk together flour, baking powder, baking soda, salt, cinnamon, allspice, nutmeg and cloves. In a large bowl, beat together molasses, brown sugar, oil, apple butter and eggs with an electric mixer until smooth. Add the dry ingredients and beat on low speed just until combined. Stir in raisins. Transfer the batter to the prepared baking pan; smooth the top. Bake for 20 to 25 minutes, or until the batter feels "set" when lightly pressed in the center.

3. Let cool in the baking pan on a rack. Cut into bars. (*Store at room temperature in an airtight container for up to 3 days.*)

Makes 20 bars.

155 calories per bar: 2 grams protein, 3 grams fat (1 gram saturated fat), 30 grams carbohydrate; 102 mg sodium; 21 mg cholesterol.

1⅓ cups all-purpose white flour

1 teaspoon baking powder

½ teaspoon baking soda

½ teaspoon salt

2 teaspoons ground cinnamon

1 teaspoon ground allspice

½ teaspoon freshly grated nutmeg

¼ teaspoon ground cloves

½ cup dark molasses

¾ cup packed light brown sugar

¼ cup canola oil

¼ cup apple butter

2 large eggs

1½ cups raisins

◆**INGREDIENT NOTE**
Spices lose their punch over time. Start with fresh ones each year.

FIG BARS

Better than their store-bought cousins, these bars have a richly flavored filling, with a little bit of crispness to the crust.

FILLING

1	cup packed chopped dried figs, stems removed
1	tablespoon fresh lemon juice
1	teaspoon grated lemon zest
⅛	teaspoon salt

DOUGH

1⅓	cups all-purpose white flour
½	teaspoon baking powder
½	teaspoon baking soda
½	teaspoon salt
1	cup packed light brown sugar
2	tablespoons butter, softened
2	tablespoons canola oil
1	large egg
1	teaspoon pure vanilla extract
	Confectioners' sugar for dusting (optional)

◆**LOW-FAT BAKING TIP**
Doughs for reduced-fat pastries can tend to be sticky, but pressing them out under a piece of plastic wrap or wax paper easily solves the problem.

TO MAKE FILLING:

In a saucepan, stir together figs, ½ cup water, lemon juice, lemon zest and salt. Bring to a simmer and stir over low heat until thickened, about 3 minutes. Transfer to a food processor and puree until smooth; set aside to cool to lukewarm.

TO MAKE DOUGH AND ASSEMBLE BARS:

1. Preheat oven to 350°F. In a small bowl, stir together flour, baking powder, baking soda and salt. In a large bowl, beat together brown sugar, butter, oil, egg and vanilla with an electric mixer on high speed until smooth, making sure no lumps of brown sugar remain, about 1 minute. Add the dry ingredients and stir with a wooden spoon until completely blended. (The dough will be stiff.)

2. To shape the dough, line the bottom of an 8-by-12-inch or 7-by-11-inch baking pan with a piece of plastic wrap; smooth out any wrinkles. Evenly press one-half of the dough into the bottom of the lined pan. If the dough is sticky, smooth it out under another piece of plastic wrap. Pick up the ends of the plastic wrap and lift out the piece of dough.

3. Lightly oil the bottom of the same baking pan or coat it with nonstick cooking spray. Press the remaining half of the dough into the pan. Spread the fig filling on top. Invert the first half of the dough onto the filling and peel away the plastic wrap. Bake for 25 to 30 minutes, or until the upper crust appears completely baked when pierced in the center with a skewer.

4. Transfer the baking pan to a wire rack and let cool, covered with a kitchen towel to help soften the top crust. Cut into bars. If desired, dust lightly with confectioners' sugar. (*Store at room temperature in an airtight container for up to 3 days.*)

Makes 15 bars.

170 calories per bar: 2 grams protein, 4 grams fat (1 gram saturated fat), 33 grams carbohydrate; 153 mg sodium; 18 mg cholesterol.

Apricot-Oatmeal Bars

APRICOT-OATMEAL BARS

These pretty streusel-topped bars are quick to make and easy to transport.
Made with unsweetened apricot preserves, they are a good source of potassium and beta carotene.

1. Preheat oven to 325°F. Lightly oil an 8-by-12-inch or 7-by-11-inch baking pan or coat it with nonstick cooking spray; set aside.

2. In a large bowl, work together oats, flour, brown sugar, salt and baking soda with your fingertips until no lumps of brown sugar remain. Drizzle oil and fruit juice over the oats and mix in until evenly moistened and crumbly. Set aside ½ cup for the topping; press the remainder evenly into the prepared baking pan. Spread apricot preserves over the top. Sprinkle with the reserved oat topping.

3. Bake for 30 to 40 minutes, or until golden. Let cool in the baking pan on a wire rack. Cut into bars. (*Store at room temperature in an airtight container for up to 3 days.*)

Makes 15 bars.

195 calories per bar: 3 grams protein, 4 grams fat (1 gram saturated fat), 36 grams carbohydrate; 55 mg sodium; 0 mg cholesterol.

1   cup "quick" rolled oats

1   cup all-purpose white flour

⅔   cup packed light brown sugar

¼   teaspoon salt

¼   teaspoon baking soda

¼   cup canola oil

3   tablespoons apple *or* cranberry juice

1   10-ounce jar apricot preserves, preferably "all-fruit" (1 scant cup)

DATE-PECAN BARS

*Here, graham cracker crumbs and dates are folded into beaten eggs and sugar to make
a wonderfully chewy date bar, with a fraction of the fat of traditional recipes.*

2   teaspoons instant espresso
    or coffee powder
2   teaspoons pure vanilla
    extract
¾   cup sugar
2   large eggs
1   large egg white
¼   teaspoon salt
2   cups fine graham cracker
    crumbs (18 whole
    crackers)
⅔   cup chopped dates
½   cup chopped pecans
    Confectioners' sugar for
    dusting (optional)

1. Preheat oven to 300°F. Lightly oil an 8-by-12-inch or 7-by-11-inch baking pan or coat it with nonstick cooking spray; set aside.

2. In a large mixing bowl, stir together coffee powder and vanilla until the powder dissolves; add sugar, eggs, egg white and salt and beat with an electric mixer on high speed until thick and pale, about 2 minutes. With a rubber spatula, fold in graham cracker crumbs, dates and pecans just until combined.

3. Transfer the batter to the prepared baking pan; smooth the top. Bake for 30 to 35 minutes, or until the top feels dry and a skewer inserted in the center comes out clean.

4. Let cool in the baking pan on a wire rack. Cut into bars. If desired, dust lightly with confectioners' sugar. (*Store at room temperature in an airtight container for up to 3 days.*)

Makes 15 bars.

130 calories per bar: 2 grams protein, 4 grams fat (1 gram saturated fat), 23 grams carbohydrate; 88 mg sodium; 28 mg cholesterol.

◆**BAKING TIP**

*Turn graham crackers into crumbs in the food processor.
Or place the crackers between two sheets of wax paper and roll them with a rolling pin.*

PROPER SCONES & TEA CAKES

There's a point in the day when you need something sweet, but not too sweet, to go with a cup of tea or coffee. This collection of scones, muffins and coffee and tea cakes satisfies just that need. There is even a doughnut recipe. Actually, the doughnuts are little cakes baked in mini-Bundt pans, but they look and taste like real cake doughnuts: instead of a dozen or more grams of fat in each one, they contain just four. Any of these scrumptious and easy baked goods will make for a healthful break during a hectic day.

Cranberry-Walnut Scones

CRANBERRY-WALNUT SCONES

In the unlikely event you have any scones left over, toast them to recrisp the outer crust before serving.

1. Preheat oven to 425°F. Lightly oil a baking sheet or coat it with nonstick cooking spray.

2. In a large bowl, stir together flour, ¼ cup brown sugar, baking powder and salt. With a pastry blender or your fingertips, cut in butter until the mixture resembles coarse crumbs. Stir in cranberries and walnuts. Make a well in the center and gradually stir in buttermilk to form a ball. Knead lightly. Do not overwork; the dough will be sticky.

3. Divide the dough in half. On a lightly floured surface, pat or roll each portion into an 8-inch round, about ½ inch thick. Cut each round into 8 triangles. Place the scones on the prepared baking sheet. Brush the tops with buttermilk and sprinkle with the remaining 1 tablespoon brown sugar. Bake for 14 to 18 minutes, or until golden brown. Serve warm.

Makes 16 scones.

115 calories per serving: 3 grams protein, 3 grams fat (1 gram saturated fat), 21 grams carbohydrate; 140 mg sodium; 4 mg cholesterol.

2 cups all-purpose white flour

¼ cup light brown sugar, plus 1 tablespoon for sprinkling scone tops

2 teaspoons baking powder

½ teaspoon salt

2 tablespoons unsalted butter

½ cup fresh *or* dried cranberries

¼ cup chopped walnuts

1 cup buttermilk, plus extra for brushing scone tops

ORANGE-RAISIN SCONES

Golden, moist and tender with a cakelike texture, these are the perfect excuse for a coffee or tea break.

2   cups all-purpose white flour
¼   cup sugar
1   teaspoon baking powder
1   teaspoon baking soda
½   teaspoon salt
¾   cup coarsely chopped raisins *or* whole currants
1   tablespoon butter
2   tablespoons canola oil
1   cup nonfat plain yogurt, plus extra for brushing scone tops
1   large egg
1   tablespoon grated orange zest

1. Preheat oven to 375°F. Lightly oil a baking sheet or coat it with nonstick cooking spray; set aside.

2. In a mixing bowl, stir together flour, sugar, baking powder, baking soda and salt. Add raisins or currants, tossing to coat. In a small saucepan, melt butter over low heat. Cook, swirling the pan, until it turns a nutty brown, about 1 minute. Transfer the butter to a bowl. Add oil, 1 cup yogurt, egg and orange zest and whisk until blended. Add the yogurt mixture to the dry ingredients, stirring just until combined (the dough will be sticky).

3. Transfer the dough to the prepared baking sheet; with floured hands, pat it out into a ½-inch-thick circle. Cut the circle into 12 wedges, leaving them in place. Brush the top with yogurt.

4. Bake for 15 to 20 minutes, or until the top is golden and firm to the touch. Serve warm.

Makes 1 dozen scones.

165 calories per scone: 4 grams protein, 4 grams fat (1 gram saturated fat), 29 grams carbohydrate; 216 mg sodium; 21 mg cholesterol.

SPICED COFFEE CAKE WITH PEARS

Fragrant pears bake under a gingerbread batter, making for a lovely presentation with a minimum of effort.

1. Position rack in the lower third of the oven; preheat to 375°F. Lightly oil an 8-inch square baking dish or coat it with nonstick cooking spray.

2. Pour butter into the prepared baking dish and tilt to coat the bottom evenly. Sprinkle brown sugar over the butter. Peel, halve and core pears. Brush with lemon juice. Cut a pear half crosswise into ⅛-inch-thick slices. Holding the slices together, slide a metal spatula underneath and invert the sliced pear half onto your hand, pressing to fan slightly. Place it, rounded-side down, on the brown sugar in the baking dish. Repeat with the remaining pear halves. Bake, uncovered, for 15 minutes.

3. Meanwhile, whisk flour, baking powder, baking soda, salt, cinnamon, ginger, allspice and nutmeg in a bowl; stir in white sugar. In a large bowl, whisk together egg whites, buttermilk, molasses and oil. Add the dry ingredients to the wet ingredients and stir just until blended.

4. When the pears have baked for 15 minutes, pour the batter evenly over the top. Bake for 30 to 35 minutes longer, or until a skewer inserted in the center comes out clean. Loosen the edges. Invert a serving plate on top of the baking pan and, grasping firmly with hands protected with oven mitts, quickly turn the cake and plate over. Remove the baking dish. Remove any pear slices that adhere to the dish and replace them on top of the cake. Let cool for at least 10 minutes, cut into squares and serve warm.

Serves 9.

215 calories per serving: 3 grams protein, 5 grams fat (1 gram saturated fat), 42 grams carbohydrate; 225 mg sodium; 4 mg cholesterol.

1	tablespoon butter, melted
3	tablespoons light brown sugar
3	ripe but firm pears, such as Bartlett *or* Bosc
1	tablespoon fresh lemon juice
1¼	cups sifted cake flour
½	teaspoon baking powder
½	teaspoon baking soda
½	teaspoon salt
2	teaspoons ground cinnamon
1	teaspoon ground ginger
½	teaspoon ground allspice
¼	teaspoon freshly grated nutmeg
½	cup white sugar
2	large egg whites
½	cup buttermilk
¼	cup dark molasses
2	tablespoons canola oil

◆ **BAKING TIP**
Where things are baked in the oven will have a dramatic effect on the final outcome. If you're after a well-browned bottom, set the shelf in the lower third of the oven. For a golden top, use the upper position instead.

BLUEBERRY COFFEE CAKE

For the best texture, do not overmix the batter or the cake will be tough.

CAKE

1	large egg
½	cup skim milk
½	cup nonfat plain yogurt
3	tablespoons canola oil
2	cups all-purpose white flour
½	cup sugar
4	teaspoons baking powder
½	teaspoon salt
1½	cups fresh *or* frozen unsweetened blueberries

TOPPING

3	tablespoons sugar
2	tablespoons finely chopped walnuts
¼	teaspoon ground cinnamon

TO MAKE CAKE:

1. Preheat oven to 400°F. Lightly oil an 8-inch square baking dish or coat it with nonstick cooking spray.

2. In a large mixing bowl, whisk together egg, milk, yogurt and oil. Set a sieve on top of the bowl and measure flour, sugar, baking powder and salt into it. Stir the dry ingredients together while sifting them into the liquid mixture. Stir the batter just to blend. Do not overmix. Fold in blueberries. Transfer the batter to the prepared pan.

TO PREPARE TOPPING & BAKE CAKE:

1. In a small bowl, stir together sugar, walnuts and cinnamon; sprinkle over the batter.

2. Bake for 20 to 25 minutes, or until the top is golden brown and a skewer inserted in the center comes out clean. (Add about 20 minutes to the baking time if using frozen berries.) Let cool in the pan on a wire rack for 10 minutes. Cut into squares and serve warm.

Serves 9.

240 calories per serving: 5 grams protein, 6 grams fat (1 gram saturated fat), 42 grams carbohydrate; 290 mg sodium; 24 mg cholesterol.

◆**GETTING AHEAD**

To save time in the morning, measure out and mix the dry ingredients the night before. Although they are best when fresh baked, coffee cakes also can be baked ahead and frozen. Defrost and warm in the oven or microwave.

PRUNE COFFEE CAKE

The delicious blending of dark, sweet prunes with a light touch of spices will make a prune lover out of almost anyone.

1. Preheat oven to 350°F. Lightly oil an 8-inch square baking pan or coat it with nonstick cooking spray.

2. In a food processor, combine ⅔ cup of the prunes and ⅓ cup hot water; process until smooth. Coarsely chop the remaining ⅔ cup prunes. Set the prune puree and chopped prunes aside.

3. In a medium bowl, whisk flour, baking powder, baking soda, salt, cinnamon, nutmeg and cloves. In a small bowl, toss 1 tablespoon of the dry ingredients with the chopped prunes. In a mixing bowl, combine the reserved prune puree, 1 cup sugar, egg whites, yogurt, oil and vanilla; beat with an electric mixer on medium speed until blended. In 3 additions, add the dry ingredients to the batter, beating on low speed between additions. Occasionally, stop and scrape down the bowl and beater with a rubber spatula. Stir in the flour-coated chopped prunes.

4. Turn the batter into the prepared pan and sprinkle 1½ tablespoons sugar evenly over the top. Bake for 35 to 40 minutes, or until a skewer inserted in the center comes out clean. Let cool in the pan on a wire rack for at least 10 minutes. Cut into squares and serve warm.

Serves 9.

295 calories per serving: 4 grams protein, 6 grams fat (1 gram saturated fat), 57 grams carbohydrate; 247 mg sodium; 0 mg cholesterol.

1⅓	cups pitted prunes
1¾	cups sifted cake flour
1½	teaspoons baking powder
½	teaspoon baking soda
½	teaspoon salt
1½	teaspoons ground cinnamon
½	teaspoon ground nutmeg
¼	teaspoon ground cloves
1	cup plus 1½ tablespoons sugar
2	large egg whites
¾	cup nonfat plain yogurt
¼	cup canola oil
1	teaspoon pure vanilla extract

ORANGE MARMALADE COFFEE CAKE

Instead of coffee, make some not-too-sweet hot chocolate to serve with the orangy cake.

1	large egg
1	cup low-fat lemon or orange yogurt
3	tablespoons canola oil
3	tablespoons fresh orange juice
1	tablespoon grated orange zest
2	teaspoons pure vanilla extract
2¼	cups sifted cake flour
½	cup sugar
1	tablespoon baking powder
½	teaspoon salt
¼	teaspoon baking soda
¾	cup orange marmalade

1. Preheat oven to 350°F. Lightly oil an 8-inch square baking pan or coat it with nonstick cooking spray.

2. In a large bowl, whisk together egg, yogurt, oil, orange juice, orange zest and vanilla. In another bowl, stir together flour, sugar, baking powder, salt and baking soda. Add the dry ingredients to the egg mixture and stir just until blended.

3. Transfer the batter to the prepared pan and bake for 30 to 35 minutes, or until a skewer inserted in the center comes out clean. Cool in the pan on a wire rack for 10 minutes.

4. In a small saucepan, heat marmalade over medium heat; simmer, stirring constantly, until slightly thickened, about 6 minutes. Spoon over the cake, spreading evenly. Let cool slightly, cut into squares and serve warm.

Serves 9.

295 calories per serving: 4 grams protein, 6 grams fat (1 gram saturated fat), 57 grams carbohydrate; 276 mg sodium; 25 mg cholesterol.

◆**INGREDIENT NOTE**

Choose a good imported marmalade made from Seville oranges. Their bittersweet quality balances the moist, rich cake.

QUICK CINNAMON ROLLS

The best thing to have on a chilly afternoon.

TO MAKE CINNAMON ROLLS:

1. Preheat oven to 400°F. Lightly oil an 8-inch square baking dish or coat it with nonstick cooking spray.

2. In a small bowl, pour ¼ cup boiling water over raisins; cover and set aside. In another bowl, whisk together flour, baking powder and salt; set aside. In a third bowl, mix together brown sugar and cinnamon and set aside.

3. In a food processor, puree cottage cheese. Add white sugar, milk, oil and vanilla and process until very smooth. Add the flour mixture and pulse 4 or 5 times, just until the dough clumps together. Turn out onto a work surface and knead several times to make a soft dough. Dust the dough and work surface with flour and roll into a rectangle, approximately 15 by 10 inches.

4. Brush the dough with melted butter, leaving a ½-inch border around the perimeter. Sprinkle with the brown-sugar mixture; run the rolling pin over the surface to gently press the sugar into the dough. Drain any liquid from the raisins and sprinkle them over the sugar. Starting at a long edge, roll up, jelly-roll fashion. Pinch the edges of the dough together along the seam. With a sharp knife, trim the ends. Slice the dough into 12 rolls. Set the rolls, cut-side up, in the prepared baking dish. (The rolls will fill the dish as they bake.) Bake for 25 to 30 minutes, or until golden and firm to the touch. Loosen the edges and invert onto a wire rack to cool slightly. Turn the rolls right-side up for glazing.

TO MAKE GLAZE:

In a small bowl, whisk together the confectioners' sugar, vanilla and just enough milk to make a nice consistency for drizzling. Drizzle the glaze over the rolls and serve warm.

Makes 1 dozen rolls.

220 calories per roll: 4 grams protein, 6 grams fat (1 gram saturated fat), 38 grams carbohydrate; 20 mg sodium; 3 mg cholesterol.

CINNAMON ROLLS

- ½ cup raisins
- 2 cups all-purpose white flour
- 1 tablespoon baking powder
- ¼ teaspoon salt
- ⅓ cup packed brown sugar
- 2 teaspoons ground cinnamon
- ¾ cup low-fat cottage cheese
- ⅓ cup white sugar
- ⅓ cup low-fat milk
- ¼ cup canola oil
- 1½ teaspoons pure vanilla extract
- 1 tablespoon butter, melted

GLAZE

- ½ cup confectioners' sugar,
- 1 teaspoon pure vanilla extract
- 2-3 teaspoons low-fat milk

APRICOT & GOLDEN RAISIN TEA LOAF

Full of tart flavor, this quick bread is great for toasting.

¼   cup chopped hazelnuts (filberts)

1¼   cups dried apricots, chopped

2½   cups all-purpose white flour

½   cup sugar

2   teaspoons baking powder

1   teaspoon baking soda

½   teaspoon salt

1   large egg

2   large egg whites

⅔   cup buttermilk

3   tablespoons hazelnut oil *or* canola oil

1   teaspoon pure vanilla extract

¾   cup golden raisins

1. Preheat oven to 350°F. Lightly oil a 9-by-5-inch loaf pan or coat it with nonstick cooking spray; set aside. Spread hazelnuts on a baking sheet and bake for 5 minutes, or until lightly toasted; let cool.

2. In a small saucepan, combine ½ cup of the apricots with ½ cup water. Bring to a simmer, remove from the heat and let stand for 10 minutes. Transfer the apricots and their liquid to a food processor and process until they form a chunky puree; set aside (you should have about ½ cup puree).

3. In a large bowl, stir together flour, sugar, baking powder, baking soda and salt. In another large bowl, whisk together egg, egg whites, buttermilk, oil, vanilla and the reserved apricot puree until smooth. Stir the apricot mixture into the dry ingredients just until combined. Fold in raisins, hazelnuts and the remaining ¾ cup apricots. Turn the batter out into the prepared pan, smoothing the top.

4. Bake for 50 to 60 minutes, or until the top is golden and a skewer inserted in the center of the loaf comes out clean. Let cool in the pan for 10 minutes. Loosen the edges and invert the loaf onto a wire rack to cool. Serve warm or at room temperature.

Makes 1 loaf, 12 slices.

260 calories per slice: 6 grams protein, 7 grams fat (1 gram saturated fat), 45 grams carbohydrate; 245 mg sodium; 18 mg cholesterol.

◆**STORAGE NOTE**
After opening, store hazelnut oil, or any other nut oil, in the refrigerator to keep it from going rancid.

Apricot & Golden Raisin Tea Loaf

ZUCCHINI BREAD

Not too sweet, and very fragrant, this is good bread to bake if you're trying to sell your house.

1	cup rolled oats
½	cup pecan halves
2¼	cups all-purpose white flour
1½	cups whole-wheat pastry flour
1½	tablespoons baking powder
2	teaspoons ground cinnamon
½	teaspoon freshly grated nutmeg
¼	teaspoon ground cloves
1½	teaspoons salt
2	cups packed light brown sugar
2	large eggs
2	large egg whites
¾	cup apple butter
⅓	cup canola oil
3	cups grated zucchini (about 2 small zucchini)

1. Preheat oven to 350°F. Lightly oil two 9-by-5-inch loaf pans or coat them with nonstick cooking spray. Spread oats and pecans on separate parts of a baking sheet and bake for 5 to 10 minutes, or until lightly toasted; let cool. Chop the pecans.

2. In a mixing bowl, stir together all but 2 tablespoons of the toasted oats, the pecans, white and whole-wheat flours, baking powder, cinnamon, nutmeg, cloves and salt. In another bowl, whisk together brown sugar, eggs, egg whites, apple butter and oil; stir in zucchini. Stir this mixture into the dry ingredients just until well combined.

3. Divide the batter between the prepared loaf pans, smoothing the tops. Sprinkle 1 tablespoon of the reserved oats on top of each loaf. Bake for 45 to 55 minutes, or until the tops feel firm when lightly pressed and a skewer inserted in the center comes out clean.

4. Let the loaves rest in the pans for 5 minutes; turn them out onto a wire rack to cool completely.

Makes 2 loaves, 12 slices per loaf.

220 calories per slice: 4 grams protein, 6 grams fat (1 gram saturated fat), 40 grams carbohydrate; 212 mg sodium; 18 mg cholesterol.

PUMPKIN & CRANBERRY BREAD

Cornmeal gives this moist quick bread a subtle crunch.

1. Preheat oven to 350°F. Lightly oil two 9-by-5-inch loaf pans or coat them with nonstick cooking spray; dust with flour and tap out the excess.

2. In a mixing bowl, combine white and whole-wheat flours, cornmeal, brown sugar, baking powder, baking soda, cinnamon, ginger and salt; mix well, breaking up any lumps of brown sugar with your fingertips. In another bowl, whisk together pumpkin, yogurt, oil, eggs and egg whites until well combined. Stir the pumpkin mixture and cranberries or raisins into the dry ingredients until completely blended, but do not overmix.

3. Divide the batter between the loaf pans, smoothing the tops with a spatula. Bake for 55 to 65 minutes, or until a skewer inserted in the center comes out clean.

4. Let the loaves rest in the pans for 5 minutes; turn them out onto a wire rack to cool completely.

Makes 2 loaves, 12 slices per loaf.

200 calories per slice: 3 grams protein, 4 grams fat (1 gram saturated fat), 40 grams carbohydrate; 224 mg sodium; 18 mg cholesterol.

1 cup all-purpose white flour

1 cup whole-wheat flour

1 cup cornmeal, preferably stone-ground

2 cups packed brown sugar

1 tablespoon baking powder

2 teaspoons baking soda

2 teaspoons ground cinnamon

1 teaspoon ground ginger

1 teaspoon salt

1 15- or 16-ounce can plain pumpkin puree (1½ cups)

1 cup nonfat plain yogurt

⅓ cup canola oil

2 large eggs

2 large egg whites

2 cups dried cranberries *or* raisins

◆**INGREDIENT NOTE**
"Stone-ground" cornmeal includes the germ and some of the hull, so it's more nutritious and has a more interesting texture. Store it in the freezer.

APPLE-CIDER "DOUGHNUTS" WITH MAPLE GLAZE

This recipe was inspired by two treats you find while touring Vermont (home of EATING WELL*): cider doughnuts and maple syrup.*

3   tablespoons white sugar (approximately) for preparing pans

2   cups all-purpose white flour

1½ teaspoons baking powder

1½ teaspoons baking soda

½   teaspoon salt

2   teaspoons ground cinnamon

1   large egg, lightly beaten

⅔   cup packed brown sugar

½   cup apple butter

⅓   cup pure maple syrup

⅓   cup apple cider

⅓   cup nonfat plain yogurt

3   tablespoons canola oil

MAPLE GLAZE

1¼ cups confectioners' sugar

1   teaspoon pure vanilla extract

¼-⅓ cup pure maple syrup

1. Preheat oven to 400°F. Coat the molds of a mini-Bundt pan with nonstick cooking spray or oil. Sprinkle with white sugar, shaking out the excess.

2. In a mixing bowl, whisk together flour, baking powder, baking soda, salt and cinnamon; set aside. In another bowl, whisk together egg, brown sugar, apple butter, maple syrup, cider, yogurt and oil. Add the dry ingredients and stir just until moistened. Divide half the batter among the prepared molds, spooning about 2 generous tablespoonfuls of batter into each mold.

3. Bake for 10 to 12 minutes, or until the tops spring back when touched lightly. Loosen the edges and turn the cakes out onto a wire rack to cool. Clean the mini-Bundt pan, then recoat it with cooking spray or oil and sugar. Repeat with the remaining batter.

TO MAKE MAPLE GLAZE:

In a bowl, combine confectioners' sugar and vanilla. Gradually whisk in enough maple syrup to make a coating consistency. Dip the fluted side of the "doughnuts" in the glaze to coat. Then set them glazed-side up on a wire rack over wax paper for a few minutes until the glaze has set.

Makes 1 dozen doughnuts.

285 calories per doughnut: 3 grams protein, 4 grams fat (0 grams saturated fat), 61 grams carbohydrate; 263 mg sodium; 18 mg cholesterol.

◆**EQUIPMENT NOTE**

Coating a mold or cake pan with sugar before adding the batter will give the outside of the cake an appealing crisp glaze. A mini-Bundt pan produces adorable doughnut-shaped cakes, but if you do not have one, you can use a regular Bundt pan and make a coffee cake; bake it in a 375°F oven for 25 to 30 minutes.

Apple-Cider "Doughnuts" with Maple Glaze

RHUBARB MUFFINS

A sweet treat from the Inn at the Round Barn Farm in Waitsfield, Vermont.

¼ cup sugar

½ teaspoon ground cinnamon

3 tablespoons finely chopped pecans

1 cup buttermilk

1 large egg

1 cup packed light brown sugar

¼ cup canola oil

1½ teaspoons pure vanilla extract

1½ cups diced rhubarb

1¾ cups all-purpose white flour

1 teaspoon baking powder

1 teaspoon baking soda

½ teaspoon salt

1. Preheat oven to 400°F. Lightly oil 12 muffin cups or coat with nonstick cooking spray; set aside. In a small bowl, stir together sugar, cinnamon and nuts; set aside.

2. In a mixing bowl, whisk together buttermilk, egg, brown sugar, oil, and vanilla until smooth; stir in rhubarb. In another bowl, whisk together flour, baking powder, baking soda and salt; add to the buttermilk/rhubarb mixture and stir until just combined.

3. Spoon the batter into the prepared muffin cups. Sprinkle the reserved sugar/nut mixture over the tops of the muffins. Bake for 20 to 25 minutes, or until the muffins are golden brown. Let cool briefly on a wire rack before serving.

Makes 1 dozen muffins.

220 calories per muffin: 3 grams protein, 6 grams fat (1 gram saturated fat), 38 grams carbohydrate; 218 mg sodium; 19 mg cholesterol.

◆**VARIATION**
Add 2 tablespoons "quick" rolled oats to the topping for a little crunch.

ICE CREAMS & OTHER FROZEN DELIGHTS

The average American eats more than four gallons of ice cream and frozen yogurt every year. Yet the first spoonful of the frosty stuff always brings a special delight that seems rooted in long-ago childhood summers. These days, it's a joy to make ice cream, ices and sorbets. Homemade ice cream used to require layering coarse salt and cracked ice in an ice cream maker and cranking until you could crank no more. The introduction in the 1980s of compact ice cream makers whose cooling units fit into the freezer changed all that.

VANILLA ICE CREAM

Commercial marshmallow creme is the short-cut secret to this ice cream's velvety texture.
The brand we use is Marshmallow Fluff.

4	cups skim milk
¼	cup corn syrup
3	large egg yolks
¼	cup cornstarch
2½	cups marshmallow creme, such as Fluff
2	tablespoons pure vanilla extract, preferably Madagascar

◆ TOP-NOTCH VANILLA

For the fullest vanilla flavor, choose a top-quality extract. Bourbon vanilla beans from Madagascar are among the finest, and extracts labeled Madagascar Bourbon Vanilla are rich and aromatic.

1. In a large heavy saucepan, combine 3¾ cups of the milk and corn syrup. Heat over medium heat, stirring to dissolve the corn syrup, until steaming. Meanwhile, in a mixing bowl, whisk together egg yolks, cornstarch and the remaining ¼ cup cold milk until smooth. Gradually whisk 1 cup hot milk into the egg-yolk mixture; then pour the egg-yolk mixture into the hot milk in the pan. Cook over medium heat, whisking constantly, until the mixture boils and thickens, 3 to 5 minutes. (Because the custard is thickened with cornstarch, it will not curdle when it boils.)

2. Transfer the custard to a large clean bowl and place a piece of wax paper or plastic wrap directly on the surface to prevent a skin from forming. Cool completely. Whisk in marshmallow creme and vanilla until as smooth as possible. (The mixture will be a little lumpy; the lumps will break down during stir-freezing.)

3. Pour into the canister of an ice cream maker and freeze according to the manufacturer's directions. If necessary, place the ice cream in the freezer to firm up before serving in chilled dessert dishes. (*Use within hours of freezing, if possible, or store in the freezer for up to 4 days. If the ice cream becomes very hard in the freezer, let it soften for 20 minutes before scooping.*)

Makes about 1½ quarts, serves 8.

240 calories per serving: 6 grams protein, 3 grams fat (1 gram saturated fat), 46 grams carbohydrate; 88 mg sodium; 85 mg cholesterol.

CINNAMON ICE CREAM

Serve a scoop of this subtly spiced ice cream with Caramelized Apple Topping (page 179) or on a wedge of New England Apple Pie (page 43).

1. In a large heavy saucepan, combine milk, brown sugar, cinnamon sticks and vanilla bean. Heat over medium heat, stirring to dissolve the sugar, until steaming. Remove from the heat, cover the pan and let steep for 30 minutes. Strain, discarding the cinnamon sticks and vanilla bean halves. (Scrape the tiny seeds inside the vanilla bean into the milk, if desired.)

2. In a mixing bowl, whisk together egg yolks, corn syrup, cornstarch and ground cinnamon. Gradually add the milk, whisking to combine, and return to the saucepan. Cook over medium heat, whisking constantly, until the mixture boils and thickens, about 3 minutes. (Because the custard is thickened with cornstarch, it will not curdle when it boils.)

3. Transfer the custard to a bowl and place a piece of wax paper or plastic wrap directly over the surface to prevent a skin from forming. Cover and refrigerate until no longer warm. Add marshmallow creme and mix with a whisk until as smooth as possible. (The mixture will be slightly lumpy, but will smooth out during stir-freezing.) Return to the refrigerator until completely chilled.

4. Pour the custard mixture into the canister of an ice cream maker and freeze according to the manufacturer's directions. If necessary, place the ice cream in the freezer to firm up before serving in chilled dessert dishes. (*Use within hours of freezing, if possible, or store in the freezer for up to 4 days. If the ice cream becomes very hard in the freezer, let it soften for 20 minutes before scooping.*)

Makes about 3 cups, serves 6.

255 calories per serving: 6 grams protein, 3 grams fat (1 gram saturated fat), 53 grams carbohydrate; 93 mg sodium; 76 mg cholesterol.

3 cups low-fat milk

2 tablespoons light brown sugar

6 cinnamon sticks, broken into small pieces

1 vanilla bean, split in half lengthwise

2 large egg yolks

¼ cup light corn syrup

2 tablespoons cornstarch

¼ teaspoon ground cinnamon

2 cups marshmallow creme, such as Fluff

♦ SUBSTITUTION

If you don't have a vanilla bean, add 1 teaspoon pure vanilla extract to the milk after it has steeped.

MALT SHOP CHOCOLATE ICE CREAM

A favorite flavor from soda-shop days can now be had in a low-fat ice cream.

1½ teaspoons unflavored gelatin

2½ cups low-fat milk

1 14-ounce can nonfat sweetened condensed milk (*not* evaporated milk)

¼ cup unsweetened cocoa powder, preferably Dutch-process

½ cup malted-milk powder

¼ cup dark corn syrup

1 ounce unsweetened chocolate, coarsely chopped

1 teaspoon pure vanilla extract

1. In a small bowl, sprinkle gelatin over 1 tablespoon water; let stand until softened, 1 minute or longer.

2. In a heavy saucepan, combine ½ cup of the low-fat milk, sweetened condensed milk, cocoa, malted-milk powder and corn syrup; whisk until smooth. Bring to a simmer over medium heat, whisking constantly. Remove from the heat and add chocolate and the softened gelatin; stir until the chocolate has melted. Transfer the mixture to a bowl. Gradually whisk in the remaining 2 cups milk and vanilla until smooth. Chill until cold, about 1 hour.

3. Pour into the canister of an ice cream maker and freeze according to the manufacturer's directions. If necessary, place the ice cream in the freezer to firm up before serving in chilled dessert dishes. (*Use within hours of freezing, if possible, or store in the freezer for up to 4 days. If the ice cream becomes very hard in the freezer, let it soften for 20 minutes before scooping.*)

Makes about 1 quart, serves 6.

320 calories per serving: 11 grams protein, 5 grams fat (1 gram saturated fat), 60 grams carbohydrate; 149 mg sodium; 16 mg cholesterol.

◆**INGREDIENT NOTE**
Look for malted-milk powder between the instant cocoa and the nonfat dry milk on the supermarket shelf.

Malt Shop Chocolate Ice Cream

LEMON ICE CREAM

With a flavor reminiscent of lemon cheesecake, this easy-to-make ice cream is delicious sprinkled with fresh berries.

1 14-ounce can nonfat
   sweetened condensed milk

2 cups low-fat milk

⅔ cup fresh lemon juice

1 tablespoon grated lemon
   zest

⅛ teaspoon salt

In a mixing bowl, whisk together sweetened condensed milk, milk, lemon juice, lemon zest and salt. Freeze in an ice cream maker according to the manufacturer's directions. (*Alternatively, freeze the mixture in a shallow pan until solid, about 6 hours. Break into chunks and process in a food processor until smooth.*)

Makes about 1 quart, serves 6.

230 calories per serving: 8 grams protein, 1 gram fat (0.5 grams saturated fat), 47 grams carbohydrate; 154 mg sodium; 12 mg cholesterol.

WHITE GRAPE ICE

Serve garnished with frozen red grapes (page 165) and a lemon wedge for squeezing over the top.

½   cup sugar

4   cups seedless green grapes
    (about 2 pounds)

1½ cups chilled white grape
    juice

1. In a small saucepan, combine sugar and 1 cup water. Bring to a simmer and stir until the sugar is completely dissolved. Let the syrup cool to room temperature, then place it in the refrigerator to chill.

2. Set a shallow metal pan, such as a cake pan, in the freezer to chill. In a food processor or blender, puree grapes until smooth; strain into a large bowl, pressing firmly on the solids. Discard the solids. Add grape juice and the chilled sugar syrup to the puree; stir until well blended and pour into the chilled metal pan.

3. Place the pan in the freezer for 30 minutes, or until ice crystals form around the edges. Stir the ice crystals into the center of the pan and return to the freezer; repeat every 30 minutes, or until all of the liquid is frozen, about 3 hours.

4. To serve, scoop the ice into chilled bowls or goblets. If the ice has become too hard, scrape it with a large spoon to break up the crystals.

Makes about 5 cups, serves 6.

135 calories per serving: 1 gram protein, 0 grams fat, 36 grams carbohydrate; 3 mg sodium; 0 mg cholesterol.

ORANGE SORBET WITH MINTED ORANGES

If they are available, blood oranges are especially striking here.

TO MAKE SORBET:

Combine sugar, honey and ½ cup water in a small saucepan and bring to a boil. Reduce the heat to low and simmer for 10 minutes. Remove from the heat and allow to cool. Combine orange and lemon juices and sugar syrup in a large bowl. Freeze in an ice cream maker according to the manufacturer's directions. (*Alternatively, freeze the mixture in a shallow metal cake pan until solid, about 6 hours. Break into chunks and process in a food processor until smooth.*)

TO PREPARE ORANGES:

1. With a sharp knife, remove skin and white pith from oranges and discard. Working over a bowl to catch the juice, cut the orange sections from their surrounding membranes, discarding any seeds. Squeeze any juice from the membranes into the bowl; cover and refrigerate.

2. About 1 hour before serving, toss the oranges with orange liqueur and chopped mint. Refrigerate. If the sorbet has frozen solid, allow it to soften for about 30 minutes in the refrigerator before serving. To serve, scoop the sorbet onto individual dishes, spoon the oranges around it and garnish each dish with a sprig of mint.

Serves 6.

170 calories per serving: 2 grams protein, 0 grams fat, 40 grams carbohydrate, 1 gram alcohol; 4 mg sodium; 0 mg cholesterol.

SORBET

- ¼ cup light brown sugar
- 1 tablespoon mild-flavored honey
- 2½ cups fresh orange juice (about 10 oranges)
- ⅓ cup fresh lemon juice

MINTED ORANGES

- 6 navel *or* blood oranges
- 2-3 tablespoons Grand Marnier *or* other orange liqueur
- 2 tablespoons chopped fresh mint plus sprigs for garnish

Cran-Strawberry Ice Pops

CRAN-STRAWBERRY ICE POPS

These ruby-red frozen treats are bursting with fruit flavor.

2   **cups fresh strawberries *or* frozen unsweetened strawberries, thawed**

¼   **cup frozen cranberry-juice concentrate, thawed**

3   **tablespoons sugar**

1   **tablespoon fresh lemon juice**

In a blender or food processor, combine strawberries, cranberry-juice concentrate, sugar, lemon juice and 3 tablespoons water. Process until smooth. Pour the mixture into individual frozen-treat molds or small paper cups. Freeze for about 1 hour, or until beginning to set. Insert frozen-treat sticks and freeze until completely firm.

Makes eight 2-ounce pops.

35 calories per pop: 0 grams protein, 0 grams fat, 8 grams carbohydrate; 1 mg sodium; 0 mg cholesterol.

◆**SMART SHOPPER**

Most kitchenware stores sell frozen-treat molds and sticks throughout the summer; craft stores sell the sticks year-round.

FROZEN FUDGE BARS

Creamy, chocolaty and just like the ones from the corner store, but better.

In a heavy saucepan, whisk together sweetened condensed milk, sugar and cocoa until smooth. Stir the mixture with a wooden spoon over medium-low heat until it comes to a simmer; continue stirring for 1 minute. Very gradually, whisk in the low-fat milk, stirring to dissolve all the cocoa-sugar mixture. Remove the pan from the heat and stir in vanilla. Pour into individual frozen-treat molds or small paper cups. Freeze for abut 1 hour, or until beginning to set. Insert frozen-treat sticks and freeze until completely firm.

Makes eight 2-ounce bars.

120 calories per bar: 3 grams protein, 1 gram fat (0 grams saturated fat), 26 grams carbohydrate; 40 mg sodium; 4 mg cholesterol.

½ cup nonfat sweetened condensed milk

½ cup sugar

¼ cup unsweetened cocoa powder, preferably Dutch-process

1¼ cups low-fat milk

1 teaspoon pure vanilla extract

FROSTED GRAPES

Frozen grapes make a cool finish to hot, spicy meals.

Wash grapes and pat dry. Place in the freezer for 45 minutes. Remove from the freezer and let sit for 2 minutes before serving.

Serves 4.

105 calories per serving: 1 gram protein, 0 grams fat, 29 grams carbohydrate; 3 mg sodium; 0 mg cholesterol.

1½ pounds red or green seedless grapes

FROZEN YOGURT SANDWICHES

Great for the kids—or the kids at heart—frozen fruit swirled into frozen yogurt and sandwiched between two crisp oatmeal/whole-wheat cookies.

COOKIES

- ½ cup packed light brown sugar
- 2 tablespoons canola oil
- 1 tablespoon low-fat milk
- 1 large egg white
- 1 teaspoon pure vanilla extract
- 1 cup "quick" rolled oats
- ½ cup whole-wheat flour
- 1 teaspoon baking soda
- ½ teaspoon ground cinnamon

FROZEN YOGURT

- 2 cups frozen unsweetened fruit, such as cherries, blueberries, strawberries, peaches, slightly thawed
- 3 cups nonfat vanilla frozen yogurt

TO MAKE COOKIES:

1. Preheat oven to 300°F. Lightly oil 2 baking sheets or coat them with nonstick cooking spray; set aside.

2. In a mixing bowl, whisk together brown sugar, oil, milk, egg white and vanilla until no lumps of brown sugar remain. Add oats, flour, baking soda and cinnamon to the bowl and stir until no traces of dry ingredients remain.

3. Divide the dough into 16 equal pieces and form each piece into a ball. Place 8 balls on each prepared baking sheet. Cover each baking sheet with a piece of plastic wrap or wax paper; with a flat-bottomed cup or bowl, firmly press each of the balls into a thin 3-inch circle.

4. Bake the cookies, one sheet at a time, for 8 to 10 minutes, or until well-browned. Remove to a wire rack to cool completely.

TO FORM SANDWICHES:

If the pieces of fruit are large, coarsely chop them. Soften frozen yogurt in the microwave at medium-low power for 30 to 60 seconds or at room temperature for 10 to 20 minutes. In a mixing bowl, swirl the fruit into the softened frozen yogurt. If the yogurt has become too soft, return it to the freezer to firm up slightly. Scoop about ⅓ cup of frozen yogurt onto a cookie and gently press a second cookie on top. Repeat with the remaining cookies and frozen yogurt. Return the sandwiches to the freezer to firm up.

Makes 8 sandwiches.

280 calories per sandwich: 6 grams protein, 4 grams fat (0 grams saturated fat), 56 grams carbohydrate; 168 mg sodium; 0 mg cholesterol.

PEACH-MELON FROZEN YOGURT

If you start with frozen fruit and a food processor, you can have fat-free frozen yogurt in only 15 minutes. Try frozen strawberries, blueberries or bananas, but avoid seedy fruits, such as raspberries.

In a food processor, combine frozen fruit and sugar. Pulse until coarsely chopped. In a small bowl, stir together yogurt and lemon juice. With the machine running, gradually pour the yogurt mixture through the feed tube. Process until smooth and creamy, scraping down the sides of the work bowl once or twice. Scoop the frozen yogurt into serving dishes, cover with plastic wrap and freeze for at least 15 to 30 minutes to firm up before serving.

Makes about 2½ cups, serves 4.

120 calories per serving: 3 grams protein, 0 grams fat, 29 grams carbohydrate; 62 mg sodium; 1 mg cholesterol.

3	cups frozen unsweetened mixed fruit, such as peaches, melon, grapes
⅓	cup sugar, preferably instant-dissolving
½	cup nonfat plain yogurt
1	tablespoon fresh lemon juice

BLUEBERRY-BANANA FROZEN YOGURT

Pureed banana gives this mixture an especially smooth texture, and orange-juice concentrate and crème de cassis add a complementary tang.

In a food processor, puree blueberries. To remove skins, work the puree through a fine strainer into a bowl. Add bananas to the food processor and puree. Add the strained blueberry puree, yogurt, sugar, orange-juice concentrate and crème de cassis or black currant syrup and process just until mixed in. If necessary, chill until cold. Pour into the canister of an ice cream maker and freeze according to the manufacturer's directions. (*Alternatively, freeze the mixture in a shallow metal cake pan until solid, about 6 hours. Break into chunks and process in a food processor until smooth.*)

Makes about 1 quart, serves 6.

190 calories per serving: 3 grams protein, 1 gram fat (0 grams saturated fat), 44 grams carbohydrate, 1 gram alcohol; 36 mg sodium; 1 mg cholesterol.

1	quart blueberries
⅔	cup sliced ripe banana (1 medium)
1	cup nonfat plain yogurt
½	cup sugar, preferably instant-dissolving
¼	cup frozen orange-juice concentrate, thawed
1	tablespoon crème de cassis or black currant syrup

Raspberry Frozen Yogurt (*right*) & Sicilian Fig Cookies (*page 110*)

RASPBERRY FROZEN YOGURT

Keep raspberries on hand in the freezer year-round so you can make this luxurious, simple dessert anytime.

In a food processor, puree raspberries with lemon juice. To remove seeds, work the puree through a fine strainer into a bowl. Whisk in sugar and yogurt. If necessary, chill until cold. Pour into the canister of an ice cream maker and freeze according to the manufacturer's directions. (*Alternatively, freeze in a shallow metal cake pan or ice cube trays until solid, about 6 hours. Break into chunks and process in a food processor until smooth.*)

Makes about 1 quart, serves 6.

240 calories per serving: 3 grams protein, 1 gram fat (0 grams saturated fat), 60 grams carbohydrate; 30 mg sodium; 1 mg cholesterol.

3	pints raspberries
2	tablespoons fresh lemon juice
1⅓	cups sugar, preferably instant-dissolving
1	cup nonfat plain yogurt

MANGO-LIME SORBET

A stunning golden-orange color, this refreshing sorbet is even more dramatic served with Strawberry Margarita Sauce (page 174).

1. Puree mangoes in a food processor or blender. Work the puree through a fine sieve. (This will remove any fibers, the amount of which can vary.) Measure out 2 cups of puree, cover with plastic wrap and refrigerate (freeze any extra for another use).

2. In a saucepan, combine sugar and 1½ cups water. Stir over medium heat until the liquid comes to a full boil and the sugar has dissolved. Remove from the heat and let cool to room temperature. Stir in the reserved mango puree and lime juice, adding more lime juice if desired. Cover with plastic wrap and refrigerate until cold.

3. Freeze the mixture in an ice cream maker according to the manufacturer's directions. (*Alternatively, freeze the mixture in a shallow metal cake pan or ice cube trays until solid, about 6 hours. Break into chunks and process in a food processor until smooth.*)

Makes about 1 quart, serves 6.

270 calories per serving: 1 gram protein, 1 gram fat (0 grams saturated fat), 71 grams carbohydrate; 5 mg sodium; 0 mg cholesterol.

3	pounds ripe mangoes (3 large or 4 medium), peeled and cut into chunks (*see tip on page 59*)
1	cup sugar
¼	cup fresh lime juice, *or* more to taste

ORANGE SMOOTHIE

Like a Creamsicle in a glass.

1   **cup nonfat vanilla frozen yogurt**
¾   **cup low-fat milk**
¼   **cup frozen orange-juice concentrate**

Combine frozen yogurt, milk and orange-juice concentrate in a blender and blend until smooth.

Makes 2 cups.

185 calories per cup: 7 grams protein, 1 gram fat (1 gram saturated fat), 36 grams carbohydrate; 117 mg sodium; 4 mg cholesterol.

STRAWBERRY MALTED

Picture this in a chrome holder set on a marble counter.

1   **cup fresh strawberry halves**
1   **cup nonfat vanilla frozen yogurt**
⅔   **cup low-fat milk**
3   **tablespoons malted-milk powder**

Combine strawberries, frozen yogurt, milk and malted-milk powder in a blender and blend until smooth.

Makes 2 cups.

180 calories per cup: 7 grams protein, 2 grams fat (1 gram saturated fat), 33 grams carbohydrate; 133 mg sodium; 7 mg cholesterol.

MINTED LIME *LIQUADO*

A bright-green cooler inspired by the light fruit-and-ice shakes of Mexico.

¼   **cup frozen limeade concentrate**
¼   **cup fresh mint leaves**
5-6 **ice cubes**

Combine 1 cup water, limeade, mint and ice cubes in a blender and blend until smooth.

Makes 2 cups.

110 calories per cup: 0 grams protein, 0 grams fat, 29 grams carbohydrate; 7 mg sodium; 0 mg cholesterol.

Orange Smoothie

PRUNES & ARMAGNAC IN FROZEN YOGURT

The pairing of prunes and Armagnac is common in southwest France. The fruit is plumped in the brandy, then folded into frozen yogurt for a simple but glorious dessert.

½ cup chopped pitted prunes

3 tablespoons Armagnac *or* Cognac

3 cups nonfat vanilla frozen yogurt

1. In a saucepan, combine prunes and Armagnac or Cognac and stir over low heat until the prunes are softened, about 1 minute. Transfer the prunes to a bowl to cool down.

2. Soften frozen yogurt in the microwave at medium-low power (30 percent) for 30 to 60 seconds. (*Alternatively, allow the frozen yogurt to soften for 10 to 20 minutes at room temperature.*) Transfer to a bowl and stir in the prunes and any liquid with a wooden spoon or whisk until well incorporated. Return to the freezer until firm, about 2 hours.

Makes about 3½ cups, serves 4.

250 calories per serving: 5 grams protein, 0 grams fat, 44 grams carbohydrate, 4 grams alcohol; 106 mg sodium; 0 mg cholesterol.

◆**FLAVOR BOOSTERS**

Nonfat or low-fat vanilla frozen yogurt is a bit bland all on its own, but a wonderful base for flavoring in myriad ways. Try adding chopped fruits, ground spices or liqueurs, alone or in combination.

SUBLIME SAUCES

A solitary scoop of ice cream or frozen yogurt makes a rather ordinary dessert. But put a little Blackberry Sauce or Praline Sauce or Passion Fruit Sauce on top, and it is transformed. Yet it's hardly any work at all.

Many of these sauces are based on seasonal fresh fruits. The sweet intensity of tropical fruits is particularly useful in dessert sauces. Quite a few of these recipes contain spirits or wine, which is an efficient way to enhance flavors without adding any fat. If you prefer not to use alcohol, it can be omitted or substituted by an equal amount of fruit juice plus a little vanilla extract for complexity.

BLACKBERRY SAUCE

An uncooked sauce with a lovely blackberry flavor; delightful over Lemon Ice Cream (page 162).

3 cups blackberries

2 tablespoons blackberry brandy

2 tablespoons fresh orange juice

3 tablespoons honey

Pick over and reserve 1 cup of the smallest and most attractive berries. In a food processor, puree the remaining 2 cups berries with the brandy, orange juice and honey. Transfer the mixture to a sieve set over a bowl. Press the puree through the sieve and discard the seeds. (*The sauce can be made up to 8 hours ahead and stored, covered, in the refrigerator.*) Stir the remaining berries into the sauce just before serving.

Makes about 2 cups.

15 calories per tablespoon: 0 grams protein, 0 grams fat, 4 grams carbohydrate, 2 grams alcohol; 1 mg sodium; 0 mg cholesterol.

STRAWBERRY MARGARITA SAUCE

Serve this spirited sauce over Mango-Lime Sorbet (page 169) or fresh fruit.

12 ounces frozen unsweetened strawberries, thawed, *or* 4 cups fresh strawberries, hulled

½ cup confectioners' sugar

¼ cup fresh lime juice, *or* more to taste

2 tablespoons tequila

1 tablespoon Triple Sec *or* other orange liqueur

In a blender, combine strawberries, sugar, lime juice, tequila and liqueur. Blend on medium speed until smooth. Add more lime juice if desired.

Makes about 2 cups.

25 calories per tablespoon: 0 grams protein, 0 grams fat, 5 grams carbohydrate, 1 gram alcohol; 0 mg sodium; 0 mg cholesterol.

MEXICAN CHOCOLATE SAUCE

Chocolate syrup makes a quick base for a delicious sauce; cocoa powder deepens the chocolate flavor and cuts the sweetness without adding fat, and orange and cinnamon lend complexity.

In a small saucepan, stir together cocoa, cornstarch and cinnamon. Whisk in orange juice and zest and stir over medium-low heat until simmering and thickened. Add chocolate syrup and stir until the sauce is heated through. Serve warm over frozen yogurt. (*The sauce can be stored, covered, in the refrigerator for up to 1 week.*)

Makes 1½ cups.

35 calories per tablespoon: 0 grams protein, 0 grams fat, 10 grams carbohydrate; 8 mg sodium; 0 mg cholesterol.

- ¼ cup unsweetened cocoa powder, preferably Dutch-process
- ½ teaspoon cornstarch
- ¼ teaspoon ground cinnamon
- ½ cup fresh orange juice
- 1 teaspoon grated orange zest
- 1 cup chocolate syrup, such as Hershey's

COFFEE-RUM SAUCE

Sliced bananas make a delicious addition to this smooth, rich and intense sauce.

In a small bowl, whisk instant coffee and rum until the coffee dissolves (small flecks of undissolved coffee will remain). Whisk in sweetened condensed milk until well combined. Serve over frozen yogurt. (*The sauce can be stored, covered, in the refrigerator for up to 1 week.*)

Makes 1⅓ cups.

60 calories per tablespoon: 2 grams protein, 0 grams fat, 12 grams carbohydrate; 20 mg sodium; 2 mg cholesterol.

- 3 tablespoons instant coffee powder *or* granules
- 2 tablespoons dark rum
- 1 14-ounce can nonfat sweetened condensed milk

APRICOT-GINGERSNAP SAUCE

Colorful, tart and crunchy.

¾ cup fresh orange juice
½ cup slivered dried apricots
1 tablespoon brandy
   (optional)
¼ cup orange marmalade
4 gingersnaps, crushed

In a small saucepan, simmer orange juice, apricots and brandy, if using, over low heat until the apricots are soft, about 3 minutes. Add marmalade, increase the heat to medium-high and cook, stirring, until the sauce is slightly thick, about 5 minutes. Serve warm over frozen yogurt, sprinkled with crushed gingersnaps.

Makes 1 cup of sauce.

145 calories per ¼-cup serving: 1 gram protein, 1 gram fat (0 grams saturated fat), 34 grams carbohydrate; 47 mg sodium; 0 mg cholesterol.

WARM LEMON & GINGER SAUCE

A final fillip for simple poached pears or a slice of Buttermilk Pound Cake (page 23).

⅓ cup sugar
1 tablespoon cornstarch
¼ teaspoon ground cinnamon
¼ teaspoon ground ginger
   Pinch of salt
½ cup apple juice
¼ cup fresh lemon juice
1 tablespoon grated lemon
   zest
2 tablespoons finely slivered
   crystallized ginger

In a small saucepan, whisk together sugar, cornstarch, cinnamon, ground ginger and salt until completely blended. Slowly whisk in apple juice and ½ cup water. Whisk over medium heat until the sauce is simmering and thickened. Cook, stirring occasionally, until the sauce has thickened further, about 5 more minutes. Remove from the heat and stir in lemon juice, lemon zest and crystallized ginger. Serve warm.

Makes 1¼ cups.

20 calories per tablespoon: 0 grams protein, 0 grams fat, 5 grams carbohydrate; 1 mg sodium; 0 mg cholesterol.

◆**INGREDIENT NOTE**
Crystallized ginger lends a peppery pizzazz to desserts.
Buy it at Asian markets or health-food stores, where it will be far less expensive.

Praline Sauce on Vanilla Ice Cream (*page 158*)

PRALINE SAUCE

A saucy version of the Louisiana confection; add a splash of bourbon if you like.

1. In a small saucepan, melt butter over medium heat. Add pecans and stir until the nuts are lightly toasted and fragrant, about 1 minute. Remove the pan from the heat; stir in brown sugar.

2. In a small bowl, stir milk, cornstarch and salt together; whisk into the brown-sugar mixture. Return to the heat and whisk until the sauce is simmering and thick, about 1 minute. Serve warm over frozen yogurt.

Makes 1 cup.

70 calories per tablespoon: 0 grams protein, 2 grams fat (1 gram saturated fat), 14 grams carbohydrate; 12 mg sodium; 1 mg cholesterol.

2	teaspoons butter
¼	cup chopped pecans
1	cup packed dark brown sugar
⅓	cup low-fat milk
1	tablespoon cornstarch
	Pinch of salt

RASPBERRY-CHOCOLATE SAUCE

Raspberry jam adds sheen and a fruity accent to this scrumptious sauce.

⅓ cup sugar

2 tablespoons unsweetened cocoa powder

1 teaspoon arrowroot *or* 1½ teaspoons cornstarch

3 tablespoons seedless raspberry jam

2 teaspoons eau-de-vie de framboise *or* Chambord (optional)

In a small saucepan, whisk together sugar, cocoa and arrowroot or cornstarch. Gradually whisk in ¼ cup water and jam. Bring to a simmer over medium heat, whisking constantly. Remove from the heat and stir in liqueur, if using. Let cool slightly. (*The sauce can be stored, covered, in the refrigerator for up to 1 week.*)

Makes ⅔ cup.

40 calories per tablespoon: 0 grams protein, 0 grams fat, 10 grams carbohydrate; 1 mg sodium; 0 mg cholesterol.

CRAN-RASPBERRY SAUCE

Fruit juice is the base of this quick sauce that pairs well with fresh fruit, frozen yogurt or a slice of pound cake.

2 cups cranberry-raspberry juice

2 tablespoons kirsch *or* orange liqueur *or* 1 tablespoon water

1 teaspoon cornstarch

1 cup frozen unsweetened raspberries (*not* thawed)

In a large saucepan or skillet, bring juice to a boil over high heat. Cook until reduced to about ⅔ cup, about 10 minutes. In a small bowl, stir together kirsch, orange liqueur or water and cornstarch; whisk into the sauce and cook until it has thickened and become clear again. Remove the pan from the heat and stir in raspberries; let stand briefly until the berries have thawed. Serve warm or cool.

Makes 1 cup.

30 calories per tablespoon: 0 grams protein, 0 grams fat, 6 grams carbohydrate; 1 mg sodium; 0 mg cholesterol.

CARAMELIZED APPLE TOPPING

Simmered in caramel syrup, the apples soften and take on an amber translucence;
spoon some over Cinnamon Ice Cream (page 159) or alongside Triple Gingerbread (page 26).

1. In a bowl, toss together apples and lemon juice; set aside.

2. In a heavy skillet, stir together sugar and 2 tablespoons water; bring to a boil, stirring to dissolve the sugar. Reduce the heat to low and cook, not stirring but swirling the pan, until the sugar turns a deep amber, about 5 minutes (if the sugar crystallizes, it will take longer, but will eventually melt and caramelize).

3. Remove the pan from the heat and swirl in butter. Transfer the apples to the pan, cover and return to low heat. Cook, stirring occasionally, until the caramel has dissolved and the apples are translucent, about 10 minutes. If using, stir in Calvados. Serve warm.

Makes about 1½ cups, serves 4.

210 calories per serving: 0 grams protein, 2 grams fat (1 gram saturated fat), 49 grams carbohydrate; 20 mg sodium; 5 mg cholesterol.

- 4 cooking apples, such as Cortland, Golden Delicious *or* Rome Beauty, peeled, cored and thinly sliced (4 cups)
- 1 tablespoon fresh lemon juice
- ⅔ cup sugar
- 2 teaspoons butter
- 1 tablespoon Calvados (*see page 10*), optional

BRANDIED CHERRY SAUCE

Try pairing this with a scoop of Malt Shop Chocolate Ice Cream (page 160).

In a saucepan, combine cherries, sugar and lemon juice. Bring to a simmer and cook, stirring, until the cherries have softened and exuded their liquid, about 5 minutes. In a small bowl, stir together brandy or orange juice and cornstarch. Stir the cornstarch mixture into the simmering liquid and cook until thickened and clear. Serve warm.

Makes about 1½ cups, serves 4.

190 calories per serving: 2 grams protein, 0 grams fat, 41 grams carbohydrate, 3 grams alcohol; 0 mg sodium; 0 mg cholesterol.

- 3 cups frozen dark sweet cherries
- 2 tablespoons sugar
- 1 tablespoon fresh lemon juice
- 2 tablespoons brandy *or* orange juice
- 1½ teaspoons cornstarch

SANGRIA SAUCE

Serve this over vanilla or peach frozen yogurt for a Sangria Sundae.

1 cup red wine

⅓ cup orange marmalade

4 clementines *or* tangerines, peeled, segmented and cut in half

1 teaspoon fresh lime juice

In a small saucepan, bring wine to a boil over medium-high heat. Cook until reduced to ¼ cup, 6 to 8 minutes. Add marmalade and cook until thickened, 1 to 2 minutes. Remove from the heat and stir in clementines or tangerines and lime juice. Serve warm or cold.

Makes about 1½ cups, serves 4.

110 calories per serving: 1 gram protein, 0 grams fat, 28 grams carbohydrate; 4 mg sodium; 0 mg cholesterol.

Sangria Sauce on Vanilla Ice Cream (*page 158*)

PINEAPPLE-MANGO TOPPING

If you have the time, toast some shredded coconut to sprinkle on top.

In a small bowl, combine pineapple, mango, brown sugar, lime juice and lime zest. Stir until the sugar dissolves. Serve over sorbet or frozen yogurt, garnished with mint sprigs if desired.

Makes 2 cups.

80 calories per ½-cup serving: 0 grams protein, 0 grams fat, 21 grams carbohydrate; 4 mg sodium; 0 mg cholesterol.

1	cup chopped fresh pineapple (¼ of a medium pineapple)
1	small mango, chopped (*see tip on page 59*)
2	tablespoons brown sugar
1½	tablespoons fresh lime juice
½	teaspoon grated lime zest
	Fresh mint sprigs for garnish (optional)

PASSION FRUIT SAUCE

Passion fruit provides concentrated tropical flavoring power, one that enhances the tastes of other fruits. Stir up this simple sauce to transform all kinds of soft fruit, such as mango, papaya, melon, strawberries, blueberries or raspberries.

Cut tops from passion fruits and scrape out all pulp into the bowl of a food processor. Process the pulp until liquefied, then strain through a sieve set over a bowl to remove the seeds. (*Alternatively, work the pulp through a sieve, pressing hard with the back of a spoon to separate the pulp from the seeds.*) Blend the juice with honey and citrus juice to taste, and rum if desired. Chill before serving. (*The sauce will keep up to 2 days in the refrigerator.*)

Makes 1 cup.

20 calories per tablespoon: 0 grams protein, 0 grams fat, 5 grams carbohydrate; 2 mg sodium; 0 mg cholesterol.

6	passion fruits
3	tablespoons honey, plus more to taste
	Fresh lime juice *or* lemon juice
2-3	tablespoons light rum (optional)

◆**CHOOSING PASSION FRUIT**
Buy fruits that feel relatively heavy. A wrinkled exterior signals ripeness.

VANILLA CUSTARD SAUCE

A lighter version of crème anglaise, *this sauce is thickened with egg whites as well as yolks, so watch it carefully to avoid curdling. Serve with poached fruits or simple desserts, such as Cranberry Baked Apples (page 64).*

½ vanilla bean, split lengthwise but left attached at one end, *or* 1 teaspoon pure vanilla extract

1¼ cups low-fat milk

3 tablespoons sugar

1 large egg

1. If using vanilla bean, combine it with milk in a small saucepan; bring nearly to a boil, stirring to avoid scorching on the bottom of the pan. Remove the pan from the heat, cover and set aside to steep for 30 minutes. (Omit this step if you are using extract; it is added later.)

2. Set a fine strainer over a bowl and reserve. In a heavy saucepan, heat the milk or vanilla milk to a simmer. In a bowl, whisk together sugar and egg until smooth; gradually whisk in a little of the hot milk to warm the egg. Pour the egg mixture back into the hot milk. Stir the custard constantly over low heat until it thickens enough to coat the back of a spoon evenly, about 7 to 8 minutes. Do not allow the sauce to boil, or it will curdle.

3. Immediately pour the custard through the strainer. Scrape the seeds of the vanilla bean into the custard, or add the extract. Cover with plastic wrap and refrigerate until chilled. (*The sauce can be stored, covered, in the refrigerator for up to 2 days.*)

Makes 1¼ cups.

15 calories per tablespoon: 1 gram protein, 0.5 grams fat (0 grams saturated fat), 3 grams carbohydrate; 11 mg sodium; 11 mg cholesterol.

VANILLA CREAM

This easy topping makes a great lower-fat stand-in for whipped cream.

1½ cups low-fat vanilla yogurt

½ cup light whipping cream

1 tablespoon confectioners' sugar

1 tablespoon Grand Marnier *or other orange liqueur* (optional)

1. Line a sieve with cheesecloth and set it over a bowl. (*Alternatively, use a coffee filter lined with filter paper.*) Spoon in yogurt and let it drain in the refrigerator until reduced to 1 cup, about 1 hour.

2. In a chilled mixing bowl with chilled beaters, whip cream to soft peaks. Add the drained yogurt, sugar and liqueur, if using; fold gently to mix. Serve immediately or refrigerate, covered, for up to 8 hours.

Makes about 2 cups.

20 calories per tablespoon: 1 gram protein, 1 gram fat (1 gram saturated fat), 1 gram carbohydrate; 9 mg sodium; 4 mg cholesterol.

RECIPE INDEX

Page numbers in italics indicate photographs

V

Vanilla beans, 10
Vanilla Cream, 182
Vanilla Custard Sauce, 182
Vanilla extract, 10, 158
Vanilla Ice Cream, 158

W

Walnuts
  Chocolate Pudding Cake with
    Coffee Sauce, 103
  Cranberry-Walnut Scones, *142*, 143
  Date & Walnut Cake, 25
  Filled Oatmeal-Date Cookies, 116
  Rugelach, 117
Warm Lemon & Ginger Sauce, 176
White Grape Ice, 162
Whole-Wheat Blueberry Bars, 134
Whole-wheat pastry flour, 8

Y

Yogurt. *See also* **Frozen Yogurt**
  about, 9
  Apricot Fool, 88
  Baked Figs with Raspberries
    & Yogurt Cream, 60, *61*
  Blueberry Torte, 16
  Chocolate Shortcakes, 95
  draining, 47, 95
  Lemon Cream Pie, 47
  Orange Marmalade Coffee
    Cake, 148
  Orange-Raisin Scones, 144
  Prune Coffee Cake, 147
  Vanilla Cream, 182

Z

Zest, 10
  zesting, 29
Zucchini Bread, 152

LOWEST OF THE LOW

While all the recipes in this book can be considered low-fat, 41 recipes stand out as being particularly low in fat and 29 have no fat at all.

VERY LOW-FAT
(1, 2 or 3 grams of fat per serving)

A Bowl-of-Fruit Cake, 14
Apricot-Gingersnap Sauce, 176
Baked Pears with Gingersnap Crumbs, 65
Baked Rice Pudding, 82
Blueberry-Banana Frozen Yogurt, 167
Caramelized Apple Topping, 179
Cherry Amaretti Gratin, 58
Cherry Clafoutis, 79
Chocolate-Dipped Apricots, 104
Chocolate Soufflé, 94
Cinnamon Ice Cream, 159
Cocoa Roulade with Raspberry Cream, 98
Cranberry Baked Apples, 64
Cranberry-Granola Blondies, 135
Cranberry-Walnut Scones, 143
Date & Walnut Cake, 25
Flan, 86
Frozen Fudge Bars, 165
Hermits, 137
Italian Cornmeal Cake, 29

Lemon Ice Cream, 162
Lemon Squares, 132
Mango-Lime Sorbet, 169
Mincemeat Tart, 44
Orange Smoothie, 170
Peaches & Dumplings, 71
Pear-Cranberry Sampler, 80
Pears Royale, 65
Poppy Seed-Orange Biscotti, 120
Provençal Pear Tart, 46
Raspberries & Cream Squares, 130
Raspberry Frozen Yogurt, 169
Roasted Pineapple, 55
Rum-Raisin Bread Pudding, 85
Sliced Oranges with Warm Raspberries, 55
Souffléed Semolina Pudding, 84
Strawberry Malted, 170
Summer Pudding, 76
Tropical Fruit Compote, 59
Vanilla Custard Sauce, 182
Vanilla Ice Cream, 158

NONFAT

Apples Poached in White Wine, 62
Blackberry Sauce, 174
Brandied Cherry Sauce, 179
Brandied Nectarines, 56
Candied Grapefruit Peels, 68
Chocolate Angel Food Cake, 102
Coffee-Rum Sauce, 175
Cran-Raspberry Sauce, 178
Cran-Strawberry Ice Pops, 164
Dried Fruit Compote, 63
Fresh Grapefruit in Honey-Thyme Syrup, 67
Frosted Grapes, 165
Melon Balls in Port, 58
Mexican Chocolate Sauce, 175
Minted Lime *Liquado*, 170

Mixed-Berry Champagne Ambrosia, 52
Orange Sorbet with Minted Oranges, 163
Passion Fruit Sauce, 181
Peach-Melon Frozen Yogurt, 167
Peppered Lebkuchen, 114
Pineapple-Mango Topping, 181
Prunes & Armagnac in Frozen Yogurt, 172
Raspberry-Chocolate Sauce, 178
Sangria Sauce, 180
Spiced Wine & Fruit, 63
Stone-Fruit Soup, 62
Strawberry Margarita Sauce, 174
Warm Lemon & Ginger Sauce, 176
White Grape Ice, 162

CREDITS

Our thanks to the fine food writers whose work was previously published in EATING WELL *Magazine.*

Nancy Baggett:
Brandied Cherry Sauce, 179.

Melanie Barnard:
Banana Spice Cake, 19; Triple Gingerbread, 26; Mixed-Berry Champagne Ambrosia, 52; Tropical Fruit Compote, 59; Huckleberry Slump, 75; Summer Pudding, 76; Sicilian Fig Cookies, 110; Peppered Lebkuchen, 114; Mexican Meringue Cookies, 126; Blackberry Sauce, 174.

Melanie Barnard & Elinor Klivans:
A Bowl-of-Fruit Cake, 14.

Nora Carey:
Candied Grapefruit Peels, 68.

Lisa Cherkasky:
Rhubarb Custard Pie, 32.

Susan Herrmann Loomis:
Provençal Pear Tart, 46. (This recipe also appears in *The French Farmhouse Cookbook*; Workman, 1996.)

Joan Nathan:
Dried Fruit Compote, 63.

Bill Neal:
Peaches & Dumplings, 71.

Mäni Niall:
Blackberry Skillet Cake, 17; Pear Frangipane, 54; Cranberry-Walnut Scones, 143.

Marie Piraino:
Poppy Seed-Orange Biscotti, 120.

Susan G. Purdy:
Ricotta Cheesecake, 12; Orange Chiffon Cake, 24; Café au Lait Cheesecake, 30; Two-Berry Pie, 33; Chocolate Soufflé, 94; Cocoa Roulade with Raspberry Cream, 98; Spiced Coffee Cake with Pears, 145; Blueberry Coffee Cake, 146; Prune Coffee Cake, 147; Orange Marmalade Coffee Cake, 148. (These recipes also appear in *Have Your Cake & Eat It, Too* by Susan G. Purdy; William Morrow & Company, Inc., 1993.)

Stephan Pyles:
Mango-Cranberry Cobbler, 90.

Richard Sax:
Upside-Down Apple Pie, 41; Spiced Wine & Fruit, 63; Souffléed Semolina Pudding, 84; Apricot Fool, 88; Vanilla Custard Sauce, 182.

Elizabeth Schneider:
Passion Fruit Sauce, 181.

Michele Scicolone:
Italian Cornmeal Cake, 29; Apples Poached in White Wine, 62; Baked Rice Pudding, 82; Pine Nut Cookies, 111; Hazelnut-Anise Biscotti, 118; White Grape Ice, 162.

Martha Rose Shulman:
Orange Sorbet with Minted Oranges, 163.

Andrew Silva:
Sangria Sauce, 180.

Lucia Watson:
Chocolate Angel Food Cake, 102.

John Willoughby & Chris Schlesinger:
Roasted Pineapple, 55.

More cookbooks
from

The Eating Well New Favorites Cookbook

More Great Recipes from the Magazine of Food & Health

From the Editors of EATING WELL®

ISBN 1-884943-07-1   (hardcover) $24.95 / ISBN 1-884943-08-X   (paperback) $16.95

The Eating Well Rush Hour Cookbook

Healthy Meals for Busy Cooks

From the Editors of EATING WELL,® The Magazine of Food & Health

ISBN 1-884943-05-5   (hardcover) $24.95 / ISBN 1-884943-06-3   (paperback) $14.95

The Eating Well Recipe Rescue Cookbook

High-Fat Favorites Transformed Into Healthy Low-Fat Favorites

Edited by Patricia Jamieson & Cheryl Dorschner

ISBN 1-884943-00-4   (hardcover) $24.95 / ISBN 1-884943-01-2   (paperback) $15.95

The Eating Well Cookbook

A Deluxe Collection of EATING WELL*'s Finest Recipes*

Edited by Rux Martin, Patricia Jamieson & Elizabeth Hiser

ISBN 1-884943-02-0   (hardcover) $24.95 / ISBN 1-884943-03-9   (paperback) $15.95